What People Are Saying About

From Hiroshima With Love

"I just gave a speech and found myself quoting what I read in From Hiroshima With Love. *Instead of twenty minutes, I talked for an hour and a half! What about? 'The vision comes first!'—proven in your remarkable history of the rebuilding of Japan after World War II.*

I spotted the first clue to Japan's rebirth early in chapter two (where your stepmother listened at Hiroshima to the emperor's broadcast) and could not put the book down until finished. Especially significant: the 'U.S. Technology Goes to Japan,' which repeats those five lines of the emperor's surrender speech and then shows how that country acted on the vision. From Hiroshima With Love *is engaging, revealing, an interesting reflection.*

Being a student of history with a background in engineering, I like From Hiroshima *because it is fact-based. While a biography of your father, Commander Wallace L. Higgins, the book will be of interest to everyone. It explains cultures, business, and history in an engaging story. I wish I had read it before seeking joint ventures in Japan six years ago. I would have been better prepared."*

> —Andrew S. Patti
> President and Chief Operating Officer,
> The Dial Corp. Consumer Products Group

*"*From Hiroshima With Love *is a delightful combination of two fascinating themes: First, it contains what I believe to be little known information about the somewhat misguided and almost disastrous post war economic reconstruction policy the United States imposed upon Japan. It details the transformation of a tough-minded American businessman, who was, like every American, shocked and resentful because of the military atrocities of the government of Japan during World War II. Given the post of American Military Governor of Hiroshima and partial responsibility for the rebuilding of Japan's business and industry after the war, Wally Higgins learned*

to appreciate and admire the Japanese people with whom he dealt. He was greatly instrumental in reestablishing the domestic economy of Japan by convincing American policy makers that the American tyrannical reparations policies and trade tariffs would crush Japanese reconstruction.

Second, the book depicts a very tender side of the tough American, who, although he had a wife and family stateside, still falls in love with a beautiful young Japanese lady, Sueno.

A delightful combination of history and love story, written by an admiring and loving son, Ray Higgins. A pleasure to read."

—Hon. Frank X. Gordon
Former Chief Justice, Arizona Supreme Court

"As I was reading I kept thinking, 'What a great move/TV miniseries this could be.' The story appears to have all the elements and potential of a mass audience appeal—intrigue, war, and moral, racial, cultural and economic values—all woven together with a great love story. WOW!"

—Muriel Barth
Retired assistant principal, Brevard NC

"The occupation of Japan by American and Allied forces following the end of World War II was one of the most remarkable events in the annals of human history. From Hiroshima With Love gives the reader an intimate view of a man who played a key role in the occupation and whose life was profoundly changed by that experience."

—Boye Lafayette DeMente
Occupationaire and author of The Japanization of America, Japanese Etiquette and Ethics in Business, and many other books

From Hiroshima
With Love

From Hiroshima With Love

By
Raymond A. Higgins

The Allied Military
Governor's Remarkable
Story of the Rebuilding of
Japan's Business and
Industry After WW II

Manufactured in the United States of America. This edition published by VIA Press, 1 E. Camelback, Suite 550, Phoenix AZ 85012-1650, 602/277-4780, 800/2 VIA NOW (800/284-2669).

10 9 8 7 6 5 4 3 2 1

Publisher's Cataloging in Publication

Higgins, Raymond A.
    From Hiroshima with love: the allied military governor's remarkable story of the rebuilding of Japan's business and industry after WW II / by Raymond A. Higgins
        p. cm.
        Includes bibliographical references and index.
        Preassigned LCCN: 95-60585
        ISBN: 1-885001-06-1

    1. Japan—History—Allied occupation, 1945-1952. 2. Japan—History—1952- 3. Japan—Economic conditions—1945-1989. I. Title.

DS889.16.H54 1995   952'.04
                                     QB195-20102

Kure-Hiroshima map on page 14 courtesy of Jinbunsha Co. Ltd., Tokyo

Book design by SageBrush Publications, Chandler, Arizona

Maps produced by Wide World of Maps, Phoenix, Arizona

Editor—Charles Sanford

CONTENTS

This book is dedicated to the millions of heroes, American and Japanese, who are dying of natural causes one by one fifty years after they might have died *en masse* had it not been for the abrupt ending of World War II by two bombs.

Preface

The Jesuit priest stopped pacing, looked me right in the eye and said, "Why, even from Hitler good things resulted!" It made instant sense to me when Father Emery Tang explained what he meant. "History shows that for every bad thing that happens to humankind, something good results, and the good usually outweighs the bad," he said.

Attending this Serra retreat in Malibu, California, gave me an opportunity to take a break from researching the story of my father's involvement with Japan and the midcentury rebuilding of the country he grew to love. I listened as Father Tang, himself of Chinese descent, describe the yin and the yang concept of the universe in which everything is a balance of opposites: darkness and light; shade and sun; death and life; bitter and sweet; bad and good. Father Tang drew the Chinese characters for yin and yang and the Korean symbol of a circle split down the middle with an 'S' shaded on one side. He discussed extremes and the gray areas between them. "One extreme leads to or follows the other. But inevitably," he added, "balance comes and brings something good."

My recent studies prompted me to offer my own example. "Never was this more true," I said, "than in the aftermath of man's first use of an atomic weapon, the bomb dropped on Hiroshima nearly fifty years ago."

"What good could possibly have come from that?" Father Tang asked.

"By ending the war early there were three to six million lives *saved* in the first two years after the bombing of Hiroshima," I replied.

I also could not help but think of my own father's experience. Although he had gone to Japan temporarily to help rebuild the country, American Navy Commander Wallace L. Higgins would meet my stepmother there. He not only fell in love with her, he also was captivated with the country where he would stay another twenty-six years, helping reconstruct Japan's industries and trade, government, and professional organizations.

During those years, from October 1945 to August 1946, Wallace Higgins served as the first military governor of Hiroshima, then as military governor of Kanagawa prefecture until December 1947. He was an advisor on General MacArthur's SCAP, or Supreme Commander of Allied Powers, staff from 1947 to 1950 and, from 1950 until 1971, became an industrial consultant to ten major Japanese companies and four American firms doing business in Japan.

These experiences—and the remarkable notes he kept during those years—proved invaluable when I started to research my father's story twenty-two years ago. As we packed his things so he could return to America to die of leukemia, I discovered his files. Until then, I hardly knew my father. Later, when I told people his story, they found the account so intriguing they urged me to write a book.

In the writing, I have drawn on far more than my own memories and those of my brothers and half-brothers. My father had preserved hundreds of pounds of records, detailed diaries, and photos, and I used these documents, as well as many other historical accounts, to tell this story. I have reconstructed the dialogue, descriptions, and actions of his world using the facts as he recorded them.

Many of the events described in *From Hiroshima With Love* have received little or no exposure until now, but that may well be because nearly all the books that cover this era have been about *war* experiences; few have been about the building of lasting *peace*.

Much more than a history, this book shares the development of this peace and the power it engendered in a people who had surrendered with dignity. That respect is epitomized by Wally Higgins's devotion to his Japanese sweetheart, Sueno, and the way he came to love his second country, to the lasting benefit of them both.

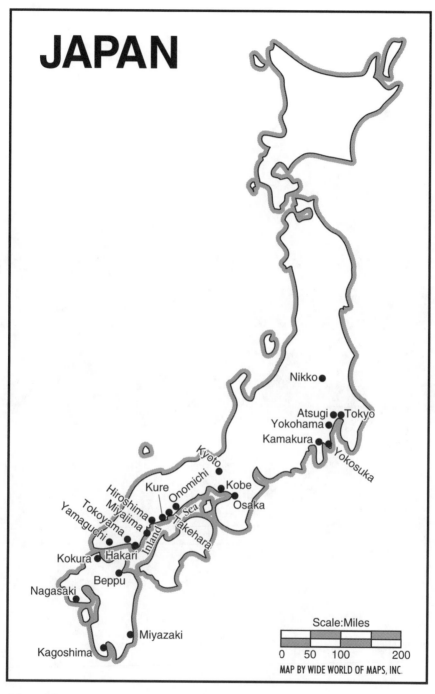

Map of Japan

ONE

Two Families at War

Wally Higgins shifted in his favorite easy chair as he scanned the front page of the Sunday *Cleveland Plain Dealer*. In Washington, there had been little progress in talks with the Japanese. In Europe, Britain seemed lost. Higgins sighed. He was discouraged after another week of his failed attempts to get Ohio companies to accept war preparedness contracts. Tomorrow he would begin another round of calls on factories for Ohio's U.S. Office of Defense Production. December had just begun, but he would be glad to get 1941 behind him.

The aroma from Adelaide's roast filled the Higgins home. Upstairs, Wally and Adelaide's son Ray was doing his high school homework, and the radio on the boy's bedroom windowsill was tuned to the swinging sounds of Sammy Kaye. With Ray's three brothers out of the house it was unusually quiet. Then it became even quieter; the music had stopped.

"We interrupt this program to bring you a special news bulletin from Washington..."

It took a moment for the youngster to comprehend the announcement.

He ran downstairs. "Mom! Dad!" he yelled. "Japan has bombed some place in Hawaii called Pearl Harbor."

"Thank God!" Wally said. "Now we can send a couple divisions of Marines to wipe out those damned Japs."

Wallace Landis Higgins went to his office an hour early that Monday. Now managers who wanted to take on war production contracts for the government were lined up outside his office. No longer did he have to sell the need for an all-out war effort.

Like many other American families, the Higginses did what they could. Adelaide went to work in a war plant while Wally and his four sons prepared to fight for their country. Back in the Navy, Lieutenant Commander Wallace L. Higgins was getting antsy over his job as executive officer of the Cleveland Diesel Engine School and pushed Washington for sea duty. During 1942 and 1943 the big, rented house in the sleepy village of Mentor, Ohio, emptied as each son graduated from high school and went off to serve. As each of her men left home Adelaide would add a blue star to the pennant that hung in the front window until there were five—and add the writing of one more V-mail letter to her evening routine.

Adelaide Petersen had married Wallace Higgins in 1919 when he graduated from the U.S. Naval Academy. Higgins left the Navy the next year and went to work as an engineer for Standard Oil of New Jersey. Adelaide produced the four boys, and Wally moved on to become director of sales with an automatic coal stoker firm in New York. In the mid-thirties, when Higgins changed to a similar job in Cleveland, the family moved to Ohio. As the threat of involvement in World War II brought an urgent need for American industry to shift to defense work in 1940, however, his company loaned Higgins to head Cleveland's War Production Board. For two years he complained bitterly about factory owners' lack of patriotism as one after another declined bids to accept war preparedness contracts.

But now, as Americans rushed to fill contracts, Higgins got half his wish. Instead of sea duty, his talents in industrial engineering and management were needed more in the military government of occupied territories. Higgins was directed to report at Princeton, New Jersey, to the School of Military Government for temporary duty on October 18, 1944.

In full dress uniform, Higgins was quite handsome. The attire also hid a slightly bulging but firm stomach, and he carried himself well. Wally walked with a decisive stride, hitting hard on his heels and springing off on his toes—a habit developed while competing for years in walking races. The "Old Man" was always in good physical shape.

Higgins completed the intensive military government course at Princeton in January 1945. At the end of the month he was transferred to the Presidio at Monterey, California, where his MG team trained. Finally Higgins was made commanding officer of Military Government Team B-12, with its medical, engineering, and other specialists from the Army, Navy, and Marines.

The Higginses had managed to get a small efficiency apartment in Carmel, California, after Adelaide left her factory job. She joined her husband at Princeton then drove to California, stopping on the way in Pasadena to visit his mother. They felt lucky to be together, especially now when so many families were separated. But the illusion of their "happy family" quickly gave way to the reality Adelaide had brought with her from Ohio.

A few days later they were driving along the Monterey Peninsula.

"I suppose you would have mentioned it if you had," Higgins began, "but did you write a thank you note to my mother?"

"No, Wally, I didn't," she answered quietly.

"Well, why the hell not? It seems to me she treats us with a whole lot more love and courtesy than you manage to show her."

Adelaide said nothing at first. "You know full well your mother and I don't see eye to eye on a number of things."

He gripped the wheel with enough strength to nearly tear it from the steering column. Fuming, his voice was measured. "I'd really like to know, once and for all, why you find it so difficult to get along with her."

"I guess you'd say we have different priorities. At least that's what she told me some years back."

"Did you ask her what she meant?"

"Yes."

"Well?"

"She said I..."

"What?" Higgins demanded.

Personal Notes

The Higgins Family (All of It) Goes to War

• • •   • • •   • • •   • • •

Father in Navy, Mother in Factory Think It's 'Privilege, Not Sacrifice,' to Have Four Sons in Service

Raymond Higgins   Wallace Higgins

Mrs. Wallace L. Higgins   Lieutenant Commander W. L. Higgins

Robert Higgins   Richard Higgins

There used to be a lot of gayety in and around the suburban home of the Higgins family in Mentor.

There were four growing boys, and you know how boys are. There were a lot of bridge parties, and you know how they are. There was lots of laughter, and love, and a friendly family comradeship, and you know how that is.

That was before Pearl Harbor. Now the house stands silent and empty in the daytime; a service flag with five blue stars flutters in a window.

The Higgins family has marched to war, gone to fighting front and home front as lightly, and as matter-of-factly, as you would walk down the street to a movie.

Lieutenant Commander Wallace L. Higgins, a veteran of the last war and now Navy executive officer of the Cleveland Diesel Engine Division of General Motors Corp., sees nothing remarkable in the family march to the colors. It's just the "done thing" to him.

And that's the way it is with his slender, blue-eyed wife, who is a war worker at the Addressograph-Multigraph Co.

Great Privilege—Not Sacrifice

Commander Higgins, who entered Annapolis in 1916 and served on convoy duty during the last war, has a new attitude for fathers of sons in the service.

"We're not shedding a lot of tears because the boys are gone," he said today. "We think it's a great privilege—not a great sacrifice. I've always been in favor of compulsory military training—and was sorry that we didn't have it."

His attitude is tinged with a military fatalism. "If their number's up, they'll get it whether they're piloting a bomber or crossing a busy Cleveland street. It doesn't do any good to worry about it. And it's a great opportunity for the boys—they come back better citizens."

Commander Higgins praises his wife for the fine job she has done in raising the boys and encouraging them in the selection of service.

Job Prevents Mother's Worry

Mrs. Higgins, however, says the credit goes to the boy's father who has set them a grand example. She is happy in her work in the assembly department, because "it keeps my mind off worries. You know how mothers are."

There is a deep pride in her voice when she speaks of her sons. "They're all fine boys," she says. "Richard, the eldest, is 23. He will be graduated as an ensign from the Merchant Marine Academy this month. Wallace Jr., 22, is a ball turret gunner on a B-17. He's been fighting in the North African campaign, and now is serving in the Sicilian campaign. I haven't heard from him for over a month, so of course I'm a little anxious."

Raymond, 19, is a cadet in the Army Air Corps officers' Training School at Keesler Field, Biloxi, Miss., and Robert, "the baby," is 17½ and has enlisted in the Reserve Signal Corps.

Couldn't Concentrate on Cards

Mrs. Higgins was satisfied with being a wife, mother and homemaker before the war broke out. "I spent a lot of time playing bridge," she says, "but I found I couldn't concentrate on the game and decided to get a war job."

After the last war, Commander Higgins was vice president and general manager of the Motostokor Corp. for eight years. Five years ago the Higgins' moved to Mentor from Westfield, N. J., and Mr. Higgins became sales manager here for the Pocohontas Fuel Co. When

war broke out, Commander Higgins volunteered for active duty and was assigned to the Diesel plant.

Commander Higgins chafes at what he calls his "policing job." "Checking on materials is not my idea of fighting a war. I've asked for active duty time and again, but they tell me I'm needed here. This is a young man's war, and the old men just have to sit back and take it."

'Bonds No Sacrifice'

He does not consider War Bond buying a sacrifice. "After all, he says, "making a fine investment is no sacrifice. People who buy War Bonds don't have a thing to brag about. They're just doing themselves a good turn."

On the other hand, Commander Higgins considers giving blood to the Red Cross for plasma one of the finest sacrifices an American on the home front can make. "Since January, we've had over 400 people from the plant here, serving as blood donors. It's a personal and real thing that all of us can do."

News clipping: The Higgins Family (All of It) Goes to War

"She told me I overindulged the boys...and didn't give you...sufficient attention."

Higgins stared straight ahead. Concentrating on the road, his face hardened, and he became the stone-cold commander. He said nothing. Adelaide took his silence to mean he agreed with his mother's assessment.

"If that's true," she said, "I didn't intend it to be that way. I didn't know how to be more..."

The tires squealed slightly as Higgins forced the car through a curve a bit too quickly.

Five thousand miles away the Kotani family had also gone to war. They were descendants of Japanese *samurai*—landowners. Iwao, the father, and Kinu, the mother, were left to till their farm on a hillside between Hiroshima and Kure when their sons, Tsuzuo and Sadamu, went off to fight in China in the Imperial Army of Japan.

Daughter Sueno joined the Home Defense Corps in her village and was trained in personal combat. A single mother with a nine-year-old daughter, Sueno had done well enough since her husband, Tadasu Yoshida, had deserted her in 1936. He had been so set on having a son that, when a second, male child died soon after birth, he banished his wife and daughter from the Yoshida family home. Such abandonment was considered the normal form of divorce in Japan, so Sueno and her daughter, "Tae," returned to the Kotani family's Hiroshima property. Although Sueno never heard from him during the war years, she learned through village gossip in 1942 that Tadasu also was serving in the Japanese Imperial Army. While others were consumed with war and its demands, Sueno, Tae, Iwao, and Kinu leased out portions of what was considered a substantial plot of land and scratched out a meager existence for themselves in the vegetable garden.

Sueno and her neighbors so feared invasion that they were trained with sharpened bamboo spears to repel attack by foreign barbarians. And when Sueno and her family heard air raid sirens from far-off Kure, they would climb to the roof and watch what happened in the city.

Like most Japanese women, Sueno was small. She had a girlish face, smooth skin, and soft, black eyes. On the morning of August 6, 1945, however, her figure was gaunt. Even in the countryside, food shortages were severe. It was worse for the people in the cities,

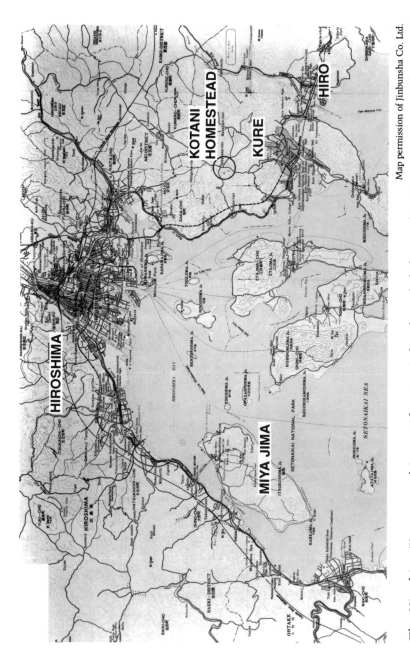

The *Hiroshima/Kure area of Japan. The atomic bomb exploded over the city at top-center. The Kotani homestead is circled.*

Map permission of Jinbunsha Co. Ltd.

Hiroshima after the bomb. The Kotanis' home is behind mountain on left.

who were called "onion people" because, to survive, they had to sell off their valuables one layer at a time, like peeling an onion, until they had nothing left.

Today was wash day for Sueno, however, and, as she busied herself hanging clothes to dry on bamboo poles, her white-and-indigo print *monpe*, or baggy work pants with a kimono-collared top, hid her thin frame.

Sueno had just finished hanging the last kimono when the village sirens sounded. Her eyes searched the sky and found a high-flying plane. She had seen many, many planes, but this huge one was alone. It turned, became a tiny dot, and disappeared. As suddenly as they had begun, the sirens stopped, and Sueno continued to stare at the place where such a large aircraft had been. Suddenly, a flash appeared over Hiroshima, brighter than the sun. It was, for a time, so bright she could not see.

A mushroom-shaped cloud appeared, churning higher and higher, bulging and billowing up over the crest of the mountain. Minutes later there came a rumbling like thunder and the boiling cloud grew monstrous as Sueno grabbed Tae and ran for the shelter.

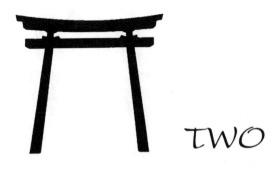

TWO

Prelude to Occupation

Sueno Kotani Yoshida pushed through the crowd of villagers to get closer to the radio placed high above the door of the small village store. It was just past noon, August 15, 1945, and the emperor of Japan had begun a special broadcast.

Speaking in the stilted dialect of royalty and his high-pitched voice, the emperor was difficult to understand. Sueno strained to grasp what he meant when he said, "...to affect a settlement by resorting to an extraordinary measure."

The entire population of this hill area twenty kilometers from Hiroshima was silent as the voice revealed, for the first time, that "...the war situation has developed not necessarily to Japan's advantage." A murmur of understanding rose from the crowd as they caught the words "...the enemy has begun to employ a new and most cruel bomb, the power of which to do damage is incalculable, taking the toll of many innocent lives."

The situation, said the emperor, called for "enduring the unendurable and suffering the insufferable!" The crowd was silent as he told his people, "Unite your total strength to be devoted to the construction of the future. Cultivate the ways of rectitude, foster nobility of spirit, and work with resolution so you may enhance the innate glory of the Imperial State and keep pace with the progress of the world."

Sueno strained to hear more, but the speech had ended. The meaning of what she had just heard sank in slowly, and her distress was so profound that she wept for days.

Just east of Tokyo Bay, on August 19, General Torashiro Kawabe's delegation of sixteen Japanese officials boarded two Mitsubishi "Betty" bombers at Kisarazu Air Base and took off, headed for a small island near Okinawa. There they left their aircraft, boarded an American C-54, and took off again. Their destination was the Philippines, to arrange the surrender of Japan.

That same day, Lieutenant Commander Higgins, in charge of American Military Government Team B-12, shipped a duffle bag containing Navy uniforms, shoes, and a winter coat to himself via APO, boarded a seaplane, and left California. Higgins's Pan Am Clipper and the aircraft carrying General Kawabe's delegation converged on the Philippines from opposite directions.

As the Clipper rose, Higgins turned from the window and removed a crisp American dollar bill from his billfold. He wrote around the margin of the series 1935 Silver Certificate:

SHORT SNORTER W L Higgins Aug. 19, 1945, San Francisco

Holding out the pen and the dollar, Higgins spoke to the man sitting next to him. "Looks like we're seatmates all the way to Manila. Before we down our first snort, would you autograph this?"

"Be happy to, Commander." The man signed "Larry Schieffelin."

The discussion soon widened as Higgins passed the bill around for signatures of others in the section. Pitt Taylor, Major Kenneth B. Burns, Major Walter McCollom were among those who signed, and soon everyone knew everyone else on board. Thus Wally Higgins began his own ice-breaking tradition, the short snorter.

Higgins arrived in Honolulu the next morning and spent the day on the beach studying his files on Hiroshima. Near midnight he left on a Naval Air Transport Service plane that stopped briefly at Johnson Island, proceeded to cross the international dateline and stopped again for fuel at Majuro. Having lost a day, it was August 21. The seemingly incessant drone of aircraft engines was interrupted at Majuro, where he swam in the lagoon and had a leisurely lunch.

The next stop was not as relaxing. At midnight August 22 they landed on Saipan. Japanese soldiers were holed up in caves on the island and continued to fight on, not believing news of a surrender. But by the time Higgins's Navy PB-2-Y approached the Philippines early Thursday afternoon August 23, General Kawabe's delegation had already taken the Allied terms of surrender and returned the papers to Japan.

When power was cut back on the approach to the Philippines, the hum of the engines suddenly changed. Higgins peered out the round porthole of the flying boat as it dropped low over Luzon and slowed as it neared Manila Bay. He saw a small village along the shoreline and rice paddies inland. Everything was wrapped in dense tropical growth. After a bumpy water landing at Cavite on the south shore of Manila Bay, the passengers carried their gear to a crash boat that took them through the harbor toward Manila.

Higgins pulled the bill of his cap down tight to prevent it from blowing overboard and scanned the harbor. He spotted a sunken Japanese ship. Then another, and another, until Higgins counted fifty sunken hulls and superstructures cluttering the outer harbor. Yes, the war had left its mark here.

Following a habit he had acquired over twenty-five years as a business manager and reinforced by his recent training for military government, Higgins made notes of the harbor's condition. Scrounging for any paper he could fold and write on, he jotted his comments.

Arriving at a table in front of a temporary tent city, Higgins logged in. The sergeant gave him Army-issued Philippines "Victory" money, and Higgins taped a one peso certificate to the dollar with all the signatures on it, his short snorter.

"Mind if I take a few sheets of this?" he asked the sergeant at the desk as he noticed a stack of typewriter paper.

"Sure, sir, all you want," replied the sergeant.

Higgins folded six sheets into thirds and added it to the papers in his breast pocket. The sergeant handed him a copy of the order:

> 3. Fol-named off having reported is asgd this hq for dy with the Military Govt Sec: (Bu Pers Restricted Dispatch 172 108 Aug 1945)
> LT COMDR WALLACE L. HIGGINS 144725 (S) USNR
> By command of General MacARTHUR

Higgins stepped out into the street and waited for the rest of the officers who had been with him on the crash boat. As he looked about, he saw Manila was a shambles. Locals swarmed about, selling the GIs all kinds of junk at high prices. The voices of young street hucksters bombarded Higgins's ears.

"Meester, Meester," they shouted.

One held up a thumb-sized banana. "Five pesos, Meester."

Many locals lay under the remains of trees and in the shadows of wrecked buildings. "Five months after liberation, and the only people trying to rebuild this place are the Army, Navy, and Seabees," he noted.

Even the old San Manila Hotel, their quarters for their stay, was a shell. The lower floors were gutted, so they climbed to the top floor where they would be sleeping in barren rooms on cots with netting but no sheets. Two improvised wash basins would serve a hundred men.

Mess, consisting of good and plentiful food, was served in the Tribune building. After an evening meal, Higgins was joined by the major assigned to the bunk next to his. The major was about thirty—little more than half Higgins's age—and his uniform bore the markings of Army ordinance. Together, they stepped out into the street.

"Care to take a walk with me? Explore the city?" Higgins asked. Dressed in his Navy tans, with World War I and American theater ribbons, he looked crisp and clean and prepared for anything.

"I was just going to ask you. Major Kerry Osterman's my name. You're Wally Higgins, aren't you?"

"That's right. I've got the bunk next to yours. Hey, would you sign my short snorter?"

The major signed the buck and handed it back.

"Thanks. I'll buy the first drink when we find one. Let's go!"

They walked a block before stopping an MP to ask directions, but they got a lot more than their bearings. "Practically everything is destroyed except big buildings which are pretty much hollow shells," the MP explained. "Inflation has spread throughout the city. One pack of cigarettes costs them a whole lot of work because pay is all out of proportion to prices. You know the Army has dropped bales of Japanese money over the cities. Maybe the Japs did the same with dollars. Anyway, there's just no confidence in paper money. Could be that's why everyone seems so lazy."

Wally made mental notes. He was beginning to see his job in Japan would require more than just technical skills. He would have to think of ways to motivate laborers as part of his military government responsibilities.

Higgins and Osterman walked about a mile, stopping to ask questions and talk to GIs, MPs, officers and Filipinos they met in the street. They quickly learned that the locals had been treated badly during the Japanese occupation. They had not only been forced to bow, but to suffer other, far more serious indignities—or be executed.

The commander and the major had come to the corner of a burned-out building and were about to turn and head back toward their hotel when a small white object fell in front of them. Instantly, two Filipino boys brushed past the officers, pounced on the cigarette butt, and ran off. Rounding the corner, the officers stopped face to face with the source of the discarded cigarette: a young GI leaning against the wall.

The GI apologized hastily. "Sorry about that, sirs!" The soldier snapped a quick, sloppy salute, then picked up his carbine and slung it across his back.

"Quite all right," said the major. "Where you from, son?"

"Chicago, sir. Rogers Park, to be exact."

The GI appeared to be about twenty, but his face was tanned and battle hardened. He wore Army fatigues and combat boots. His helmet was tilted back, exposing a shock of light brown hair that stuck forward, wet from sweat.

"How long you been here?" Higgins asked.

"Six months. We came in that way." The GI gestured with his hand in a sweeping motion. "Swept that part of the city."

"I'm Commander Higgins and this is Major Osterman. What's your name?"

"Kubec, sir. Private First Class Casey Kubec. You two headed this way?" He pointed.

"Actually, we're looking for the way back to the San Manila."

"That's this way," the GI said. "I'll walk you there."

The threesome stepped around some debris, dodged a Jeep full of Filipino girls, and walked together in the direction of the hotel.

"Private, what do you think of the Japs...or is that a fair question?" asked the major.

"Ha! Fair enough, sir. Funny people. Tough fighters. But they must have a good sense of humor. When I was on a sweep of the outlying area about six months ago, I ran into a Jap soldier. I'll never forget it. I stepped out from behind a bush, my rifle at the ready, and there he was, on the low branch of a tree with his pants down at his feet. Just as I let go with my M-1, he smiles at me with a silly grin. Must have thought it was funny that I caught him in such an embarrassing situation."

The major chuckled. "Sounds to me like a crappy war story!"

The commander laughed.

The private moved a few steps ahead of the officers, turned, and walking backward, said, "Hey, no, I'm serious. If it'd been me up there, I'd have reached for the rifle. But this Jap just sits there and laughs, 'Ha-ha!' like he's saying, 'It's funny!'"

Private Kubec turned and dropped back to walk alongside the officers. Some time passed without anyone speaking. The only sound was the passing traffic.

Higgins suspected the young soldier might be troubled by the memory. "Does it bother you?"

"Naw, not after seeing what the Jap marines did to the Filipinos...especially those trapped here in the city while we were trying to reoccupy it. They were fanatical."

The three Americans waited for four Jeeps to pass before crossing the street.

"Out in the countryside," the private continued, "it was a different matter. Out there, the Filipino guerrillas harassed the Japs and kept the natives from working for them. The Japs couldn't even operate the sugar mill since the natives wouldn't cut the sugar cane."

They reached the San Manila Hotel.

"Well, it was nice talking with you, gentlemen." They shook hands with the private, saluted, and walked on. Higgins and Osterman watched as he quickly disappeared into the darkness.

The next morning, just as Higgins got his turn at one of the wash basins, he was told they would be leaving right after breakfast. By noon August 24 Higgins had arrived at San Fernando—Sixth Army headquarters. He dropped his gear in the one of the stilt-supported local huts where the officers were quartered. With sides woven like baskets and floors of bamboo sticks, the huts did little to fend off the terrific heat. After a shower, Higgins went to the supply tent for salt tablets. He was also given Atabrine to fend off malaria.

"Hey, how come there aren't many flies around here?" Higgins asked the supply sergeant. In spite of unsanitary conditions, he had noticed there were surprisingly few insects.

"It's the DDT, sir. They sprayed the Army areas and Manila with it right after securing the region."

The heat, however, was stifling. Higgins tried taking four showers a day, but soon admitted, "You can't fight the heat, so just resign yourself to it." A long line formed in front of the Red Cross wagon and they waited an hour for a cold drink. Bottled water and Coke were fifty cents each. Never without something sociable to say, Higgins bantered with the Womens Army Corps soldiers in line behind him. They returned his good-natured kidding and let him know that they were unhappy with this rough-and-tumble front line duty. At the officers club later that evening Higgins found things more to his liking. This club was better than the one at the Presidio, with plentiful gin at thirty-five cents a drink.

In discussions with Sixth Army commanders, Higgins learned the strength and locations of military establishments in the three largest cities of Tokyo, Nagoya, and Osaka. They considered the potential problems of governing the Japanese while disarming the troops.

Commander Higgins, a lieutenant colonel, and three majors left San Fernando on August 27 for a day in Manila, piling into a truck for a smelly, dusty ride. Passing many locals—sometimes slowly—they could hardly miss the flirtatious girls with their beautiful, white-toothed smiles and clean cotton clothing.

After several hours, they arrived in Manila and had lunch at the Tribune Building. At Navy small stores, Higgins and the others each drew sheets and towels, barracks bags, a gun, knife, and other Army supplies.

The group of Americans was supposed to meet at the Avenue Hotel at 1600 hours for the ride back to San Fernando, but the driver did not show after two hours, so Higgins and Major Osterman decided to hitchhike. They got their first ride at 1830, but it dropped them off just ten miles from Manila. The waitresses at a nearby local roadhouse hut watched as the Americans waited for hours. As dusk began to settle, one of the girls left her post.

"Hi! My name's Gloria. We felt sorry for you, so I brought you a cold drink."

"Gee, thanks," Higgins said.

They made small talk for a few minutes, then, quite grateful for the drink and attention, Higgins gave her the lei of flowers he had bought in Manila. "We've got to get back to San Fernando. I sure wish we could get a ride."

"I'll fix that!"

A short time later, three Aussie officers picked up the Americans. But Higgins's luck didn't last long. Their lights failed, and it took an hour to get them fixed. Trucks and Jeeps refused to stop to help, even though by then the rain was falling heavily. Since the car had no windshield wipers, they were obliged to stop every time another vehicle approached, a frequent occurrence as convoy after convoy whizzed past. A twenty-mile detour when the driver took the wrong road could have been too much of a bad thing, but Wally Higgins was enjoying the free-wheeling times that he had only dreamed of in faraway Ohio.

Still, Higgins had work to do. He continued to study the local economy as he explored the town. Gambling was everywhere, all the time, on the side of the road and in the streets. Six-year-old boys bet up to five pesos in a game using a bird cage and three dice. He watched cockfights, finally decided to bet, and lost a peso.

At camp, the officers drew cigarettes at the Red Cross wagon and took salt tablets and Atabrine. Since it was still stiflingly hot, they lay around in shorts. Higgins preferred the officers club, which was decorated in the red and white colors of the Sixth Army. The club's large windows were propped wide open with bamboo poles for ventilation. At the bar, where nudes adorned the wine glasses, Higgins listened to a combat veteran dish out advice to newcomers. "The Japanese come down from the hills at night and set booby traps for stragglers," he declared. "They haven't learned that the war's over. No one should go out after 8:30. You know, six Jap officers were captured today in the hills, just ten miles away. And one American was killed with a samurai sword!"

Kerry, the major who had made the all-night trip through the jungle with Higgins the previous night, let out a sigh and chanted, "Golly, golly. Jesus Christ!"

Higgins laughed, picked up the chant, then broke into a song. Others joined in and soon there was a big crowd at the bar. Higgins led the singing. Since he was far outnumbered by Army officers, he picked his songs carefully, avoiding his Navy favorites. The sing-along lasted for hours.

The next day he had to get moving. Orders had been cut transferring him from headquarters at San Fernando to Tenth Corps at Del Monte, so he busied himself packing for the trip to Mindanao.

At 0430 Higgins left for Clark Field. There, amid other passengers, he searched for their C-47. They loaded their gear on board, climbed up, and in a few minutes the engines sputtered, backfired, and roared. With no waiting or formality, the plane just rolled past destroyed Japanese planes and took off. Ten minutes later they had landed. The passengers looked out their windows, then at one another, wondering what was happening. This was a different field, but Mindanao was surely further than this! Then, as two females got aboard, everything became clear. The pilot and copilot had stopped at Nicholson Field in Manila to pick up their dates, a nurse and a WAC corporal.

"First things first!" the pilot announced.

The C-47 landed at Del Monte on Mindanao at 1140 where they were introduced to Tenth Corps staff. Higgins drew majors Carmon and Kenneth B. Burns as tentmates.

The two atomic bombs dropped on Japan had made the planned September 5 landing on Kyushu—and the projected November 1 all-out assault on Japan's main island of Honshu—unnecessary.

Tenth Corps was told it would go into Japan on the third phase about October 15. It was also announced that Lieutenant Commander Higgins of the Tenth would be military governor of Hiroshima. His team would be composed of men from all the services. In the meantime, he was assigned to work as labor officer in the staging area.

After the briefing, Higgins and Burns walked out into the adjoining pineapple plantation. Because of wartime neglect, the pineapples were small. A group of Moro, or Muslim, Filipinos were harvesting with large bolo knives. Using his Army knife, Higgins cut a pineapple in half and shared it with the major. They discovered how delicious a ripe, fresh pineapple can be.

"Eats like a watermelon!" Higgins exclaimed. As the juice ran down their faces, Higgins looked around for some way to wash up. He saw a fast-moving stream, where a truck was taking on water for the camp. He and Burns got down on the bank and drank the cool, clear water, then followed the truck back to camp.

They weren't there long when Higgins got a taste of how knotty his administrative problems could be. Word reached the camp that Japanese were beginning to come in from the hills to surrender. As rain pelted their tent, Higgins, Commander Jennings, and the two Army officers deliberated: What kind of terms should the Japanese be given?

Higgins spoke first. "I ran into one guy who should know. Lieutenant Commander Goodman. He expedited my clearance in San Francisco and got my reservation on the Clipper. He's lived in Japan." Higgins was on his feet, pacing in front of his cot. "He's not all that concerned about military prisoners. He believes the powerful industrial families should be our real target. He says they need to be broken up, then raise the standard of living in Japan."

"There's a word for them," Burns asked. "*Zai...*"

"*Zaibatsu*," said Higgins.

"Right. Industrial control."

"Not just industry," Commander Jennings said. "They also dominate commerce and finance."

"That's all well and good as far as the big picture," said Burns. "But what do we do with these Jap soldiers?"

"I sure as hell don't think we should coddle or feed the Japs," said Jennings. "I say we send the POWs back at once on Jap ships. We take all the stores that have been in Jap-held areas and sell the surplus materials to natives in the Pacific area."

Major Carmon turned to Higgins.

"What's your personal opinion?"

"Me? I really don't know! All this military government training I've gotten has been aimed at helping the civil population to function, to get it back on its feet. There was a clear line drawn between how to treat civilians and how to treat POWs. It looks like that's got to change. We're going to have to help both of them in peacetime."

"I'd say," said Burns, "that how we're going to treat these POWs today is a far cry from how I wanted to treat them a month or two back." The four officers murmured their agreement.

By now Higgins was lying on his cot, his hands folded behind his head. A part of his mind was watching drops of moisture merge into tiny rivulets on the inside of the tent canvas. "I'll tell you what, gentlemen. I'm just damn glad this war is over with none of my sons killed."

⛩

Up early on September 2, Higgins stared at his closet. It amused him to think that some GI had the ingenuity to make a closet from the bullet-shaped belly tank of a Japanese plane. He pulled his khakis from the rack and dressed.

While the surrender ceremony was taking place on the deck of the USS Missouri in Tokyo Bay, Higgins explored the area around Del Monte on the island of Mindanao. He hiked out into the countryside, climbing a hill to an American radio telephone center. He didn't find an incoming wire for him, so he sent an inquiry to San Francisco about the baggage that had failed to catch up to him. Higgins noticed that Allied forces were still using high frequencies so the radio telephone messages could not be intercepted by the Japanese.

With a seasoned military man's sense of respect, he explored the edge of the battle area with a feeling for the violence that had just taken place. From the entrance to a tunnel near the top of a hill he could see the entire valley.

Downed Japanese planes were strewn all over the landscape. About half a mile away he spotted a lone Grumman Wildcat, its tail rising from the earth, missing one of its stubby wings. As he neared the American warplane he saw the fighter pilot's freshly dug grave. He kneeled, removed his cap, lowered his head and whispered: "Our Father, who art in Heaven..."

Nearby, Higgins found ripe pineapples and sweet potatoes. He took out his Army knife and cut into a pineapple. Savoring its sweet taste and breathing deep the fresh air, his eyes were drawn back to the field of destruction where he had walked a short time before. "Abandoned fields of war have looked like that for a long time," he thought. "I wonder what Hiroshima will look like."

Back in camp, Higgins was asked to prepare a speech on Hiroshima ken to present to the Tenth Corps. He dug into his portable files and began outlining his talk.

Wally Higgins climbed into the front seat of the truck. As it pulled out it was joined by escorting Jeeps. There was a bumpy ride of more than an hour, mostly downhill, then north to the shore of Mindanao. When the motorcade reached the POW camp at Bugo, they interrogated a Japanese major and a second class officer. The interpreter was a young Nisei, or first generation Japanese American, an Army corporal.

"Ask about their situation," Higgins said. To his surprise, rather than showing resentment, the two prisoners were polite and cooperative.

"The senior officer says there are two thousand Japanese troops in the hills within six miles of this camp. Most of them are unable to travel. They have no supplies, no medicine, no ammunition. They know the war is over. *Banzai* battle cries have been replaced with *hárikari*."

"Ask them where they are from."

"*Jusho wa doko da?*"

"The major is from Tokyo, thirty years old, a career officer from a military academy."

To Higgins he looked to be in fine shape.

"He tells of having two children and says they are all anxious to get back to Japan. The other says he is twenty-five years old, a university graduate."

Later, Higgins and the interpreter visited the pens of prisoners. The forty officers appeared healthy, but the enlisted men were a sorry lot. Undernourished, they were covered with body sores, dressed in shreds of loincloths or tattered rags. None had shoes. The contrasting conditions of the officers and enlisted men disturbed Higgins. "The officers lie around most of the day, sleep a lot, and complain they don't get any exercise," the Nisei remarked with a shrug.

As the two Americans left the tent of more Japanese officers, the corporal laughed. "A few days ago we gave the complaining officers seven shovels. So far they have not been touched."

"Better hope they don't use 'em to dig their way out," Higgins cautioned.

The corporal laughed again. "There have been no attempts to escape. They haven't eaten so well in years!" The POW camp had limited cooking facilities, but the prisoners dined on canned, boned American turkey.

There was one Japanese naval doctor in the POW compound. As the Americans approached, he saluted the corporal.

The Nisei laughed, turned to Higgins, and explained. "The doctor apparently doesn't know American ranks. I think he's afraid of officers."

Higgins watched as the prisoners filled in a swamp area. "From the way these Japanese work," he told the corporal, "one prisoner is equal to five Filipino laborers."

They walked through the camp until Higgins stooped to look into one of the shelters. He noticed that ten cots were crowded into a pyramid tent that would normally house four GIs. The enlisted Japanese prisoners stood and bowed. As the two strolled outside the prison compound, Higgins noticed that Filipino girls, allegedly selling fruit, were walking right into the GI tents.

Higgins spent the next morning researching Hiroshima and writing his speech. He followed a case study format he had used at the MG school to describe the infrastructure of a model city, estimating how many refugees the town could support.

His investigations occupied him off and on during the next four days and involved several trips to G-2 (Intelligence). Not for the first time in his military experience, Higgins kept getting blank stares and noncooperation. He was given a good map of Hiroshima prefecture only after considerable explanation, then insistence, then pulling rank. It was not large enough to use as an exhibit, so he gathered materials with which to make his own map.

His two tentmates kidded him about his cartographic skills. "It's nutty," Higgins muttered. "Just because they give you an area, you're supposed to be an expert!"

"What did you get from Intelligence?"

"Not very damn much! It's like pulling teeth to get data from that outfit."

Dressed for a call on the Del Monte plantation, Wally knocked at the front door of the main house.

"Come in, Commander. My name is Taylor. I'm manager of the plantation. What can I do for you?"

"Wallace Higgins. I just wanted to talk about the area. I'm going into Japan as a military governor, and I'm interested in your experience with the Japanese."

When they had settled in with cool pineapple drinks, the manager began to speak. "Before the war, the natives were all good workers," he said. "Until the Japanese came, there were a thousand Filipino employees and nine Americans with their families. Since then, the Filipinos have been following the ways of armed gamblers and thieves. Most of them are no longer eager to work. Right now there are twenty-thousand acres of pineapple in need of workers. I'm trying to use piecework as an incentive. The eight-hour day has been cut to six hours. Many workers have gone home, because for ten months of the year there's been no harvest. Right now we're spraying pineapples with hormones, hoping to get a normal crop." Taylor stopped, took a deep breath, and momentarily stared blankly at the floor. "We'll see. Now, about the Japanese..."

Higgins spent Saturday morning copying a map of the seaport town of Kure. For the first time since his arrival, he found dry ground and took a walk to see if there was any news.

He noticed a commotion as he approached the bulletin board. A hand-printed sheet was tacked to it:

NOTICE

Sept. 8, 1945
TO: ALL HANDS
1. Sunday Sept 9, 1945 will initiate "TRY TO BE KIND TO HIGGINS WEEK"
2. The least you can do is say "Good-morning Commander." It you don't feel that you can honestly wish HIM a good morning just pretend you're commenting on the weather. (If it should be raining it is good for the crops.)
3. It will not be necessary to shine his shoes nor place your coat in puddles for him to walk upon, however, all hands will refrain from holding him underwater in the swimming pool—more than 10 minutes at a time.

Signed: Personnel under obligation to Higgins and those who are looking for future favors from the Navy.

Higgins was privately pleased that his government team would make him the focus of good-natured razzing. The bulletin board also had an announcement about campaign medals. The notice said they would be entitled to the Philippine Liberation Medal with two bronze stars and the Pacific Theater Medal with two stars.

At assembly time Sunday afternoon, Higgins was ready. Major Burns helped him carry the maps to the edge of the low platform. Army officers and GIs filled the benches, sat on helmets and the grass. The crowd noise quieted as Lieutenant Commander Wallace Higgins was introduced. He stepped to the microphone.

"I've never been to Japan. As Will Rogers said, 'All I know is what I read in the papers.' I've gathered data from many sources, mostly prewar, plus intelligence reports. I hope it is more accurate than was compiled before the Okinawa engagement." Some of the combat veterans snickered. A few even laughed.

"My pronunciation may be off—like the sailor who said, 'I ain't never been to none of them there land-guage schools!'" As laughter spread through the crowd, Higgins grinned widely, and the sun reflected off his gold tooth.

"The present condition of the area we are going into should be in fair shape, outside of Hiroshima shi and Kure shi."

Higgins's large map of the prefecture was placed on the easel. He used a pointer to indicate areas of bomb damage to the cities and described conditions they might find.

"I am going to tell you the following things about Hiroshima ken: location, physical characteristics, size, climate, natural resources, industries, public utilities, agriculture, transportation, communications, public safety, public health, public welfare, labor, legal, education, forestry and fishing, banks, and government."

Higgins stepped to the map and traced the borders to be occupied by the Tenth Corps. "Location: These are the boundaries of the area we will occupy. Over here, the Fifth Division will occupy the Daizamo castle grounds.

"Size: We will occupy an area eighty-seven by seventy-five miles. That's about two-thirds the size of New Jersey. Before the war there was a population of 1,890,000. Hiroshima had 343,000, Kure 276,000, Fukuyama 63,000, Onomichi 48,000, Mihara 2,000 to 10,000.

"Physical characteristics—geographical and political: There are five cities, fifteen counties, or five towns and fifteen villages. The difference between Japan and the United States is that cities are not part of counties.

"Military: Hiroshima prefecture was a feudal headquarters. We know there are several military establishments." He pointed them out.

"Climate: The latitude of Norfolk with the climate of north Florida. The mean temperature is never below thirty-two or above eighty. Oranges are the principal fruit crop. Humidity is high in the summer rainy season. The growing season lasts 225 days.

"Natural resources: Forests, water power, cold springs, iron, copper, zinc, and fisheries. Three power plants on sixty-cycle three-phase 220 and 440 volts. There are twenty-five water systems.

"Industries: Forty-one percent is agricultural. The farms are small. Thirty percent is manufacturing: chemicals, textiles, rayon, abrasives, munitions, shipbuilding, food processing, machinery, metals, lumber, brewing, ice manufacturing, marine products, fruits, vegetables, and ceramics.

"Public utilities: There is gas in all the cities, but sewers in only three. Adequate water systems are in all cities, with twenty-five in the prefecture and two each in Hiroshima and Kure. We will find twenty-one electric generating stations, fourteen hydroelectric, six steam, one diesel. One produces fifty-one-thousand kilowatts."

Higgins paused a moment. "Are you all taking notes?"

After a ripple of laughter he plunged ahead.

"Agriculture: Although forty-one percent of the population is engaged on small farms, food is deficient. They raise rice, wheat, barley, vegetables, soybeans, fruits. As I say, our area is deficient the equivalent of about 200,000 tons of food per year. It will always be a deficient area, but this is not serious in view of easy water transport from surplus areas. In livestock, this is the largest cattle producer in Japan. They also raise hogs, horses, chickens, and rabbits. Most are tenant farmers. Those of you from American farms may understand this next set of data: There are sixteen-thousand horses—and seventeen thousand tons of "night soil"! Of course it's not all from the horses!

"Transportation: In the province there are fifteen railroads, Sanyo being the main line, then Sango Line, Geibi, and Saushin. There are two double tracks, thirty-two tunnels, 105 bridges. Six are electric, nine steam. Eight are government owned, five are private railroads, and two belong to the prefecture. All told, there are 360 miles of railroad in Hiroshima ken. There is a roundhouse and marshalling yards in Hiroshima. They have a good network of roads: 2,330 miles maintained by the prefecture, 114 miles of national, and 143 miles of village streets. Plus, there's a very extensive system of inland water routes.

"OK, let's look at communications. With twenty-five-thousand subscribers, we have a ratio of 1.25 phones per 100 population. There are two radio stations of ten-thousand watts. Newspapers: nineteen dailies, but some are only a single sheet. The province has 352 post offices.

"Public safety: There is one chief of police for the province, nine superintendents, forty-three wings, ninety-four assistants, 208 sergeants, and fifteen-hundred Jinsa—one for every 1,256 of population. At the prefectural level there are thirty-six police stations and ninety-five substations. The area has 415 call boxes, four prisons. The 399 fire departments have fifty-one trucks and several hundred pumps."

And thus it went. For the next twenty minutes, Higgins itemized data. When he finished, the audience applauded.

Later, as he sat enjoying the evening movie, *The Thin Man Returns*, several men stopped by to congratulate him on the talk.

Back in their tent, Major Burns joshed, "Boy, for a guy who starts out, 'All I know is what I read in the papers,' you sure can talk long!"

Added Carmon: "'Don't know much about Hiroshima.' Hah!"

"What the heck," Higgins replied. "Now I'm an *expert*. All I did was gather the information and pass it out!"

At Zamboanga on September 12 Higgins, Commander Morton and some other officers were given a who's who explanation of the groups going into Japan. Higgins was asked to repeat his talk on Hiroshima and Kure, and then some colonels joined the discussion as they were shown recent aerial views of Kure and Hiroshima. It was clear that Hiroshima had been leveled.

When Higgins got back to his tent, he learned that one of his military government team had arrived on a B-24 and the others would meet them at Okinawa.

At the Navy Club, Higgins was introduced to Mrs. Ambrosia MacCrohon. He ordered her a drink and pulled up a wicker chair. During the pleasantries, it became obvious to Higgins that she was a Filipino woman of some refinement.

"Have you lived here all your life?" Higgins asked.

"Yes, I was born right here in Zamboanga."

"Family?"

"I have three boys, ages eleven, thirteen, and fifteen."

"Hey, that's great! Would you believe I've got four boys, all in the service?"

The inevitable wallet-size pictures were brought out and examined. "I'm having a big birthday party on Tuesday at our home. Would you join us?" asked Mrs. MacCrohon. "I'd like to have you meet the boys."

"That's very gracious. I accept." After a moment, Higgins said, "Perhaps you could tell me about this area better than anyone I've met. What was it like here before...?"

"Before the war," she replied, "there were more Christians here than Moros. Now the Moros outnumber the Christians. The Moros played along with the Japs. Many of the Christians were killed...by guerrillas, by Japs, and by Moros."

"I'm awfully sorry!"

"A lot of my people...my friends...fled to the jungle."

"Maybe now they'll come back."

They talked more about families, and war, and hopes for the newfound peace. Higgins promised to visit even before the birthday party.

Later that afternoon, Higgins was introduced to Dick S. Kawamoto, his language instructor. A good-looking Oriental man about thirty years old, Kawamoto was a corporal in the United States Army. "I'm a naturalized citizen," he said, answering the question in Higgins's eyes. "Live in New York." Kawamoto had been born in Japan near Hiroshima, and educated at a school on the Inland Sea. He could obviously help with more than language, Wally noted.

On September 15 Higgins went to the local market with a Colonel Hamilton, who watched as the lieutenant commander stopped at one stall after another. Hamilton understood some of the purchases, like cigars and candy. But then Higgins bought flowers.

Hamilton's curiosity took over. "Now you're buying flowers? What's all that for? Have you found something interesting to do that the rest of us should know about?"

"Nothing of the sort!" Higgins laughed. "You recall I said I'd met a Mrs. MacCrohon the other day?"

"Right."

"I'm going to pay her a visit this afternoon, and the candy and flowers are for her."

"And she smokes cigars?"

"For her husband, of course."

They walked on a few paces before Hamilton spoke. "You really go out of your way to be sociable, don't you?"

"I try to do that, yes."

"Seems to me that going out of your way to meet people and get them talking would take a whole lot of extra energy."

"Not really. I enjoy it. I've always found I can learn more and get more done in my work if I get to know people and they get to know me."

Later, Higgins called on Mr. and Mrs. MacCrohon at their bamboo hut. He presented the gifts and met the rest of the family.

Early on, Higgins noticed a tension. As everyone became more relaxed the reason became evident: The MacCrohons needed to explain that they hadn't always lived so humbly.

"This hut is worth only 450 pesos," said Mrs. MacCrohon.

"Our former house burned down," added her husband. "It was worth fifteen-hundred pesos. I worked for a warehousing company before the war. Now I make $105. Twenty-one pesos per month."

By the end of his visit, Higgins had made more friends, had learned more about the Philippines, and was looking forward even more to the birthday party. On his return to camp, he regretted not having asked Hamilton or Burns or one of the others to accompany him on this social call. "They miss so much," Higgins thought, "by not seeing how others live."

Higgins also was determined to understand and speak some Japanese by the time he arrived in Hiroshima. The morning of Saturday, September 16 was an example. He filled pages and pages of practice paper, writing an English word and its Japanese equivalent.

ache — *itamu*
angry — *okotta*
also — *mo*
always — *itsumo*

Higgins got up to stretch and stepped out of the beachfront tent. Along the length of the bay, as far as he could see, were ships. Hundreds of Moros paddled their dugouts around the ships and dove for coins tossed by the Americans on board.

A seaman stopped in front of Higgins's and Morton's tent. "Grab your things, sirs! You're going on a two-day excursion."

Morton looked at his fellow officer. "What's this about?"

"No idea," Higgins said. "But I'm ready for a break from this language study. Let's go!"

They boarded a PT boat and soon they were skimming through the waves at breakneck speed. When they reached the island of

Basilan, their sixteen-foot boat was tied alongside a hundred other similar vessels.

Higgins and Morton were assigned to Raymond tents, two cots per tent. Inside, they found iceboxes, an RBO-2 radio, bedsheets, pillows, an electric fan, chairs, tables, and a stove.

"Eeow!" yelled Higgins. "All the comforts of home right here in the jungle."

In the head they found washbowls and mirrors.

"And look," exclaimed Morton, "showers, just like stateside!"

Their quarters were on a hill, overlooking the harbor. It was warmer than at Zamboanga, but there was cool spring water and plenty of cold beer. At mess, they dined on hearts of palm salad.

Back in their tent, Higgins turned on the radio and out came the strains of the Wayne King orchestra and the voice of Betty Grable. Higgins stood in the doorway and watched the harbor below as a PT boat went racing by, with Filipinos riding as passengers. That evening, a local band played in the officers club.

The next morning Higgins was awakened by a PA blaring reveille and a speaker announced, "All hands hit the deck!" The officers were free to relax or explore. Higgins spent one day visiting a rubber plantation and a second day just wandering and assessing the military presence.

As their sleek PT boat raced across the water on the way back to Zamboanga, Higgins imagined how nice it would be to own such a craft. "I'd sure like to have one of these some day!" he shouted to Commander Morton.

"So would I! Plans are to decommission them by the middle of November. The hulls are going to be abandoned or blown up."

"That's a damn shame!" Higgins yelled.

"Maybe not such a terrible loss when you consider each one of them costs four hundred bucks an hour to run."

Higgins had lunch aboard the USS Cecil, the destroyer that would take him to Japan. The next afternoon, September 18, he attended the MacCrohan birthday party. This time he was determined to bring some of his countrymen. He was accompanied by five other Navy men and three GIs. The MacCrohons had gone to considerable lengths to make their American guests welcome. They dined on chicken livers, fried duck, roast pig, tomatoes, cucumber salad, and biscuits. As daylight faded the local girls began dancing with the GIs.

Vincinetta, Mrs. MacCrohon's fifteen-year-old sister, becomingly dressed in a sarong, approached Higgins. "You like to dance, Pop?"

Although unfailingly polite, he later noted in his diary, "She was not a very good dancer."

With Higgins aboard, the Cecil headed due east on September 20 and laid off the war-ravaged island of Leyte all the next day. Two days later it was underway at 0600. The Cecil had become part of a twenty-five-ship flotilla and made its way between two flattops. The war may have been over, but no one was sure that some dissident *kamikaze* wouldn't attack in final desperation.

Still in equatorial waters the next day, Higgins found a stretcher, pulled it onto the after gun-deck to sunbathe, and watched the other twenty-four ships stretched out in formation as they raced north, headed for Okinawa.

Higgins continued his lessons with Kawamoto and studied Japanese for long periods. Sitting on the deck one evening, waiting for it to get dark enough for the evening movie, he admired the silhouetted ships. "Six weeks earlier," he thought, "this flotilla would have been under terrifying *kamikaze* attacks. But now, everything is serene. God, I wish all my friends could share this experience!"

Thirteen miles from the place the bomb had exploded over Hiroshima and seven miles from Kure, the young mother placed some sweet potatoes from the Kotani family garden on a square cloth and added a few meager belongings. She carefully tied the four corners of the *furoshiki*, or all-purpose carrier, so she could carry it.

For the second time in her life, Sueno Kotani Yoshida prepared to journey down to Kure and report to the police. Just a few years earlier she had been trained with sharpened bamboo spears as a volunteer in the Home Defense Corps to protect her country from the invading foreigners.

Now the war had ended, and the occupiers were coming soon. Heeding her emperors request to "endure," she would not fight them. But the military was pulling out of the huge Kure Naval Base, and the call had come for civilian *kamikaze* volunteers to meet the barbarians wherever they landed. Fujiwara-san, the local police chief, himself had sent word to her village of the urgent need.

Her mind was made up. Sueno would volunteer. She left her nine-year-old daughter and family, and headed to the city below to help the authorities.

On September 26 the USS Cecil was among hundreds of ships laying off Okinawa, spread out in the harbor as far as the eye could see. As the day began, Higgins counted six aircraft carriers against nature's magnificent backdrop, a beautiful double rainbow before a retreating rain squall.

Higgins studied Japanese all the next morning and went ashore at noon with a small party. He discovered hundreds of LSTs and LCIs along the beach, Jeeps and all kinds of trucks, and mud everywhere. A four-Jeep tour of Okinawa took them into the cave-honeycombed hills surrounding the harbor.

"Look at all the graves!" Higgins exclaimed.

"Okinawans bury the dead for three years," an escort told the occupants of Higgins's Jeep. "Community virgins then scrape the bones and lay them away in vaults as a form of ancestral worship."

Higgins knew that the war had added tens of thousands of Americans to the dead on this island alone—and a hundred thousand Japanese soldiers.

Higgins was wondering whether he would ever see Japan. These side trips were instructive and some were enjoyable, but he was getting more and more impatient to see Hiroshima's condition firsthand and take up his duties. September 28 began with a debarkation drill. Everyone went over the sides on nets. Higgins enjoyed the climbing exercise and was amused as he listened to a chaplain complain throughout the drill. By 1400, the ship was underway, but not toward their destination. A typhoon was coming and to avoid it the Cecil and a host of other ships laid off.

Higgins awoke to discover the Cecil was seventy miles southwest of Okinawa. When the sun broke through, they headed back eastward, following the edge of the storm. Higgins sunbathed and pencilled a summary of the past month and a half:

2 days flying time
1 day in Hawaii
2 days in Manila
7 days at 6th Army Headquarters in San Fernando
10 days with Tenth Corps at Mindanao
10 days with the 41st Division at Zamboanga
10 days on ship to Japan
2 days at Okinawa

Have met Generals Krueger, Seibert, , Boyd, Admiral Rogers, Captains Carry and Pope.

In the Harbor at Okinawa, the missing members of Higgins's Military Government Team B-12 caught up with their commander and came aboard for a joyful reunion. The USS Cecil sailed out of the harbor and joined a mighty armada headed for Japan.

In Mentor, Ohio, Adelaide Higgins repeatedly read her husband's letters, but she still couldn't believe what she read. He informed her he would not be home for a year, perhaps more. Not even a short leave. On top of that, her children, all grown, had written of their plans to attend college on the GI Bill.

"Men are supposed to come home after a war," she thought. "They aren't supposed to wander off." She found herself roaming from room to empty room. Then she would sit at the big kitchen table with her coffee, angrily jabbing at the ashtray with half-smoked cigarettes. She had very much hoped that when the war ended all her men would come home. There would be the familiar warmth and laughter, and a feeling of usefulness. Instead, she was alone, and the house was too large to manage by herself and too full of memories.

She sold most of the furniture, packed her things, and moved into a small cottage around the corner. It was certainly big enough until Wally returned from Japan.

THREE

Into
Hiroshima ken

One group of thirty-five ships in the American flotilla peeled away from the formation as it passed Kyushu, the southernmost of the Japanese main islands, leaving twenty-five ships carrying the Tenth Corps, the Forty-first Infantry Division, and Military Government Team B-12. They all turned into Bungo Suido, the straits that separate the islands of Kyushu, Shikoku, and the main island of Honshu. Protected by carrier air cover, none of the feared *kamikaze* planes appeared as the ships entered the Japanese Inland Sea.

On October 5 the ships lay off of Hiro, at the foot of hills facing the Inland Sea. From the deck of the Cecil, Higgins studied the map he had obtained to accompany his talks and compared it with what he could see. He had scurried for more detailed information when he heard the name Hiro. At first he thought it might be a contraction for "Hiroshima." Then he learned of a town called Hiroo, but that turned out to be in northern Japan. Hiro was simply what Higgins would call a small suburb, a mile east of Kure.

A hilly peninsula protected Kure Harbor, the nearly landlocked anchorage of Japan's largest naval base. Kure and Hiroshima were close, near the southern end of the main island of Honshu. The

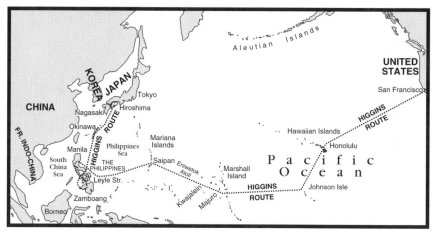

Map of the Pacific and Higgins's route

Inland Sea cut a twenty-five-mile wide crescent into the land. At the middle of the curve, beyond the mountain to the west, lay Hiroshima.

The signal was given for the advance party to go ashore, and Higgins descended to the landing craft. As the landing boats touched the shore at Hiro, soldiers of the Forty-first Division dashed ahead to establish a defense perimeter. When, just moments later, a sergeant waved all clear from the far side of the beach, Commanding Officer General Jens A. Doe of the Forty-first, Lieutenant Commander Higgins, and Corporal Kawamoto stepped down the ramp and onto the beach.

There was no resistance—in fact, there was no visible life of any sort. The village was eerily quiet, the streets deserted, with the homes' and shops' *amado*, or wooden doors, tightly closed. To hide from the horrible treatment that was sure to befall them, young women and children had fled to back country hills or concealed themselves deep within the buildings. Adjacent to the beach, rows of barracks stood empty. The only movement was a slight breeze blowing through the deserted buildings.

As they neared the center of the village, a small delegation approached the Americans. Doe, Higgins, and Kawamoto were met by police, a few government authorities, and the kamikaze corps of volunteers who had agreed to face death by serving as domestics and laborers for the invading barbarians.

Pretty thirty-two-year-old Sueno Kotani Yoshida and her friend Nobuko were among the volunteers. Hiding at the back of the small group, hoping not to be noticed and dreading the worst, they wore the baggy *monpe* work clothes of domestic laborers. Sueno tried to keep her eyes cast downward, but curiosity finally overcame her. During the brief moment when she looked up to witness the aliens, she caught the glance of the one in the Navy uniform. A jumble of fear and fascination flew through her, and, mortified, her gaze returned to the ground.

At the front of the Japanese delegation, volunteer interpreters Elsie Yamamoto and Takeo Yamamura introduced Fujiwara-san, the local chief of police. Dressed in a black uniform, the small but muscular chief removed his billed cap with a sweeping motion and bowed low to the Americans. Higgins was also cordial, for he knew that it was not the Japanese army or navy the Allies would be dealing with, but the Japanese police. Although he was only in his mid-thirties, the chief wielded influence Higgins respected.

Fujiwara-san led the delegation in bowing and welcoming the Americans. *"Kangei shiteorimasu! Dohzo yoroshiku."*

"Welcome. I am happy to meet you!" Kawamoto translated.

As Kawamoto helped Higgins converse with the police chief, everyone came to understand it was the American's intention to

Kure as seen by occupation forces, October 5, 1945

A Japanese aircraft carrier rests on the bottom of Kure Harbor.

move to a suitable headquarters in the Kure area. Doe, Higgins, Fujiwara-san, and Kawamoto crowded into a Jeep and led the procession of Army trucks and Jeeps around the small mountain toward Kure. As men of the combat-savvy Forty-first forged ahead to secure the road from Hiro to Kure, they discovered the entire route was already guarded by Japanese police standing at fifty-yard intervals. Higgins could say nothing to the men in the Jeep, but the positioning of the police intrigued him. They faced the countryside,

Japanese Midget "suicide" submarines being burned out before they were cut up for scrap.

as if to protect the invaders—as though fearing nothing from the Americans. It would not be the last time Higgins wondered at Japanese courtesy and logic.

The end of the three-mile trip around the mountain to Kure was littered with debris from conventional bombs. Out in the harbor they could see, jutting from the water, the twisted superstructures of Imperial Navy battleships, cruisers, destroyers, and aircraft carriers that had been bombed by the U.S. Army Air Corps or scuttled. Four dozen midget suicide submarines, neatly tied to the docks, caught the attention of the Americans.

Kawamoto explained that the whole harbor area at the foot of Kure had been occupied by the naval base. The road to the barracks crossed a narrow bridge so their procession slowed, and Higgins had plenty of time to see there was much to be done. Bombing and the typhoon that had hit just days earlier had left the deserted base in ruins, but Higgins was able to set up shop in one of the buildings near the edge of the complex.

General MacArthur's orders to mete out severe penalties for rape or pillage had encouraged the Americans to return the Japanese people's courtesy in kind. And it worked: GIs were businesslike and friendly to any Japanese who ventured out. In Higgins's opinion, these first occupiers were behaving magnificently. The supreme

The city of Hiroshima, October 8, 1945, as seen by Commander Higgins

commander had issued another order, however, that was somewhat unusual for occupying forces. Americans were to subsist on their own rations and were prohibited from taking any local food supplies.

Working around the clock, it took the team two days to reconnoiter and set up the Kure area. They established their billets on the North Camp area at Hiro. The military government headquarters, the labor camp, and occupation headquarters were set up on the Kure Naval Base.

It was just nine weeks after the August 6 explosion when Higgins led the first Allied inspection trip into Hiroshima. Approaching the devastated area of the city on the morning of October 8, he noticed that one side of everything left standing was blackened. Stubs of trees, telephone poles, posts, solid buildings, walls, chimneys, and all wooden structures were incinerated.

Their vehicle stopped in a leveled area, and Wally got out to kick aside some debris. He bent down and picked up a small dish. One side was beautiful—white, with part of a flower painted on the ceramic. The other side was gnarled, black, and further blemished with a puffy, purple blister.

"Look at this," he said, showing it to Kawamoto, his driver.

"What is it, Commander?"

From rubble under the overhang of a damaged building in Hiroshima, Wally retrieved a blistered dish, which he later shipped home to Ohio.

"Just a saucer. But it's so beautiful on this side, and you turn it around to the part exposed to the blast, and it's so damned ugly." Higgins dropped it into a bag.

"What're you going to do with it?" Kawamoto asked.

"Send it back to the wife. Souvenir."

The corporal started to say something, but decided to let it go.

The city of Hiroshima appeared increasingly flattened as the motorcade moved toward the bomb's epicenter. Most corpses had been removed, but many gruesome sights remained. Higgins's nausea grew as they passed dazed survivors stumbling along, a few pushing carts of meager belongings.

Moving away from the levelled part of the city, the inspection team stopped to visit a hospital. The crowded wards were full of patients with burns. Higgins thought how some wounds resembled the blister on the ceramic dish in his bag. As they left the hospital he remarked, "Hard to miss that place lacked sanitation."

"You're right," said General Doe, "but that seems to be true throughout the area."

"Everywhere you look, open ditches are being used as toilets. This whole Hiroshima area needs sanitation facilities, procedures."

"You've got my support. Go ahead and get something built!"

Back in Kure, Higgins started the requisitions and paperwork. Using the Japanese word for toilet he called it The Benjo Project, and ordered modern latrines for the base and the cities of Kure and Hiroshima. Cement for the foundations came from a prefecture plant, and lumber was brought in by the Americans. It was the beginning of a long list of projects Wally jotted in his book:

> Recruit laborers, electricians, carpenters, drivers, interpreters and others for the immediate job of cleaning up damage caused by the recent typhoon. Provide living quarters for the military units. Secure all Japanese military installations. Collect small arms. Destroy heavy armament and ammunition. Check hospital facilities, water supplies, sanitary conditions.

Laborers were recruited through Kobayashi-san, the local labor representative. From the volunteer corps of civilians, Higgins found

seven who understood both Japanese and English, and established
the Military Government Section Interpreters.

Before long, the local people realized the victors had not come to
punish them at all. Children began peering from the corners of buildings
and smiling back at the grinning GIs. Civilians began appearing on
the streets, and stores began opening for the sale of daily necessities.
Soon the GIs had enticed out the kids with candy bars and gum, and
word spread of the Americans' visits to hospitals with food, medicine, and kindness. No one smiled wider than Wally Higgins, who
eagerly passed out American candy and an occasional C ration.

One day when investigating an abandoned building on the naval
base, Higgins found a document that looked especially interesting.
When he had it translated, he realized how right he was. The pages
described the Japanese version of the start of war with the United
States. Higgins read with interest.

> Dec. 8, 1941
>   11:45 a.m. An Imperial Edict declaring war on the U.S.
> and Britain was issued.
>   3:05 A.M. (Hawaiian time 7:35 a.m.), our Navy attacked
> the Pearl Harbor and exterminated the US Pacific Fleet.
>   Our Army and Naval Air Forces carried out surprise
> attacks on various air-fields in the Philippine Islands.
>   At Shanghai, our Navy bombarded and sank a British gun
> boat, Petrel, while the U.S. gun-boat surrendered. Our forces
> occupied the Foreign Settlement of Shanghai.
>   At dawn, our Air Force attacked Hongkong.
>   The US marine corps in Peking and Tiensin were dis-
> armed.
>   Our troops peacefully entered Thailand.
>   At dawn, our army forces landed in Malay Peninsula in
> the face of the enemy.
> Dec. 10
>   The Emperor praised our Navy for its great achievements
> in Hawaii sector, bestowed an Imperial Edict on our Com-
> bined Fleet.
>   Our army and naval forces, conjointly, landed at Guam
> Island and also in the northern sectors of Luzon Island.
>   Our air-force sank the British battle-ships, Prince of Wales
> and Repulse, off the east coast of Malay Peninsula.

Dec. 12

The Emperor praised the extermination of the main force of the British Far East Fleet and again gave an Edict to Admiral I. Yamamoto, Commander-in-chief of our Combined Fleet.

The Guam Island was completely occupied. The crack forces of our army and navy land in the southern sectors of Luzon Island.

One day, as he plunged into the ever-increasing flow of papers on his desk, Higgins discovered a formal-looking envelope. The invitation from Fujiwara-san stated that Higgins's entire military government team, the provost marshall, and the commanding officer of the infantry division were invited to a sake party. After checking with the others to make certain they could attend, he sent word of their acceptance.

Early on, the police chief let Higgins know he wanted to show his gratitude for the humane treatment and cooperation shown by the occupation authorities and by the military government team in particular. So for the party, Fujiwara-san, his assistant, and the other city officials had gone all out. A long, low table down the center of the eighty-mat *tatami* room in one of the surviving large buildings groaned under the weight of chicken, sake, baked tai, beer, sukiyaki, fruits—and more beer and more sake.

The Americans sat amongst their Japanese hosts, and a geisha attended each guest, endlessly filling the sake cups. For several hours there were countless toasts. "To a long and lasting peace." "To the Americans." "To MacArthur." "To the hosts." Regardless of how many times they were drained, the beer glasses and sake cups always seemed to be full.

The geisha began performing their traditional dances at the end of the room, but as the drinking continued they outdid themselves with some not-so-traditional risque interpretations. There was loud and boisterous singing, much of it led by Wally Higgins.

Suddenly there was silence. All eyes stared at the spot where a geisha had just been dancing. The police chief stood there, completely disrobed except for a loincloth, going through strange motions and grunting.

"What's he saying?" Higgins asked the interpreter next to him.

American guests arrive for a sake party on October 10, 1945, in the largest surviving building in Kure.

"Ahhh...Fujiwara-san is the judo champion of the prefecture. He is probably too drunk to know what he is doing."

"I can see that, but what the hell is he yelling about?"

"Actually, he is challenging one and all to a wrestling match!"

The explanation was passed to all the Americans in the room while the other Japanese officials tried to discourage the chief. One attempted to pull him down, but failed.

Higgins looked around. Since MG officers were not selected for their athletic abilities, it was obvious that none of the American officers present was about to take up the challenge. He looked at the infantry CO. In his fifties, he obviously had never been an athlete. The provost marshall had been called out of retirement for the war and was well beyond the age for physical competition. Higgins reasoned that the older man might have taken on the chief in his younger days, but this particular night he was too busy trying to find out, as he phrased it, "what makes a geisha tick." The medical officer was young enough, but he was a little guy and looked scared to death. Higgins's director of the economy seemed busy taking inventory of food and drinks, trying hard to completely ignore the proceedings. The remaining guests were either out cold or playing dead.

At forty-seven, Higgins was no youngster. With a potbelly and completely bald head, he looked entirely out of shape. But in his case, looks were deceiving. Only two years earlier he had been top man in the Great Lakes Naval District strength test, which all officers and men were supposed to take monthly. He had scored 426 points of a possible five hundred, highest in the district, regardless of age. Wally also had been a runner all his life and had recently been swimming a mile or so a day. After leaving the U.S. Naval Academy, where he was on the wrestling team, he had wrestled competitively for a number of years. Then, too, he outweighed Fujiwara-san by thirty pounds.

In his drunken stupor, Higgins figured the odds were all in his favor. He got to his feet, undressed down to his shorts, and walked to the improvised ring area at the end of the table. There he began to mimic the antics of the Japanese chief. Laughter rose from some of the American guests; others groaned. A few applauded. All drinking stopped.

As the two combatants circled one another, it occurred to Higgins that the chief was not wearing the traditional Judo wrestling jacket that, with its waistband, could have given the commander a leverage advantage. Both were obviously pretty drunk. They grappled, then fell to the mat. The American shifted his hold from a headlock to a reverse nelson and body hold, giving him the leverage to exert enormous pressure on the chest and stomach of Fujiwara-san, whose shoulders were now pinned to the mat. Higgins used his weight and strength to apply more than the required punishment, then shifted even more weight and leverage onto the Japanese.

Fujiwara-san grunted as he exhaled. *"Iki ga kurushii!"* ("I can't breathe!")

"Give up?"

"Hai!"

The American released his hold and staggered to his feet, grinning. It had taken only a minute.

Gasping for breath and shaking his head, the loser rolled over and got to his knees. He rested a moment, then let out a hearty laugh. *"Ya-a-ah. Tanoshikatta."* ("That was fun.")

The Japanese police chief slowly got up, rubbing his side. He was smiling from ear to ear. Fujiwara-san had obviously enjoyed the contest. *"Ha ha! America-jin no kachi!"* The chief bowed to the American, threw his arm around his shoulder, and proposed a toast.

From that moment on, Fujiwara-san and Higgins built a lasting friendship.

The morning after the party Higgins was in a vile mood. The Americans needed six-hundred laborers.

"Must say very sorry," said Kobayashi-san, the labor representative. Smiling his best toothy grin, he continued to apologize to the American labor officer. "Can get maybe about three-hundred workers for tomorrow."

Suspecting Kobayashi-san of passive resistance, Higgins exploded. "If there are not six-hundred laborers reporting here tomorrow," he shouted, shaking his fist in the face of the Japanese, "I will personally push every tooth down your throat!"

On October 12, 625 laborers reported for work at the American camp. Higgins wondered if Fujiwara-san might have passed the word about the wrestling match, but, when they met later that day, Fujiwara-san never mentioned it. Instead, the chief told him he had a surprise. Fujiwara-san was obviously enjoying himself as he recounted the events of the previous night to all within earshot. He raised Higgins's hand in the air, mimicking a referee announcing the victor, and laughed.

"The chief would like to reward the champ with a boat," Kawamoto translated. He explained that the Japanese had scuttled eight new forty-five-foot diesel-powered motor launches at a secret location. The launches had been used to ferry naval officers and midshipmen from Kure to Etajima, where the Japanese naval academy had been located.

"The motor launches have inside cabins with a seating capacity for fifteen passengers," Fujiwara-san explained. "I shall raise one and have my men recondition it for the champion of Hiroshima ken!"

The two Americans and the Japanese police chief got in Higgins's Jeep and wound their way down to the water's edge of a narrow inlet. At first, Higgins only observed that other Japanese warships were being stripped and carved for scrap. Tied to their pens in the harbor, smoke erupted from the interiors of the one-man submarines. The torches of Japanese workmen and American Seabees were burning them out and cutting them up.

Fujiwara-san led him to a spot on the bank and directed his attention almost straight down. He made out the shapes of eight wooden motor launches resting in ten feet of water.

"That one would be easiest to get." The chief pointed and Kawamoto translated. "But you pick any one you want."

"That one will do very nicely," Higgins agreed.

Back at the naval base, Higgins asked the commanding officer of the Kure area for permission to raise a launch for his personal use.

"That'll be OK," the CO said, "provided you also have one conditioned for me."

Within a week, Higgins's launch was being repainted and made ready to go back in the water for testing. The engine had been overhauled and reinstalled. Higgins decided to name it The Good Ship Titanic in honor of his favorite Navy party song, and Fujiwara-san had the name painted on the bow in English.

During the week after landing on Japan's shore, Higgins made inspection trips to factories in Kure, Hiroshima, Onomichi, and Takehara. He was bowed to and flattered by managers of shipyards, steel plants, rayon works, machine shops, and chemical complexes. Everyone was struggling with poor conditions.

Everywhere he went the Japanese were exceptionally friendly and cooperative. No one was more helpful than Fujiwara-san, who could be counted on at any time to give the military government commander the truth. His tips were invaluable, like the time the chief led him to a cache of ninety cases of what Fujiwara-san described as "good old Suntory!" A Japanese naval officer had hidden the supply in a farmhouse several miles from Hiroshima. Half of it was in half-pint bottles, spiked for the use of *kamikaze* pilots who drank it before they made their strikes.

Higgins used these bottles to barter with the Navy supply ships off Kure in exchange for beef, turkey, fresh vegetables, officers mess gear, china, table and bed linens, and other items the Army club could not get.

When Fujiwara-san presented the Titanic to Higgins it had been completely reconditioned as a pleasure craft with bunks to sleep four passengers plus the crew. Fujiwara-san thoughtfully provided an engineer and two deckhands, who always seemed to be on hand

The Good Ship Titanic, with the services of chief Isamu Shoji and its crew of three, was given to Wally Higgins for winning the wrestling match at a sake party during the first week of the occupation.

when the commander wanted to cruise the Inland Sea or make an inspection trip. Try as he might, Higgins was unable to find out if the crew had any duties away from his boat. He reasoned that just maybe they had no better place to live.

On the last day of October 1945, Higgins sat in his office late at night. It bothered him that in less than a month Allied soldiers were behaving in ways that revealed a lack of understanding of Japanese customs. Accustomed to walking in the narrow streets, Japanese civilians were in danger from Jeeps and trucks driving on the wrong side. Innkeepers and shop owners winced as Americans walked inside their establishments with heavy shoes and combat boots, cutting the fragile *tatami* mats.

He wrote:

> I wonder how we would feel if a force of arrogant occupation troops came into our cities—occupied all our important buildings, drove pedestrians off streets—sat around offices with feet on desks—destroyed all our resources? How do the Japanese actually feel? Their attitude is one of complete subjugation and cooperation. But I cannot forget that only a few short months ago the nation was united in fanatical support of the war. Volunteers were numerous for suicidal efforts to win. Kamikaze planes and suicide submarines. What goes on

inside these people? Are they sincerely repentant? Or is it a game to get rid of occupation early? Or are they that sold on the emperor that they blindly follow and obey?

What about Kato, Hattori, Ohbayashi and others: heads of plants; former kings of all their domain; used to being bowed to—why do they bow to our crude handling? Will it last? Or, are "fires" being kindled inside? Do we care? We have an opportunity to show the Japanese how good or how stupid we are.

We may want a strong ally here against Russia. The Japanese cannot like our cutting up their ships for scrap. But, then, neither does Russia. Perhaps it is just as well not to have the ships available for "reparation." Maybe we will need Kure and the Inland Sea sooner than we think. Maybe we will need the Japs here also!

In a makeshift shelter a mile from Higgins's office, Sueno Kotani Yoshida kept waking from a fitful sleep in the cramped quarters of her friend, Nobuko-san, who also worked for the occupation force, cleaning buildings at the navy base. Sueno had moved in with her friend after it became clear that the charcoal-burning bus that traveled the seven miles from the Kotani home to the base was entirely unreliable. Because the cleaning never seemed to end and the long walk over the mountain was difficult, she had managed only one visit home on a rare day off. She wanted her daughter to be with her, but where could they stay? There was hardly room for two in Nobuko-san's meager shelter, much less three. She had made it this far, though, "working with resolution" as the emperor had instructed.

FOUR

Winter of Hardship

By the beginning of November 1945, much of the debris from the *pika don*—or flash bang—and the additional damage from the recent typhoon had been cleared away, and the devastated metropolis of Hiroshima was reawakening.

Higgins hunched over his desk at the military government office in Kure, developing a list of his priority projects for the prefecture. His main concerns were the Benjo Project, lumber and firewood shortages, a mess hall and food for Japanese workers, disposition of ammunition, and road repair. The list included the need for a policy regarding reconversion and reparations of Japan Steel, Hikari Naval Arsenal, Kure Naval Base, the Eleventh Navy Aeronautical Base, and Mizuno Shipyard. He reminded himself of the need to inspect and inventory all plants and warehouses, and noted there were no Navy clubs on shore for officers or enlisted men.

Higgins folded the paper and stuffed it in his breast pocket so he could revise it on the go. Although he chipped away at them daily, the problems at the landing area of Kure and the southern part of the main island of Japan only intensified over the winter.

Dick Kawamoto tapped the door frame as he entered. "Commander, excuse please. This was hand delivered this morning."

His interpreter gave Higgins an elaborately decorated folder containing an invitation to a party that evening sponsored by the Japanese Businessmen's Organization of Hiroshima ken.

Higgins examined the invitation for a moment. "Dick, give this to Major Renchard and tell him I'd appreciate it if he'd go as the military government representative." He handed the invitation back to Kawamoto. "And Dick, call and convey my regrets that I'm unable to attend personally."

His recent experience with this group was all too fresh in his mind. The organization, similar to a chamber of commerce, had invited leaders of each section of the American occupation forces to a party at the bazaar in Hiro. Seven American officers attended. Higgins had stayed in his quarters at North Camp in Hiro that night to write letters and pack a box of souvenirs.

The Japanese hosts made a big mistake: Contrary to normal custom, they failed to pay the geisha girls, who, as professional entertainers, were traditionally paid to dance, sing, serve, and flatter the guests. When the geisha found out they weren't going to get paid, they proceeded to get drunk. As soon as one girl passed out the party was over.

At 9:30 p.m. the quiet of the bachelor officers quarters was shattered. Five American officers and five Japanese girls barged into Higgins's quarters, arguing and yelling. By 11:30, he had managed to get the two Navy commanders to the boat and return to the BOQ. All was quiet by midnight, but he had decided right then that he must move to quieter housing off base as soon as he could find a suitable home. And he had vowed to be friendly, but circumspect, with the Businessmen's Organization of Hiroshima ken.

Higgins paused at Kawamoto's desk as he prepared to leave.

"Corporal, I'm taking the Jeep over to Takehara. I'll be back late this afternoon."

"Ah...sir...will you need me to go as interpreter?"

"I don't think so, Dick. I'll be meeting Ohbyashi-san, and he speaks good English. Besides, it'll give me a chance to test my Japanese." Higgins had noticed that Dick and another interpreter had been spending time together both in and out of the office. Higgins paused, and, with a wry smile, asked, "You need some work?"

"No, Commander, I've got lots of translation to do…"

"With Takeo Yamamura?"

"No, sir. That would be with Miss Yamamoto."

"Miss Yamamoto?" He pretended not to place the name.

"Elsie, sir."

"Ah, of course. Elsie." Higgins swung his Navy cap low to the floor, bent in an exaggerated bow, and, emphasized each syllable. "*Sah-YOH-nah-rah!*"

At Takehara, he had lunch with Mr. Ohbayashi, a well-educated businessman in his fifties. The characteristic that fascinated Higgins was a streak of silver that ran from the middle of Ohbayashi-san's forehead back through his full head of dark hair. His square face sported a small dark mustache.

Higgins trusted Ohbayashi to some degree because he had been most cooperative in assisting the occupation and had taught Higgins a lot about Japanese customs and local industries. The two conversed in English, but once in a while Higgins tested his limited Japanese.

After lunch, accompanied by additional managers, they went to a warehouse that was being cleared of rifles, caissons, mortars, and precision instruments. Higgins noted the inventory of linoleum, felt, and rubber being left in the warehouse. As they discussed the problems of what products were needed and possible to produce in the plant with the dawn of peacetime, Ohbayashi's business acumen proved far more helpful than Higgins's other translators. The Japanese businessman's insight was the very thing Higgins needed to help him effectively govern the province.

After the meeting they walked alone a distance from the warehouse. "Ohbayashi-san," Higgins said, "I need you to come work for me at Kure as labor officer. Please think about it."

As he drove back to Kure, admiring the mountains and small farms to one side of the road and the sea on the other, Higgins recalled something Ohbayashi had said: "The nice thing about Japan is you're never out of sight of the mountains or the sea."

Throughout the Inland Sea area of Japan, which was being occupied by a huge fleet of American and Allied naval ships, there was no club for visiting sailors or officers. Launches discharged naval personnel with nowhere to go and nothing to do. Local establishments were overwhelmed. Higgins stopped at the club under construction and was pleased to see it was nearly finished.

Higgins, "Red" Hilliard, and Dick Kawamoto were late getting started to Onomichi. The drive was difficult, what with the narrow roads without guardrails and Dick fighting the sun's glare off the Inland Sea as he drove the Jeep northeast. They stopped briefly at a kimono shop in Takehara where Higgins bought several kimonos for Christmas gifts. After they had checked into the hotel, Higgins located the local police chief, and they walked through the colorful bazaar, where the commander bought more souvenirs.

Mr. Ohbayashi, the police chief, the labor chief, and six Japanese girls joined the three Americans for a sukiyaki dinner. When they had finished eating, they all stayed seated on the padded floor and began to sing. The Americans went first.

"Now you sing to us," Higgins urged the Japanese. "Sing a local song."

When they stopped, he said, "Please, sing that one again."

They sang it again.

"Once more," Higgins asked. "Slowly." He turned to Kawamoto. "Dick, get these words written down."

The translator looked at his supervisor quizzically.

"I don't mean in real Japanese. Phonetically, so I'll have a reference."

Dutifully Kawamoto transcribed the lyrics as best he could, but his boss would have to remember the melodies. On their way back to the hotel the translator asked the commander, "Why do you want all these words to songs?"

"Something happens when people sing together." Higgins smiled his wide, gold-tooth smile. "I've had a passion for group singing ever since I sang in the glee club at Annapolis during the first war. Call it morale, camaraderie, or whatever. I'm pleased the Japanese share my enjoyment."

Higgins stood in the Japanese bath house, lathering his body. He had reached for rinse water when a girl approached and began to scrub his back.

"Not bad!" he thought.

She poured hot water from a gourd-shaped ladle over his back. Then, lifting the ladle higher, she poured some over his bald head and giggled.

With the soap rinsed from his body, Higgins slowly entered the very hot water and settled in up to his neck. The girl sat on the side of the pool.

"Watashi Onomichi Hatoba no umare yo..." Higgins began to sing.

When he paused the girl sang the next phrase of *Onomichi Ondo*: *"Defune Irifune mite kurasu yo."*

Together, his rich baritone and her sweet soprano reverberated off the walls of the small bath house and completed the duet.

They sang another song, then he motioned an invitation for her to join him in the pool. She dropped her kimono, washed, and casually entered the bath.

When he crawled onto the futon that night, Higgins still felt the heat within his body. He slept soundly, Japanese style, on the floor.

Higgins continued his team's inspection tour at the Onomichi Shipyards.

"This yard can turn out a two-thousand ton merchant vessel every six months," said the yardmaster.

"Very impressive," Higgins told him. "By the way, I want to compliment you on your command of English."

"Thank you. I lived in America for seven years."

A short Jeep ride took the party of Americans and their Japanese guides to an industrial stamping plant. When introductions were completed, Ohbayashi explained, "The plant is seeking work."

"Why not try pressing out helmets for pails?" Higgins suggested.

"Ah, so!" the manager replied. "Everybody in Japan needs pail to carry water. We have many helmet. Ahh, we may! *Yoshi. Shohchi shimatshita.*"

Despite the retooling in some arenas the Japanese maintained other successful—and innovative—production methods. One day at the hotel, Higgins, Hilliard, and Kawamoto breakfasted on C rations, steak, onions, potatoes, and synthetic coffee. Although the C rations and coffee were nothing to mention in a restaurant review, the steaks were extraordinary.

"You know why these steaks are butter tender?" Kawamoto asked.

Knowing they were letting themselves in for a small lecture, Hilliard and Higgins looked at the man of two worlds. "Why, Dick?" they asked in unison.

"In this beef-raising part of southern Honshu, the farmers take the cattle into their homes a month before the steer is ready for slaughter. They feed it a beer diet and apply hand massages daily."

"You're kidding!" Red looked at Dick in disbelief.

"No, I'm not. The beer is massaged all through the muscles of the steer, and it tenderizes the steak."

"Tender meat from contented steers!" added Higgins. "Come to think of it, I'd get pretty tender, too, with that treatment!"

Leaving Onomichi they stopped to pick up Ohbayashi at his home. The three Americans were introduced to Mrs. Ohbayashi, who gave the commander flowers, an antique ceremonial headdress, and a scarf. As they drove off in the Jeep, Higgins put the headdress on his bald head, then wrapped the scarf around his neck and, waving to Mrs. Ohbayashi, called, *"Sayonara!"*

Later, in his diary, he wrote:

> Riding through town like a conquering hero...another perfect day!

But other days were not so perfect. At the office, Higgins had bumped up against a typical interservice problem. The clubs for officers and enlisted men on the Hiroshima ken shore were complete, yet inadequately supplied. His command was under Army jurisdiction, but he had managed to get Navy service clubs built on Army territory to be used by the visiting fleet. So, the Army reasoned, stocking the Navy clubs was not the Army's responsibility.

On the afternoon of November 6, carrying a load of *kamikaze* Suntory, The Good Ship Titanic and its crew were called into service by Lieutenant Commander Higgins to take a tour of ships in Kure Harbor. He knew that a Navy supply ship lay at anchor, laden with supplies. Onboard the American ship, the commander promised Higgins he would send eggs and spoons ashore. Some Suntory was brought aboard and the commander continued his tour.

Higgins also had other bartering tools. During the winter of 1945, nearly all the swords in Japan were collected and shipped back to America as souvenirs. General MacArthur's concern was that taking the million or more swords from the Japanese might pose a threat and cause unnecessary loss of face, so he announced that the Japanese could sell or give their swords to American servicemen voluntarily. As the military governor of Hiroshima prefecture, Higgins did his share by collecting and distributing dozens of the swords to the skippers, executive officers, and supply officers of ships that called at Kure. In exchange, his forty-five-foot motor launch carted goods to shore that Army clubs, personnel, and Japanese friends could not otherwise obtain.

Still, everything seemed to be an uphill fight. "What a hell of a way to run a railroad!" Higgins muttered as he sat at his desk in Building 8, working through one knotty labor problem after another. Lumber trucks were late, so work on his Benjo Project had halted.

While his instincts drew him to inspect factories and other business operations, Higgins forced himself to also tour hospitals. He invited Mr. Ohbayashi to drive with him on such a visit in Itsukaichi, on the east side of Hiroshima. Higgins still hoped Ohbayashi would become his assistant and take over labor affairs.

They had just finished going through one of the hospital wards when the military governor took a doctor and some nurses aside for a private conversation. As Higgins left the floor, Ohbayashi hung back for a quick word with one of the staff.

"What was that about?" he asked.

"The commander wanted to know about her," the nurse said, motioning toward a girl. "Her condition is very poor, and there is no money for her operation or her care."

"What did the commander say?"

"He said to go ahead, that he would pay from his own pocket."

On the drive back to Kure, Higgins figured that since Ohbayashi had not come forward to accept his job offer, he would give it one more attempt, and then give up.

"You know," Higgins began, "things are getting complex. We've got many projects underway."

"Yes "

"By the end of this month the labor count is going to be over three thousand."

"Yes."

"I guess you've forgotten about my request."

"To join your staff?"

"That's the one."

"To the contrary. I would be honored."

In his desire to move out of the BOQ, Higgins had found a small house and moved in. He would use it for entertaining until General Doe was transferred and his house became available. The new director for labor matters in Hiroshima prefecture had also moved, and Higgins decided it was fitting that he introduce him with a party at Mr. Ohbayashi's own house.

The gathering was for Americans and Japanese involved in the labor needs of the occupation. More and more frequently, Higgins brought Japanese authorities and businessmen together socially with American occupation leaders. When he did he would pick up knowledge—and songs. At this event a former Japanese naval commander taught Higgins another Japanese song: "*Chan nuge—Chan nuge—Chan—Chan Nuge Nuge—Changa naga hada...*" Higgins wrote down the words to the entire song.

Arriving at Miyajima, Americans were startled to see women doing the heavy work, such as carrying fifteen bricks at once.

The massiveness of the war munitions that Japan had held in reserve—and that could have been used against American invaders—was brought home to Higgins when he went to Miyajima in late November. Ohbayashi and Kawamoto accompanied him to a former powder plant on the island where munitions were being gathered from all of southern Japan.

They walked into a beehive of activity. Everything up to sixteen-inch shells was taken apart and destroyed. The powder was burned, holes were drilled in the casings, and the shells and primers were dumped. Five-hundred men were at work on the three-month project of destroying a portion of Japan's stockpile.

Back at Kure, Higgins was taken by The Good Ship Titanic to greet classmates from his Naval Academy days who were in the harbor aboard the USS Baltimore. He found Captain Olsen and Admiral James Forrestal. Higgins invited them to a party for fourteen officers.

Then it was persuasion time. Higgins called on the chief. The fact that an admiral would be at the party was enough to convince Fujiwara-san he should sponsor the party at Konoie's, a restaurant

A geisha serve Admiral Forrestal, Captain Olsen, and other officers from the USS Baltimore at Konoie's restaurant in Aga.

with a large private room. Everyone had a good time, judging by the laughter when all the geisha girls ganged up on the admiral as he attempted to eat an egg with chopsticks.

Within a day, Higgins received requests from three generals who wanted parties. "Is this what a military governor is for?" he mused.

When sirens wailed at 0735 on December 7, 1945, Higgins was reminded it was the anniversary of Japan's attack on Pearl Harbor four years earlier. Some high-up Japanese authorities had scheduled a meeting with the military government up north so Higgins ignored the order to stand on station and took his MG team by train to Onomichi to inspect shipyards.

The American shore patrol intervened. "Didn't you know there was an alert?" Determined to proceed, Higgins rode in a motorcycle sidecar to the SP shack, where he engaged in a heated debate with top brass via telephone.

"But, sir," Higgins insisted, "the Japanese home minister, ship-yard owners, and the police chief arranged this weeks ago. It would be an insult not to show up."

Permission was given for Higgins to go ahead with the shipyard's interpreter, but the rest of the military government party had to return ASAP to Kure.

On the island, the lone American commander was partied, bathed, massaged, and put to bed. In the morning the group visited two shipyards. The officials said they could not get workers under current conditions because of the lack of food and quarters. General MacArthur's order to convert the aircraft carrier Honshi into a passenger ship—to get the troops home from around Japan's former empire—was being delayed. They were in need of some materials, and the small yard needed machines. Higgins' inspection of the Honshi revealed it had been gutted, its guns removed, and bunks were being installed.

Meanwhile, the point system was decimating occupation forces. Many had already left and, when Higgins got to work December 9, he found most of his office staff deep into planning their departure. The Forty-first was going home and would be entirely deactivated by the beginning of 1946.

At the end of the day, Higgins looked at his calendar. "Twenty-two days and they're gone," he thought. He reflected, "Nobody cares about nothing. It's very difficult to get any work done by GIs and officers, and the Japs are being spoiled by lack of supervision."

Sueno had been sleeping on a futon next to the door in Nobuko's shelter. It had been cold and cramped for several weeks. As she prepared to enter the office of the military governor on December 11, her assignment was to wash the windows of all the offices in the complex. Among the cleaning crew Commander Higgins had a reputation as a bear, so she had to be careful. With water pail and washrags the diminutive woman in the working kimono took a deep breath and backed into the office.

Square and plain, the room was larger than others in the building. Four metal folding chairs faced the American naval officer who sat at the four-by-six-foot table that served as a desk. Two black telephones were at his left elbow. The nameplate proclaimed *Comdr. Wallace L. Higgins* in both English and Japanese. The wall behind him held two windows with closely-spaced iron bars, and Higgins had made no effort to hide the obtrusive black electric cables hanging from the socket high on the wall between the windows.

Wally Higgins in his Hiroshima office

Wearing his black uniform with starched white shirt and black necktie, Higgins munched on C rations as he worked on reports. When he heard Sueno Yoshida shuffle to the window behind him and set down the bucket, Higgins turned and smiled.

"*Gomennasai, gomennasai,*" she said, and bowed.

Their eyes met in an instant neither would ever forget.

"*Donata desu ka?* What's your name?"

"Yoshida. Me Yoshida," she replied, shyly.

"Yoshida? Yoshida-san. That's a nice name," Higgins said. He struggled for something appropriate to say in Japanese, but gave up. He gestured, indicating he was offering leftover food to her. He was getting better at estimating people's age in this part of the world. About thirty, he figured.

"*Iie,*" Sueno responded, as she declined the offer and backed away. Her eyes and body language continued to reveal her hunger, and the commander insisted she take the food. Sueno tried to appear reluctant as she accepted the scraps of food and pretended to eat.

As she backed up, he noticed that she carefully slipped most of the C ration into an inner pocket of her kimono.

"*Arigato, arigato gozaimashita.*" She bowed, then turned and diligently resumed the task of washing the windows.

Higgins marvelled at how the two windows sparkled when she finished. She gathered up the rags and moved into Dick Kawamoto's area.

"Dick!" When the translator appeared in the doorway, Higgins said, "Find out from that cleaning woman why she didn't eat the food but instead hid it in her clothing."

The translator stepped back into his own office and conversed with the Japanese domestic.

When Kawamoto explained to Higgins that the cleaning woman had a nine-year-old child who was hungry, Higgins reached into a drawer of his desk, removed another C ration tin, and took it to the woman who was then cleaning the last window in the building. He pressed the tin into her hand and returned to his desk.

When she had left, Kawamoto appeared again in Higgins's doorway. "I forgot to tell you. I think she's sleeping in the street with a friend."

"Damn!"

Wallace called on Fujiwara-san and arranged to have the domestic named Yoshida removed from the compound cleaning crew and assigned specifically as live-in housekeeper of his Hiro quarters.

Sueno was summoned to the police station before work the next day.

"The American officer Higgins wants you to be his housekeeper," Fujiwara-san told her.

The woman was terrified and stood as still as bamboo on a windless day.

"Well? What have you to say? You should be most pleased."

"I...do not believe I would be a good housekeeper to one of such high rank." By now she was literally trembling at the prospect.

"You will do well. This is a great honor."

"But what if I fail? I do not speak his language."

"This is a very important man," said Fujiwara-san. "Commander Higgins is learning Japanese, and, in time, you will pick up enough of the English language to manage. Remember," he said, dismissing any further discussion, "it is your duty to treat him very, very nice!"

Bowing, and with many *arigatos*, Sueno backed out of Fujiwara-san's door and hurried down the street to Nobuko's shelter. If she could keep from fainting on the way, she would tell her friend of her good fortune.

Higgins was pleased when the chief confirmed arrangements for the housekeeper. Otherwise, things were not going the way he would have liked. He made a difficult trip to Shobara to track down a rumor about a large supply of shells, army clothing, and food hidden by former Japanese officers. They had mysteriously disappeared. Then he learned that while the Japanese were going hungry, the Kure port commander, a lieutenant general, had dropped twenty-six-hundred pounds of beef over the side of a supply ship into the bay. Higgins and others had missed important labor meetings due to misunderstandings. When he found out there would be an inspection the next week he exploded. "One long series of misses—damned SNAFUs!" he fumed. When Higgins had his blood pressure checked at the aid station, it was up twenty points. He went out in the bay to Ship 163 and got drunk.

After work the next Saturday he was told that his interpreter, Kawamoto, was being rotated back to the States. That night he got drunk again, managing to drag two of his fellow officers home at 2:00 a.m.

*The military gover-
nor with his new
h o u s e k e e p e r ,
Yoshida-san (Sueno
Kotani Yoshida) in
December 1945 in
front of the bachelor
officers quarters at
the Kure base.*

On Sunday, Higgins had a hangover and slept until lunch. At the office, he learned that the admiral had canceled, because "a visiting British admiral has dropped in."

"Perhaps things are turning around," Higgins thought that evening, as his new housekeeper served the four officers he had invited.

"She's delightful," one guest pointed out to Higgins.

"And very pretty!" said another.

The mid-December weather was cold, and the military governor was busy with many tasks. There was the furnishing of a hospital wing and visits to young patients, a trip to Hada regarding Japanese businesses, and chilling, soaking trips out to the supply ships for things needed on shore. He went to the shipyards, to Kure arranging for oil for boats, inspected the Tanabe cement works, collected information on Japanese companies and their managers, and put together economic forecasts for MacArthur. Higgins toured the airplane factory the Japanese had built in deep caves near the area of Hiroshima leveled by the atom bomb. Walking through what seemed like miles of underground tunnels with complete machine shops and a parts warehouse, he concluded it could have survived a direct hit.

Higgins left the office to visit the now-complete Brass Hat Room at the officers club. It was December 20 and it was apparent that the Twenty-fourth Division was moving in.

When the USS Oklahoma had sailed for America on November 29 it carried twenty Christmas boxes from Higgins to his wife, his family, and his many friends stateside. This December 24, he sat wrapping presents for his new Japanese friends. There were many packages for children: the eight girls in the Tanabe family, the Hattori family, several youngsters in Hiroshima and Kure hospitals, and his new housekeeper's family. Recalling good times from Christmastimes past, Wally realized all six members of his family had not been together since the war started. "Well," he thought, "at least three of my boys will be home with Adelaide this Christmas."

On Christmas Day Wally accompanied Sueno to the Kotani family home. Sueno's mother, who was called "Grandma" Kinu Kotani, Tae, and Sueno's father, Iwao Kotani, were all pleased with his presents, especially Kotani-san, who devoured the chocolates.

Higgins made himself sick eating two turkey Christmas dinners, one in Hiroshima and another aboard ship off Kure.

When he returned home he found a package on his doorstep. The daughter of the Onomichi police chief had sent him a gift much cherished by the giver, one of her baby dolls.

In America, Adelaide prepared the first Christmas dinner of her married life without her husband. She was happy, however, to have three of her four sons out of the service. "Bud" Wallace Jr., Ray, and Bob had made it home to Mentor for the holidays. The oldest, Dick, was still at sea.

The small house on the edge of Johnny Cake Ridge Road overlooked a snow-covered, peaceful view of farm fields across the seldom-traveled avenue. Inside, the two-bedroom cottage was filled with good-natured kidding—and all the furniture Adelaide had kept. The large wooden box from Japan had been unpacked a week earlier, and the unopened presents were piled against the tree. Before the family attacked the huge turkey with all the trimmings, they unwrapped the gifts from Dad: kimonos, flags, swords, a ceremonial headdress, vases, parachutes, silk, and money.

After dinner, Adelaide retrieved a small dish from a display shelf. As it was passed around the table, she explained it was from the box of souvenirs from Wally. They all thought it was quite curious—half beautiful, and half ugly.

In the last days of 1945, Higgins received a sixty-foot boat for official military government business and so no longer needed his own Titanic for work in the Inland Sea. His staff was getting larger: five on the boat crew, three housekeepers, an interpreter, a driver, a mechanic, a club bartender, and five club kitchen personnel.

He also learned that he was qualified for spot promotion from lieutenant commander to commander. It was not yet a fact, but there was the possibility.

Amid much confusion a new MG team moved in on December 29. Starting in 1946, the prefecture would be occupied by a multinational force of Australians, British, and Americans.

For the Americans occupying Hiroshima, the New Year's Eve party was one tempered by mixed emotions. The Forty-first Division was being deactivated as of midnight, and many friends were saying goodbye. At midnight, everyone sang *Auld Lang Syne*. General Doe, CO of the dissolving Forty-first, wept. To get the party back on a cheerful note, Higgins led the singing of *Sink The Ship Titanic!* and finally closed the club at 3:00 a.m.

On New Year's night, he wrote:

> This is a tuff, tuff New Years! As I sit writing, next to a good radio with the usual good Holiday programs, a box of good Stateside candy on the table, three Japanese women awaiting my every command, one beauty (Sueno) sitting at my side, it is almost like Spring out—so colorful, with the children dressed in bright kimonos—the house decorated for Christmas. Well, somebody has to do the dirty jobs!

Not long afterward Higgins drew a Jeep from the motor pool and visited Chief Fujiwara-san. When they had finished speaking of labor matters, Higgins said, "I want you to know my new housekeeper is working out just fine!"

At home that evening, Sueno was especially attentive. She served Higgins warm sake, rubbed his back and sat at his side as they stared into the warm coals of the hibachi fire. Softly, she began to sing a love song in Japanese. He had her sing it again so he could learn the words. Together, they sang the song until he had it memorized.

"What do the words mean?" Wally asked Sueno. The petite woman hung her head in embarrassment. She did not know how to say it in his language, so she pantomimed what came to mind, pointed at him, then herself, and to her heart. Like children, they played a guessing game while singing, until the touching turned into the understanding of adults. Wally's hands slid around her waist. Her head rested on his shoulder. He gently pulled her closer. His hand in her kimono discovered her heart was beating as wildly as his. The *tatami*-matted floor was soft and comfortable under their bodies as they embraced. Her futon, in the back room where fellow housekeeper Sadae Sato slept, remained empty until early morning.

Higgins wrote in his diary, "Love is wonderful in any language!"

Years later, Sueno would recall, "At first, I try only to carry out orders from Japanese officials to be very nice. But soon I find myself falling more and more in love with this wonderful, kind man from America."

Something was different about Higgins that Thursday morning. Although it had been raining outside, he was unusually cheerful. Kawamoto contained his laughter until safely out of the commander's office.

Hurrying over to Elsie Yamamoto, he told of his suspicions. "I think the boss man has lost his mind! He is going to check on the status of his request for extended Japan duty."

"*Wakarimasen...dohshita no desuka?*" ("I don't understand, what is the matter?")

"I think he is in love!"

Kawamoto failed to recognize the pained expression on Elsie's face. She had feelings of affection for an American, too, but her secret love wanted to go back to America. She bit her tongue, and when Kawamoto had returned to his own desk she cried softly.

Higgins agreed to stay on duty for 180 days after being eligible for discharge as part of the process to qualify him for the rank of full commander. He could use the extra pay, and he was painfully aware that many of his Annapolis classmates had made captain or admiral.

There was a party for Dick Kawamoto and a sergeant who was also leaving the MG team. Higgins would have to depend on a new interpreter, a native of the area, to translate. He was grateful for the help Kawamoto had provided in his struggle to learn the language, but somehow he enjoyed his language study more with his local interpreter and Sueno.

When Higgins got home, Sueno and Sadae were bantering in Japanese. Higgins was delighted to discover the two servants, who shared the small room at the back of his quarters, having genuine fun. Many evenings at the Higgins house had been devoted to teaching Sadae and Sueno how to cook American style. To Higgins this meant barbequed steak alternated with various chicken dishes. The servants practiced on two stoves: one M-42, one Sears Roebuck. By the third week in January, they had not only mastered the art of cooking chicken and steaks, they had become a proficient team of food and drink servers to Higgins's many guests.

Late at night, however, Sadae retired to the back of the house as Higgins studied his language lessons. Sueno sat next to him, coaching him in pronunciation.

But Sueno Yoshida was crying when Wally arrived home one evening. A friend had told her she was the subject of gossip in her village, that her father was upset over her growing relationship with the foreigner. Higgins decided it was time to try to win over Sueno's parents. Early the following morning, armed with food and a box of American candy, he drove Sueno to the Kotani home above Hiroshima.

As it turned out, he needn't have worried. Sueno told her parents of the orders she had received from Japanese officials, and after that Higgins was a popular weekend guest.

At work, however, Higgins had bigger worries:

> Why all this emphasis on "Points?" The war is over six
> months and we've decimated our forces in Japan! Nobody
> wants to do nothing—except get home! What if something
> happens? China is going Communist. The Russian Bear sits
> watching us, licking his chops. Rebuilding the peace will be
> tough enough without everyone jumping ship!

At the close of January 1946, though, Higgins was well pleased
with his circumstances and accomplishments. General Doe turned
his house over to Higgins, and it became known to Higgins's many
guests as Higgins Manor. Sueno and Sadae prepared delicious
dinners, and for the next seven months Wally entertained with
lavish meals, served his One-Two drink, with its veiled reference to
the world of boxing, and led songfests nearly every evening. Sueno
had diligently followed her orders to help smooth the occupation. In
the process, she devoted herself to the gracious service and tender
loving care of Higgins. Sadae and Sueno were gracious, retiring
servers. "Unspoiled jewels," he called them.

At work, Higgins was supervising the conversion of a mess hall
for Japanese workers. He was busy with warehouse inventories,
meetings at the Home Ministry in Kure, and at the Thirty-fourth
Infantry. Higgins also was asked to be both labor officer and head of
the Ninety-seventh Military Government Company. "I must really
be coming up in the world," he mused, when he was offered his
choice of two Nigata-based boats.

As March bloomed, Higgins took Sueno for a boat ride on the
Inland Sea. They stopped at a small island and admired the flowers.
He was attentive and kind, just as he had been since she had first
met him. Sueno had expected the worst when she volunteered to
meet the barbarians on the beach at Hiro, and she continued to be
overwhelmed by the kindness shown her, and with Higgins's genuine interest in her country.

A few days later, he received a note he kept close from that day
forward:

> Thanks you very much to be take care of me frequently, and
> gives to me good every time. I am cordially grateful and desire

if I could speak English language. I won't to express one's thanks to you. I don't no your language and I am hart to understand but I no you are very very kindness to me and I am very glad in my hart. In this time please continue your favours toward me.

Yoshida (Sueno)

FJVE

The Secret Mission

Displaying its Military Government sign, Building B-10 on the sprawling naval base at Kure had changed little in the five months of American occupation.

Inside, Lieutenant Commander Higgins swiveled in his office chair and opened the file marked *Personal Correspondence*. He slipped the handwritten note of admiration from his servant into the folder and smiled. The pretty Japanese domestic made his Asian duty enjoyable, but as military governor and labor officer of Hiroshima prefecture, he had to be careful. Though ignored by some of the occupation forces, fraternization rules were strict, and besides, he had a wife back in the States.

He thought of his recent diary entry:

> She surely makes my few spare moments of free time a delight—looking for flowers—cruising the beautiful Inland Sea—lounging before the warm hibachi—sharing Japanese-English language lessons. She and Sadae make entertaining a pleasure, be the guests Americans, Japanese, Brits, Aussies, Dutch or Indians.

He closed the file drawer and turned to the stack of military government work on the desk. This March Monday morning, emergency orders for labor were all fouled up. Higgins's smile quickly fell. Changes in the occupation forces of Hiroshima ken were causing some dramatic reactions from the Japanese as some of the Americans were being replaced with a mixed force of Australian, British, and Indian troops.

The British were moving into buildings 3, 6, and 8, and Higgins was getting acquainted with some Australians who were taking over the security of Hiroshima prefecture from the Forty-first Division. The advance party of Aussies was at Higgins's house the evening of January 4, and there was a party for them three days later. "The officers I have met so far are not very high grade," he observed. The incoming British and Australians treated the Japanese quite differently than had the Americans. Higgins noted that the Aussies' attitude was possessive and antagonistic. They did not feed their own workers, so the Japanese worked feverishly to get all the goods out of their warehouses before the Australians officially took over. At one point, the port director issued a directive stating the area was a "Non-Aussie Area unless on official business." A British commander arrived at Kure expecting to take over all mess gear and food and demanded the generators from the bomb disposal group. Japanese house girls were very unhappy, and Nobuko, envious of the respectful treatment Sueno was receiving, begged for a job with the Americans.

As each new group of British and Aussies arrived, Higgins invited the officers out to his house, fed them, entertained them, and worked for a smooth transfer of responsibility. By adding a porch, a brick patio with dance floor, an awning, outdoor lights, and an enlarged kitchen, Higgins had transformed his off-base house. The Higgins Manor staff was increased when Nobuko and Annie Ikemoto were hired to assist the live-in staff.

As Higgins was released from Tenth Corps and reassigned to the Seventy-sixth Military Government Company—a move that delayed any possible promotion—he reflected on his first five months in Japan:

> The people of these islands intrigue me by their charming ways...by their seeming enthusiasm for the occupation. From

the time of our landing five months ago, all Japanese have welcomed our occupation with what seems to be as much enthusiasm as they had shown in fighting the war! I wonder what the Emperor told them that caused the Japanese so enthusiastically to turn in and help destroy their tools of war?...Just look at how quickly they have cleaned up the bomb damage and cut up their warships!

After the wedding of their son Ray Adelaide packed her clothes, closed up the house in Ohio, and went to New Jersey to live with her aging parents.

On the noon train bound for Tokyo, Higgins found his compartment, pushed the door open, and stepped in. A study in contrasts, it had running water, was well arranged, and it was dirty. Precisely on time, the train moved out of Hiroshima's cleaned-up station, left the war-torn city, plunged through several tunnels, and sped across

Trolleys were running again in bombed-out Hiroshima March 27, 1946, as Higgins headed for the train to Tokyo.

the green countryside of southern Honshu. Throughout the afternoon, Higgins studied Japanese and watched the landscape, surprised by the lush vegetation and the profusion of gardens.

After a sound sleep, he woke at dawn as the train slowed and
jostled its way through the remains of Yokohama. Most of the city
had been the target of incendiary air strikes, and the resulting
firestorm had incinerated everything in their path as they swept
from the center of Tokyo southward through much of Yokohama.
"As bad as Hiroshima!" Higgins noted. Only the New Grand Hotel
and a "Westernized" section of the city, located atop a hill, were
spared.

Higgins was riveted to the window as the train passed crews of
men, women, and children cleaning bricks. Others were rebuilding
structures of which only chimneys now remained. All the way from
Yokohama into the southern half of Tokyo the scars of the firestorm
were apparent, but buildings in the center of the city were relatively
undamaged.

The next afternoon he arrived at COM NAV JAP, Commander
of Naval Activities in Japan headquarters, and took a seat by the
reception desk. A lieutenant came out of the office. "The captain
will see you now."

GIs surrounded by Japanese boys in Tokyo, March 1946

"Lieutenant Commander Higgins reporting. I am requesting extended duty to July 1947, sir." He handed over a document along with a copy of ALNAV 235 and copies of his previous requests.

The captain looked briefly at each, glanced up and smiled. "This should get you that long overdue extra stripe for sure, and damned quick! Congratulations, Commander!"

They shook hands, then saluted.

Wally left feeling much better.

Higgins wanted the phone call to go well. Mr. Tsuneo Hattori, head of Harima Ship Building Company of the Mitsubishi conglomerate, was to be in Tokyo also, and had suggested dinner with a friend from government.

"Moshi, moshi, Mitsubishi." He had the right number.

"Moshi, moshi. Is Mr. Hattori there? Tsuneo Hattori, please."

The friendly Japanese industrialist brought along Mr. Furuichi from the Japanese embassy staff. They took Higgins to a Japanese hotel where they treated him to a lavish dinner, complete with high type Tokyo geisha. It was a memorable evening, and one of his first contacts with highly positioned Japanese.

Feeling assured he would make commander, Higgins took a side trip to Yokosuka for a new uniform. His request ran into some opposition, however. "Hell, it must take an act of God to get rules changed!" he grumbled. He had his uniform by early afternoon and returned to Tokyo.

March 31 was the Sunday that Higgins met a Mr. Pierce from SCAP, Supreme Commander of Allied Powers. They spoke of Japan's recovery as their lunch was served, then Pierce expressed his reason for getting together.

"You seem to be well accepted by Japanese business leaders. What's your secret?"

"Ha! I guess my experience in industry helps," Higgins answered.

"For example?"

"Well..." Considering that Pierce was an advisor on General MacArthur's staff, Higgins was fully aware that whatever he said about himself might be carried to others. "I left the Navy right after the academy at the end of the First World War, in 1919. Went to work for Standard Oil. Then hitches at Babcock Wilcox, Motor Stoker Corporation, Pocahantis Fuel Stoker Division, and the War Production Board. I've been through all levels and functions...engineering, manufacturing, sales, and general management."

"Interesting...and impressive," Pierce summed up at the end of the meal. "I hope we meet again soon, Commander."

The brick patio at Higgins Manor was crowded. Four SCAP officials were among the twenty-four dinner guests. As usual, Higgins's household staff served the Allied officers with courtesy, charm, and good food.

"Got a surprise for you, Higgins," Commander Raleigh broke the news to Wally. "As of Monday you've got the job of head of Industry and Commerce. Congratulations!"

The MG team started singing, "For he's a jolly good fellow..."

On Monday, Hattori, and Furuichi expressed their delight with developments. Higgins would need to move north to be closer to SCAP headquarters in Tokyo and work with staff members. He was now responsible for all military government matters of industry and commerce in Japan.

The following day, he sought out Commander Raleigh to talk about his July 1 relief, but Raleigh had another matter on his mind.

"You made it, Higgins! You are now full commander. Congratulations!"

"This calls for a celebration!" Higgins exclaimed to everyone at MG headquarters. "You're all invited out to dinner at my place tonight."

When the guests arrived, Higgins was wearing the uniform he brought back from his Tokyo trip.

"OK, Higgins, you look great," one of the guests offered. "But isn't it a bit much to be wearing your new chickenshit hat in the house?"

As usual, the party began with laughter and ended with singing.

That same week, General Tilton from SCAP came to Higgins Manor for dinner and asked Higgins about his prewar industrial experience. The questions indicated Pierce had passed along Higgins's background.

Higgins dressed in his new uniform immediately after being promoted

On April 12, General George C. Stewart, General Tilton, and a Major Richard Rasmusen came down from Tokyo. Commander Higgins ushered the three high-ranking officers into his office. Rasmusen closed the door, and the three pulled their chairs unusually close to Higgins's desk.

"Commander, we're here to request your assistance on a secret mission," General Stewart said. "We want you to do some bird-dogging in Yamaguchi prefecture." He leaned forward, lowered his voice even further, and continued. "Major Rasmusen will accompany you in a search for uranium ore we think the Japanese have hidden near Tokuyama. The purpose, and your findings, are to be kept confidential and reported to me personally in Tokyo."

Rasmusen picked up the conversation on Stewart's cue. "Lieutenant Nagano, a Nisei, heard it through the Japanese grapevine. Apparently there is a quantity of uranium stored somewhere in Yamaguchi prefecture."

"Uranium could be used to make an atomic weapon," General Tilton added. "With your acceptance by the Japs, and your industrial civilian experience, we figured you're in a better position to find it than the MG team in Yamaguchi."

"Sounds interesting," Higgins said. "What should I be looking for? Do you know what the stuff looks like?"

"Just that it's a thousand pounds of ore. That's really all we know, and so far it's just a rumor," Tilton answered. "When I told the supreme commander, he hit the ceiling! If the Japs are hiding it to make atom bombs we've got a major problem!"

"Wow!" Higgins reached for his calendar and flipped it open. "I can run down there Monday. Major, pick you up about nine in the morning."

On Sunday Higgins pored over a map of Yamaguchi prefecture and got out the encyclopedia. He found very little information under "ores" and "mining."

Dressed in her best kimono, Sueno lugged the heavy encyclopedia to the Jeep and placed it under the passenger seat. Wally stowed his gear and climbed in. All Sueno knew was that he was off on a trip to Yamaguchi. "Part of the new job," she was told, "is to inspect industries in that area of Honshu." She bowed, then waved a polite *sayonara* as Higgins drove off. Sueno continued waving until he was out of sight. Her chest heaved with a sigh as she stepped out of her sandals and entered Higgins Manor. It would be quiet and cold for the next few nights.

Major Rasmusen was waiting when Higgins arrived. In addition to his luggage he had a strange, long-handled gadget. "A Geiger counter," he explained. Gear stored, they roared down the road from the western edge of Hiroshima and along the coastline of Hiroshima Bay. The air became colder as they turned inland at Iwakuni, climbed some hills, and caught a glimpse of the ruins of Iwakuni Castle.

"Hey, Higgins, what the hell does this uranium look like?" Rasmusen shouted above the rumble of the down-shifted engine.

"Frankly, I'm not quite sure! There's an encyclopedia under your seat, but it doesn't give a description."

Rasmusen struggled to read in the bouncing Jeep.

When they stopped for lunch in the small town of Shuto they were joined by an Aussie officer who bought them a beer.

"What you mates 'ere for?" he asked.

"An industrial inspection trip," Rasmusen answered. "Commander Higgins is head of the industries and commerce section."

The Australian tipped his hat and left after ten minutes of discussion about the Japanese. "Well, enjoy the beer, mates."

Higgins and Rasmusen climbed the hills of Kanozama and reached Murozumi. They entered the beautifully furnished hotel lobby via a bridge that crossed a shallow pond stocked with brightly colored carp called koi.

"Dick, let's meet in the lobby at five o'clock for dinner," Higgins told his companion as they headed for their rooms. "The CIC guy should be here by then."

After a bath and a nap, Higgins was on the path in front of the hotel, watching the fish and waiting for his companion. The squeal of a Jeep's brakes and a loud voice shattered the quiet.

"*Boi-san! Boi-san!* Bellboy! Goddamn it!"

Higgins turned to see the American Nisei get out of the Jeep. The short, dark-haired lieutenant strode toward him. "*Boi-san!*" At the same time, Rasmusen exited the hotel.

"I'm Commander Higgins, and my friend here is Major Dick Rasmusen," Higgins said as he returned the lieutenant's salute and offered a handshake. "You are...?"

"Lieutenant Jack Ogami, Counter Intelligence Corps, out of Yamaguchi HQ."

The three Americans agreed to have dinner together as soon as Ogami returned from his room. Higgins and Rasmusen had quite a wait because Lieutenant Ogami wanted a large room with bath and was shown three before he was satisfied.

At dinner, they talked of the mission.

"I've been threatening native Japanese whom I suspect know something, but so far, shall we say, nobody will talk." Ogami apparently knew no more about the rumor than the commander or the major.

Higgins had an upset stomach and could not eat the raw sea fish known as *sashimi*, but even more unpleasant to him was the behavior of their CIC companion, who demanded all kinds of extra service.

Ogami asked what they planned to do, specifically.

"We're over here on orders from General Stewart of SCAP to talk to some of the Japanese plant managers," Higgins told him. "We want to get a feel for what's going on...and run down the rumor. Dick is down from SCAPJAP to accompany me."

"Well, damn it, as CIC, you should have let me know what you were going to do! I plan to go out on my own tomorrow."

Higgins and Dick looked at each other and winked as the Nisei lieutenant turned away to demand more beer. *"Motto biiru!"*

On the way to their rooms, Higgins and Rasmusen were alone in the hall. "What do you think of our dinner partner?" the major asked.

"Change his name to Jack Ass! Well, at least he seemed to swallow our explanation of what we plan to do. He sure hasn't found anything yet, and no wonder. That bastard needs to be sat on!"

Higgins was sick all night and was grateful the next day that Major Rasmusen drove their Jeep well as they climbed over the hills of Kanazama from Murozumi and downhill toward the coast. At Tokuyama, the two Americans found the local police station.

Tokuyama Police Chief Takenaka was very cooperative, and brightened when Higgins spoke, in Japanese, of his close friendship with Fujiwara-san.

"Takenaka-san, do you know what's in the naval arsenal?" Higgins asked.

"Iie, no," the chief answered. In broken English, he explained that civilians and police had been barred from entering the arsenal for years.

The Americans got in Higgins's Jeep and followed the chief to the arsenal. There were no Japanese naval personnel available for questioning, but the chief helped Higgins obtain a *Survey of Natural Resources* from the arsenal files. Studying the paper, Higgins's finger stopped at a listing of *Ores In Kyushu.*

"This looks interesting. Pitchblende!"

Rasmusen's look indicated he was not on board.

"The massive form of uraninite," Higgins explained.

They went into a warehouse with the Geiger counter, found some manganese, and took a small sample.

"Takeda Chemical Company is taking over part of the plant," the chief told them. "They may be able to analyze your samples."

The Americans left the arsenal and drove back to Kanazama, where they found nothing. They turned west on a bumpy trail to Yamaguchi, the prefectural capital, to check in with Commander James M. Boswell and Lieutenant Button of MG.

"Nice quarters!" Higgins muttered as the two visitors were led into a building of American architecture and Japanese interior design. The area surrounding the headquarters had not been bombed. Boswell and Button welcomed the visitors and showed them around the elaborate quarters.

"It's good to see you again, Higgins," Boswell said. "What brings you out of Hiroshima ken?"

"Glad you asked. I've been given the industries and commerce job and wanted to make contacts with plant managers over here." Higgins gestured, indicating the surroundings. "You seem to be well situated with quarters."

"All except our feeding facilities. Our mess is a mess. Never did get half of what we needed."

"Hey, that's why I'm here," Higgins said. "I've got a direct pipeline into the fleet at Kure. You just tell me what mess gear you need, and I'll get it sent to you."

Boswell made out a list on the spot and handed it to Higgins.

"Oh, by the way," Higgins said, "we ran into your CIC, Jack Ogami, last night at Murozumi."

"Yeah, he said he was going to stay there last night."

"Is he always so obnoxious?"

"He's out scaring the hell out of the natives all over the prefecture," Boswell replied. "He's a bull in a china shop!"

When Higgins and Rasmusen arrived back at the hotel at Murozumi they were told Lieutenant Ogami had checked out. Higgins and Rasmusen got out the encyclopedia and discussed what to do next.

"It wouldn't be so bad if we had some guidelines as to what to look for," Rasmusen said.

"A top-secret search for a material that's so exotic no one can describe it or tell us where to look. Maybe we should get hold of a chemist."

They drove from Murozumi to Hakari, and again found nothing.

"Another damned blind alley!" Higgins growled as he climbed into the Jeep.

They drove down from the hills once more and checked in at the Tokuyama Matsuzukan Hotel, a converted home run by a group of brothers.

"A chemist?" one of the brothers said. "You could try Takeda Chemical Company. Mr. Nakamura, the plant manager, might help."

"*Konnichiwa, Nakamura-san,*" Higgins began. He quickly discovered Mr. Nakamura spoke English.

"Uranium?"

"Uranium oxide or any derivatives," Higgins answered. "I think it may be found in some manganese compounds. We have several samples we would like very much to have analyzed."

"*Hai...*yes, of course!" They soon had their analysis. The Takamori samples contained ferro manganese magnesium, manganese carbon dioxide, rose pyrosine, copper, silver, gold, and lead. The sample from Kanayama was manganese.

Nakamura retrieved two small samples of compounds from a storage cabinet. "These may be of interest," he said. "We keep samples of every ore produced or processed in the area." Analysis revealed they were fifty percent clay, thirty percent copper, twenty percent uranium oxide.

Higgins and Rasmusen stood frozen, staring at the samples.

"By God!" yelled Higgins.

They turned to their Japanese hosts, but neither officer could ask *the* question.

Without waiting, Mr. Nakamura said, "This is all we have."

The host, seeing the disappointment on the Americans' faces, added, "But I know where a lot more is stored. We can arrange for our chemists to go with you to the fuel depot tomorrow. There are six barrels in Osakoda Warehouse Number Six."

"That would be...appreciated!"

At the depot, Higgins and Rasmusen found twenty-four boxes and six large bottles of a compound like the lab sample. The chemists assured the Americans the lot would contain twenty percent uranium oxide.

"Mission accomplished!" Higgins roared, pounding the major on the back.

Estimating the ore's weight at about a ton, the chemists retrieved lumber from the warehouse, recruited a carpenter to enlarge the cargo area of the Jeep, and helped load and secure the jars and boxes.

With Higgins at the wheel, the Americans began the difficult drive to Yamaguchi. The front of the overloaded Jeep rode high, making it difficult to steer. A spring broke when they hit a pothole halfway to the prefectural capital. The Jeep sagged and slowed as Higgins nursed the heavy load past Taiunji Temple on the approach to Yamaguchi.

"How the heck are we going to keep this secret from the local MG team...and that snooping CIC guy?" Rasmusen asked.

Higgins shifted to first gear and turned down a side street, away from the building that housed Boswell's MG group and the CIC.

"Hell, let's see what our Allies can do about shipping some clay to SCAP headquarters in Tokyo."

Higgins stopped in front of British headquarters of the Allied Occupation Forces. A most understanding commanding officer from New Zealand took over the Jeep and promised to ship the valuable cargo under guard to General Stewart at SCAP.

"My friend, your secret is safe. I shall even have your Jeep repaired and sent back to Kure. Why don't you two plan to return by train? I'll arrange your passage."

General Stewart had ordered Commander Higgins to report to a Colonel Newberg in Yokohama. Newberg wanted to know where the uranium ore came from, if there was any more, how long it had been in the Osakoda warehouse, and who put it there.

"I'll go back to Tokuyama and see if I can find out," Higgins said.

Higgins prepared to go back for answers, knowing that, as a lone occupation authority, he might not get straight answers from the Japanese. They would, he reasoned, probably open up to a respected, well-known Japanese, but most top industrialists were in prison under suspicion of aiding the Japanese war effort.

Higgins, however, knew a Japanese manager who was second in command at Japan Steel Works. Mr. Satoshi Nii was highly educated, spoke both languages fluently, and Higgins could trust him as a friend of America. He made arrangements to meet the Japanese industrialist in Tokuyama.

Higgins left the port of Kure on the port director's boat at 0930 April 29 and headed for Hikari. He walked from the dock to the police station and was greeted by a lovely Japanese girl.

"Haroh, Komanda Higgins-san! Sorry, but chief is waiting for you at railroad station."

"You speak very good English, Miss!"

"Oh, thank you. I study your language at girl's college before I marry naval officer. I am Mieko."

They chatted until a short time later when the chief returned from the train station. Mieko assisted with translation as the two men talked about the ore in the warehouse.

"The chief says that the ore was brought there only a month ago," she related. "Excuse me, but I may know where it came from. My husband talk about cave with his Japanese navy friends."

Higgins and the chief listened as the girl described a cave near a certain house in Kanoyama. "I will take you there and help you find cave."

The chief drove his secretary and Higgins from Hikari to Kanoyama, and they began to search for the house. It was hard to find, and they searched for long time. When they finally found it, it took another hour before they spotted a cave.

"Achira ni!" The chief pointed excitedly to diggings near the back of the cave. He held up a lighted match.

There were cavities in the floor that indicated a number of square objects and six round ones had been removed. They combed the dirt, but Higgins finally decided there was nothing left. "Nothing more we can do here."

When Higgins and the industrialist Satoshi Nii arrived at Tokuyama they were met by Chief of Police Takenaka. They obtained light bulbs and went to the Osakoda warehouse where they illuminated the storage area for the first time since the fall of Japan.

But that is not all that would be exposed to the light. Commander Higgins had brought together Japanese chemists, people from naval ordnance, police, representatives from the Home Ministry, industrialists, and warehouse workers, all of whom contributed to the understanding of what had happened here.

Takenaka-san and the chief from Hikari were exceptionally helpful during the questioning, and the full story finally was revealed. When Japanese scientists examined fallout from the Hiroshima bomb and determined it was fueled by uranium, that

Notes of Apr. 16-20: Higgins's diary during the time of the secret mission to Yamaguchi to search for uranium ore. Separate notes contained test results of ore samples.

information went to the Imperial Navy. After the surrender, a small group of dissidents removed a thousand pounds of uranium ore from the Osakoda warehouse and secretly buried it at Kanoyama. When word of the misdeed got out, civil authorities pleaded with the ringleaders to return the ore. It was dug up at the end of March and shipped to Tokuyama, where it was locked up in the Osakoda warehouse with the other thousand pounds of ore. The first load of ore—which Higgins had taken to SCAP in Tokyo—was all there was in the area.

Higgins shook hands with everyone, offered many *arigatos*, and was bowed to as each conferee left the warehouse. When Mr. Nii and the Hikari chief were the only ones left, Higgins asked, "Sake? Whiskey?" After many toasts the chief took Higgins and Mr. Nii back to Hikari.

The boat was waiting at the Hikari dock. Higgins hurried onto the boat, retrieved some food and sugar from his cabin and returned to the chief. *"Hai, kore wa anata no desu...satoh!"* ("Here, this sugar is for you...!")

"Well, that closes that assignment!" Higgins said. By noon the boat was underway with Mr. Nii on board as Higgins's guest.

 *SIX*

From Hiroshima to Kanagawa

The rain of the previous twenty-four hours stopped just as Higgins picked up the large silver shears at 11:00 a.m., May 2, 1946. Decorated with bunting and streamers, a brand new merchant ship stood in the large dry dock. He cut the ribbon, and the ship Tokitsumaru was launched at Habu from the island of Ino Shima in the Inland Sea. More than five-thousand citizens cheered as the huge ship slipped stern-first into the water. The Japanese band playing American music reminded Higgins of a junior high school group from his youth. At the same time, he watched as a large balloon opened and dozens of pigeons flew out. He had mastered the inscrutable smile, and this was an occasion to practice it.

Higgins turned to the shipyard manager. "The rain...er...ah: *ame tomaru!*" ("Rain stop.")

"Ah, *so desu ka*...yes, Commander. We have never had a launching in the rain!"

Higgins looked around at the crowd. Hundreds of women stood with children tied to their backs.

"Most impressive," he told his host. "I thank you for inviting me to last night's party and today's launching. Now, I must get back to Kure."

As Higgins returned, Sueno walked the downhill mile and waited at the dock.

A few days later, Mr. Nii was standing in the doorway of Higgins's office, holding two boxes. "Ahh, good morning, Commander! I have a gift for Yoshida-san..." he placed the smaller package on Higgins's desk, "...and a gift for your wife." The industrialist opened the lid of the larger box and showed it to Higgins. It was a bolt of Japanese silk. He placed it alongside the other package.

"*Ohayo gozaimasu*, good morning! And *arigato*." Higgins replied. "May I peek at the one for Yoshida-san?"

"*Hai!*"

Higgins lifted the cover of the smaller box and found yard goods, enough for a summer kimono. "Yoshida will be thrilled! *Arigato*, thank you."

"Are you ready for lunch with Mr. Ohbayashi? He is waiting for us."

Higgins placed the boxes aside and retrieved his hat.

Sueno Yoshida in a kimono made from the bolt of silk given to Higgins by Mr. Satoshi Nii.

Arriving home early, he gave the smaller of the two packages to Sueno. When she saw what was inside she clapped her hands and hopped up and down, as if on a pogo stick.

"Kirei desu ne!" ("How beautiful!"). "Ahh." She impulsively hugged Higgins, and he hugged back, kissing her gently on the forehead as he continued to hold the trembling, doll-like woman. His plan to leave at midnight on the boat for Kobe changed. He decided to wait and leave for Kobe early the next morning.

"Hey, we've got all kinds of food and gear up north," Major Hull had offered. "Why don't you come up to Kobe and pick out what you need?"

Higgins had quickly accepted. The three-man crew of the Titanic was waiting when he and Commander E.J. Ellsworth arrived at 0600. The diesel engine powered them east-northeast up the Inland Sea. At noon they enjoyed the lunch Sueno had packed, and leftovers were stowed for later.

As Higgins sunbathed, Ellsworth looked up from the book he was reading. "How do you decide whether you're going to use your official boat or this unofficial one?"

"Depends on the activity," Higgins said.

"Well, what's this trip supposed to be?"

"Getting supplies for the clubs? I'd call it a little Navy business and a little pleasure cruise."

"Want to know what I'd call it?" Ellsworth asked.

"I don't know. Do I?"

"I'd call it monkey business. The Navy would no more authorize transportation for the stuff we're going after..."

"There you are. It's not really Navy transportation. Also, I didn't ask the Navy, did I?"

"Wally, you're amazing. You have no authorization whatsoever to go around trading and bartering. God knows you've accomplished a lot for the good of morale and international relations, but..."

"But what?"

"But it's been completely outside your duties."

"I do my job first, then this."

"Yes, you do. I guess I've just never met another officer who goes quite so far out of his way to promote good will."

"Hell, it's fun, Ellsworth!"

It was late at night with a bright moon shining when they pulled into Kobe Harbor. From Hiro, near the southwest end of the Inland Sea, to Kobe, at the northeast end, they had covered nearly 250 kilometers. The two commanders slept comfortably in the bunks of the boat's main cabin.

By 0430 the next morning, all food, provisions, and gear had been stowed and tied down. The weather was bad, but they still shoved off. Out in the channel, the wind increased, and the weather worsened. They could no longer see land as the wooden forty-five-foot boat heaved and wind-driven saltwater sprayed over the cabin. Higgins held on tight and admired the skill of the crew as one tended the churning engine, one steered, and the third rode outside, pointing the way. They encountered rough seas all day, bouncing from the partial shelter of one island to another. It rained intensely all afternoon and evening. Just before dusk the sea was still running rough, and the boat came down especially hard off a swell.

"Ha, maybe I shouldn't have named this boat the Titanic!" Higgins laughed.

"I hope to Christ it gets us all the way from one end of this puddle to the other!" his passenger answered.

The anguished eyes of the Japanese woman watched as the fiercely driven rain threatened real damage to the porch of Higgins Manor.

"Ohh...! Higgins-san *o ushinatte shimatta kamo shirenai!*" ("My Higgins-san might be lost at sea!")

Sueno resumed her shuffle from one end of the porch to the other. She had been pacing ever since Eddie Nakashima called at noon with news that Kobe reported the boat had left before dawn.

"Ohh...!"

The ringing of the phone startled her. Lifting the skirt of her kimono, she hurried inside. Trembling, she squeezed the heavy black earpiece against her head and listened.

"*Moshi, moshi!*" Her worried frown changed to a smile, and her eyes widened as she recognized the familiar voice in the earpiece.

"Ahh...so, Higgins-san!" she answered. *"Yokatta!"*

Standing in the shack on the Hiro dock, Higgins looked at his watch. It was 1900. He swayed slightly on his sea legs as he spoke with Sueno in Japanese.

"Yes, this is really me, and I'm OK."

Sueno kept interrupting to ask where he was and when he would be home.

"I'll be home very soon."

He hung up the phone and returned to the boat. "Boy, was Yoshida excited!" he told Ellsworth. "She was worried about the weather."

Before going home, Higgins made a hurried trip to his locker at the officers club and visited the kitchen. He returned to the boat and presented gifts of sake, beer, whiskey, and beef to the crew. "You are a good bunch!" he told them.

Later that week, Higgins delivered the loot from Kobe to the service clubs in the Hiroshima area.

Higgins had a full schedule with many days consumed by inspections of industrial plants like Moriaso Drill Company, Harima

Machinery from industrial plants had to be dug out of sand and caves, refurbished and reinstalled.

Upon the reopening of steel plants, large delegations of industrialists inspected work in progress. At one plant Higgins found lathes bigger than anything in America. They had produced eighteen-inch cannons for the military.

Shipbuilding Works, Mitsuko Industries, Amagasshi Steel Works, and Japan Steel. He visited some plants several times in efforts to help them return to peacetime work. Sometimes he made additional inspections simply to keep track of developments, as at Mizuno Ship Company, where he noted they were doing a good job digging machines out of the sand and reconditioning them.

In Hiroshima, Higgins inspected Nippon Steel, Nakahio Industries Company, Toda Manufacturing Company, Toya Cotton Spinning Mills, and Fujikawa Steel, Hiroshima in a single day.

Higgins began noticing the ties between companies, as when he discovered salvaged boats had been taken from Nippon Senkai by shipping control, repaired, and given to other Amagasshi companies.

He also was learning about the Japanese male ego. The manager of Mitsubishi #20 and Mitsubishi Shipyard in Hiroshima had invited Higgins and his new translator to dinner at his house. In no time at all, their host dragged out an album of photos, many taken in America. There were two pictures of his wedding, one of his wife and kids, and Higgins counted nearly sixty of his host.

The social aspects of the inspection trips far exceeded anything Higgins had known stateside. "You must favor me with a visit to my home," his contacts would say.

He accepted the invitation from the manager of Naha Iron Works, whose plant was located on the Inland Sea. Arriving by boat, Wally and Eddie were taken to the manager's new home in Naha. The host took his guests on a walk around the gardens before they entered and were introduced to the manager's sisters. Sake appeared, then dinner, served by the sisters, who treated their guests to a feast of thick steak, chicken, tai, cucumbers, sukiyaki, and clam soup. As the evening continued, the sisters entertained as geisha.

Higgins and Eddie, the manager, and his sisters then went to the Fujisan Hotel in Onomichi where they attended a party. Higgins was impressed with the excellent music and the attire of the girls, who wore a variety of long dresses, kimonos and street clothes. When his Japanese companions left, Higgins retired to his room for a massage by a *mamasan*.

He awoke to a soft, female voice. *"Ohayohgozaimasu."* Wally looked up at a very pretty young lady in a short dress.

"Who?"

"I your *mamasan* last night," she said, kneeling beside him and hiding her disappointment.

"I was a bit groggy," Higgins explained.

As she began to sing softly, she removed his bedcovers and gently massaged his back.

"I bring breakfast if you like."

"Yes."

As he attacked the steak and eggs, Higgins enjoyed the mixed conversation of Japanese and pidgin English with the delightful girl.

While Higgins enjoyed his time in Japan, he never seemed to forget the feelings of his "hosts," especially on May 24, 1946, Empire Day. "What are the feelings of the natives about this 'Empire Day' holiday this year?" he pondered in his journal. "They have fought a long and bloody war...and lost! For the very first time in modern history, a foreign force occupies the main islands of Japan. The former empire is gone, and Japan's warriors are disarmed and coming home...one whole boatload is due in Onomichi this very day!"

Later, as Higgins's crew tied the MG launch to the Onomichi dock, a shipload of repatriates—Japanese servicemen—disembarked from a large ship, docked alongside. They formed up in groups and walked by, escorted by Australian troops.

"A husky and formidable lot!" Higgins commented to Eddie Nakashima. Higgins and his interpreter followed the group to the camp, where they called on the Australian CO.

"Rough looking bunch you've just taken in," Higgins commented.

"Right you are, Commander. It's the officers I feel sorry for. They already know about the post-surrender directive barring them from responsible jobs. They're a pretty sad lot."

"Did you know their army and navy pensions were cut off, too?"

"More than 200,000 of them. What can I do for you, Commander?"

Higgins explained the reason for his call: the need for cooperation with nearby plants.

By greeting and entertaining the officers of each arriving ship, Higgins kept up with the news and widened his circle of friends. His local tours, superb food, good-natured songfests, and gracious Japanese servers made the days and nights at Kure a pleasant part of Far East duty for the visitors. During a stretch of four days and five nights in late May 1946 while the USS Chicago was in port there were parties at Higgins Manor, the old Forty-first club, a new restaurant in a bombed-out factory in Hiroshima called Mr. Furukawa's, the Army mess, and Higgins's favorite restaurant, Shogun's.

Some time was spent alone with Sueno, too. On the afternoon of the May 30, Higgins found himself somewhat bored with catching up on chores around the house.

"Would you like to climb the mountain behind the house?" he asked Sueno.

"Kanari tohkutemo ikimashoh." ("Let's go, even if it is far.")

Sueno took his hand as they made the long climb to the top. It was the first time Higgins had explored the area, and he found the view spectacular. They saw the port of Kure and Hiro below, and parts of Hiroshima and its harbor to the west. Nearly surrounding them, at a distance, they saw the Inland Sea and many of its islands.

"Damn!" Higgins exclaimed.

"What wrong?"

"Nothing, really. I'm angry with myself for not bringing a camera."

They noticed a breastwork of sandbags at the crest of the mountain and climbed to it. Higgins was a bit unnerved to discover a Japanese emplacement with five-inch antiaircraft guns. They had not been enough to protect Kure and Hiroshima, just fourteen kilometers away, from the high-flying B-29s. Higgins made sure that the guns had been disabled.

The next day after work, Higgins climbed the same mountain and took pictures.

By June 2, the rainy season had begun, but in spite of the drizzle, Sueno, Eddie, Annie Ikemoto, and Higgins took a boat ride for a Sunday of shopping on the island of Miyajima. Higgins went on a buying spree, including purchasing a Western-style suit for Sueno. Anne and Eddie observed the two as Higgins smiled broadly and Sueno seemed about to jump out of her skin with joy.

"Sueno behave like a child," Anne whispered to Eddie.

"He makes her happy."

"Sueno Yoshida is always a companion to Higgins-san. How do the Americans call that?"

"Going steady."

From Tokyo, Higgins carefully followed the directions he had been given as he guided the Jeep to the entrance of the Decker mansion. He was right on time for his lunch date with Captain Benton W. Decker, an Academy classmate. Decker met him at the door.

"Hey, Wally, good to see you!"

"Benny, it seems like a hundred years since I last saw you!"

Their handshake was cordial.

"Come on in."

"You've certainly got impressive quarters here," Higgins said as they walked through the beautifully decorated entrance hall.

"Thanks, but the credit really goes to Edwina. She persevered until she found this place. Of course, these hallway pieces are all Japanese paintings and artifacts."

"Well, it looks like her search was very successful." Higgins had been caught off guard. Had someone told him Decker's wife had come to Japan? Maybe, but he wasn't yet accustomed to thinking about the presence of American wives, and he'd let it slip by.

Presently, Mrs. Decker joined them for lunch in a formal dining area that looked to Higgins like it was straight out of a senior officers mess.

"Goodness," she said, "how long has it been since we were all together at the last reunion?"

"The incredible class of 1919," said Higgins, hoping that idle chatter would steer them away from his domestic situation. By her use of the word "all," Higgins was quite aware that she was referring to the absence of his wife. "It's been a long time."

"Understandable," Decker said. "You were out of uniform in business all those years."

While Higgins wondered whether Decker looked upon his absence from the Navy as a truancy or an advantage, Edwina delivered her real question. "How is Adelaide?"

"Fine," answered Wally too quickly. "I haven't seen her in over a year."

"Benny and I got accustomed to those long absences when he pulled sea duty."

Higgins smiled and ate. "Good," he thought. "She isn't going to reminisce about being a bridesmaid at our wedding."

"But I can understand," she continued, "you not being used to those prolonged stretches. It must be very lonely for you."

"I'm sure Wally will fill us in with all the news from Adelaide and the boys when he's good and ready," Decker chided.

"Damn!" thought Higgins. "They're both on this fishing expedition."

"All I know," Higgins said, "is what I read in her letters. Last I heard she was doing fine... *is* doing fine."

Captain Decker moved on. "Have you had occasion to get to know this prefecture, Wally?"

"I've been to Tokyo, but my work down south has taken most of my attention."

"You'll just love it," Edwina broke in.

"For God's sake, Edwina!" Decker said, half smiling at his wife's forthright approach. "I haven't mentioned anything to Wally yet." After a brief pause, Decker continued. "Kanagawa ken takes in half of Tokyo and the area just to the south...Yokohama and Yokosuka."

"The naval, commercial, and industrial heartland of Japan," Higgins added.

"Precisely. And as commander of fleet activities my job is to oversee the activities you just enumerated."

"Benny is running the show around here, and he wants you to come and help him," Edwina contributed.

There was a pause, then they all laughed.

"What about it, Wally?" Decker asked. "How about you moving up here to handle military government for me?"

鳥

Higgins had just pulled the Jeep to a stop in front of Higgins Manor when a Japanese man burst from the front door and stomped down the sidewalk. Wally watched with increasing concern as the stranger approached, arms flailing, stopped in front of him, and grunted and mumbled as he jumped about like a tantrum-throwing child. Then, almost as suddenly as he had appeared, he walked off down the street. Higgins watched from the Jeep until the man was out of sight. Hearing sobbing from the house, Higgins hurried inside. Sueno Yoshida was on her knees, weeping.

"Who was the man?" Higgins asked.

"Husband," was all Sueno could blurt out for several minutes. "Tadasu wants her back," she finally said.

"He wants who back?"

"Tae. He want my daughter."

"You told me he deserted both of you."

"That is true. He leave us nine years ago. Now he come back from Imperial Army. He find out from people in village Sueno well off, working for important American. He not want me back, but Yoshida family nag at him to come tell me to stop working for barbarian. Tadasu demand I go back to work in Yoshida family house."

"My poor Yoshida-san," Higgins comforted the sobbing woman, "*Iku tsumori des ka?*" ("Do you intend to go?")

"*Iie!*" ("No!"), wailed Sueno. "*Ano hito wa itsu de mo yakusoku wo mamoranai kara. Mo iya ni natte shimatta!*" ("That man never keeps his promises, I'm disgusted with him and I'll have nothing more to do with him!")

Higgins had been in Japan long enough to know that loss of face was extremely important. From what he could piece together, Tadasu's family felt some loss of face, as most Japanese men shun deserted or divorced women. And the Yoshida family may have resented the commander's attention to Sueno, especially after Tadasu had rejected her.

Late in June, Sueno and Sadae watched as the Indian chef from the officers club taught Higgins's new cooks, Nobuko-san and Annie Ikemoto.

While taking the chef back to his quarters after an evening meal, Higgins and the Indian saw an American in the process of picking up two nurses.

"You Americans get everything!" the Indian said.

"It does look like that fellow's going to have a good time tonight," Higgins replied.

"Americans are so lucky! In India, we had enough of the Brits taking everything at the expense of Indians."

The chef paused before he said, "There is one thing that I cannot understand...your attitude of not wanting to rule the world!"

Higgins received word on June 27 that Decker had officially requested his presence in Yokosuka. He would be released thirty days after they could find a suitable replacement for him. Although he was excited by the prospect of moving on, Higgins planned to "keep an anchor here."

Sueno clutched the trinkets and dresses Wally bought her that morning. She and Eddie were at the railroad station in Hiro to see Higgins off on his trip to Yokohama.

"*Sayonara!*" Sueno called as she waved to her departing boss, lover, and friend.

The train stopped at Ofuno (Kamakura) the next morning and Higgins got off to await transportation to Yokosuka. He sat on a bench and watched the faces of the many Japanese paying homage to a huge Buddha. Taking out the folded papers in his pocket, he brought his diary up to date:

> The country sure is united in its action and makeup. Will it be cooperation or resistance? I don't like the idea of a resistance movement. I also don't like the looks on the faces of a lot of the Japs nowadays. There are many thousands of returning repatriots who will aggravate the situation. Our Military Government under the present conditions is a farce! There is constant turnover of personnel—100% every three months so far.

While Higgins was having breakfast at the Yokosuka Naval Base Officers Club, Captain Decker approached him, followed by Edwina. Higgins rode to Yokohama with them in their staff car to view a parade, then on to Tokyo for lunch with what Higgins called the brass hats.

A viewing parade on July 4, 1946, in Yokohama. Right to left, Commander Higgins, Captain Benny Decker, Edwina Decker, unidentified family members, Marine Colonel Jeff Jefferson, and an interpreter.

In the afternoon Higgins went to Admiral Momsen's home for drinks and was back at Decker's mansion for dinner. After finishing his dessert, Decker napkin-dabbed his mouth, pushed back his chair, and turned to his former classmate.

Higgins glanced at Edwina, who looked slightly bored, as if she knew the drill.

"Higgins, I'm going to make rear admiral any day now, and I need you here. You must come to Yokosuka to run the military government for me. How about starting August first?"

"Well, I can't say I especially care about the Army's job at Kure," Higgins admitted. "And Yokosuka is a Navy area. I think I'll take you up on the offer."

"Good, then it's settled!"

"I just love the formalities you Navy big shots go through," Edwina teased. "I told Benny you'd come up here when he first suggested it. We're glad you've agreed, Wally. It means a lot."

"How very helpful a clever wife can be," Higgins said to himself.

As the Deckers drove Higgins to Ofuna to catch the Allied Limited back to Kure, Higgins noticed the time. "Gosh, I'm late! We'll miss it by ten minutes."

Nearing the station, they saw the train still standing there.

Higgins bid a hasty goodbye and ran for it.

"Do not worry, Commander," the conductor said by way of greeting. "We hold the train for you!"

As they rolled across the Japanese countryside, Higgins mused, "Well, I guess I'll have to abandon 'Higgins Manor,' become a sub-sub-Lieutenant under Captain Benny Decker and live an honorable, civilized life. That is not good. Poor Yoshida-san. When she gets the news she'll be so sad!"

Sueno and Eddie met Higgins at the Hiro station. For the next week, he took daily swimming and inspection boat trips. At night they entertained large groups of officers with dinners and songfests at Higgins Manor. He mixed work with play, winding down his tour of duty in Hiroshima. On many of Higgins's boat trips around the Inland Sea, Sueno Yoshida, Eddie Nakashima, and Annie Ikemoto went along. Higgins appreciated the Japanese girls' many little acts of courtesy.

His opinions regarding differences between Japanese and American women were taking solid form. When several American Red

Cross girls from Kobe visited, he had Eddie take them to Miyajima, where they toured the Itsukushima Shrine, among the most beautiful in Japan. When they got back from the island, Higgins bought them a good dinner at the club.

"There's nothing special about them," he thought. "Like all other American women they can't compare with Japanese women for graciousness. It seems to me the women here are far superior to the men. They not only work better, they talk differently...when answering the telephone, for instance. Japanese women almost sing their conversations. I look forward to tomorrow night, studying Japanese and songs with Sueno Yoshida. Only fifteen more days to change of duty. Hate to tell her."

Starting early in the morning, Higgins took Sueno to her parents' place above Hiroshima so she could help her mother with the cleaning while Higgins visited with Kotani-san, Sueno's father. As they left, Higgins insisted that Sueno try to drive the Jeep.

"Oh, no!" she protested.

"Go ahead."

The Jeep lurched and stopped, then lurched again, and started to gain speed. Sueno looked at Higgins for instruction.

"Don't look at me! Watch the road."

Not able to follow what he was saying but thinking he was giving her directions, she totally disregarded her driving and tried to comprehend Higgins's words. Even amid the confusion, Higgins thought how youthful and joyful the petite, frightened woman looked.

"Help me, please!" She had let go of the wheel and was screaming.

Higgins leaned over and slammed the brake to the floor, whereupon the Jeep careened into the side of a house. While Higgins laughed, Sueno climbed into the back of the Jeep and covered her face. Higgins drove away, still chuckling.

They spent the rest of that long day on the Inland Sea, fishing, swimming, and exploring a small island.

Higgins's next trip to Yokosuka was by night train on July 24. The beauty of the next morning did little to change his disgust with the train's late departure or with the broken screen in the window of his berth funneling soot on him all night as the train chugged north.

He began the day by reviewing intelligence reports:

> Concerned by evidence of the self-fulfilling prophesy that American Intelligence sees what it looks for. Japs seem to be starting passive resistance by appearing to perform duties diligently. Maybe Japanese workers are confused over American preachings of democracy. Japanese farmers in the fields are wearing veteran's patches on their backs.

On his arrival at Yokosuka, Higgins spent several hours with Captain Decker, and his new orders were cut.

"This assignment won't be so bad," he thought. "Benny is ambitious, but for a good cause."

On the train back to Hiro, his sleeper car was in second class and full of drunken, rowdy GIs. Seven months into 1946, nearly all the original occupation troops with combat experience had gone home and been replaced by fresh draftees. The new recruits were fond of bragging about how they beat the Japs.

Higgins had become concerned with the demeanor of occupation troops. Some of them did not even try to understand the island nation. At a concert at the finest enlisted men's club in the Far East, with its theater, dance hall, beer garden, billiards, library, gym, private rooms, and snack bar, he watched as the number one Japanese singing star performed and was booed. "What a disgraceful exhibition!" he had thought. "What must the Japanese think of our rudeness? Maybe we don't care, but the day may come when we will be glad to have them as our allies!"

The first warnings came when ominous clouds formed the afternoon of July 28. Higgins entertained twenty-two for dinner and enjoyed a good songfest until 11:00 p.m. The next morning, when he went to the club to secure his boat and help shutter the windows against the wind, the water was beginning its turbulent dance of warning. Higgins made it home by noon, and immediately the lights went out. He called Kure Naval Base, and just as he confirmed that emergency relief for the Kure-Hiro area had been mobilized, the phone went dead.

Higgins and Sueno ate lunch by the light of a Coleman lamp and listened to the wind intensify. The main force of the typhoon struck at midafternoon. They sat close on a futon and watched through the narrow slits of the shutters as trees bent so low they were nearly level with the ground and sheets of rain slammed against the house.

The weather cleared the next afternoon. After dinner, Higgins and Sueno sat alone.

"I have to tell you something that distresses me."

She smiled at him with her uncomprehending look.

"Distress means not easy...hard to do."

"You have hard-to-tell news?"

"I have, yes."

Sueno's smile remained, though was slightly deflated.

"I am being transferred to Yokosuka."

"You take more trip to Yokosuka?"

"No. I'm moving there. To live there...all the time."

"Ohh..." Sueno's face went white, and as much as she attempted to hide it, her whole demeanor changed. *"Yokosuka anata desu ka?"* Her words were more like a cry of anguish. "I have much sadness," she finally admitted. "Like a year ago, when emperor talk over radio."

During the next few days, the staff of Higgins Manor went into an emotional tailspin. Whenever Higgins came into the same room with the head housekeeper, she disappeared.

"Eddie, what the hell is going on with her?" Higgins asked.

"She's afraid to ask if she will be going with her master. She says if she doesn't ask, she won't be told bad news. So she avoids you."

Higgins was beginning to feel it: The fun was over. The occupation of Hiroshima prefecture had become "very GI," full of rules and regulations and a tighter chain of command. Activities like bartering booze for steaks out in the harbor were things of the past. The enjoyment Higgins had experienced as military governor—managing without being tightly controlled—was at an end. The last day of July was also his final day of official duty in Hiroshima ken. With Brigadier General Frederick M. Hopkins, Jr., a major and three colonels aboard, Higgins motored to Kanawa Island, inside the port of Hiroshima. He was less than totally enthusiastic about reviewing his plans for turning over his boat. The Titanic was to be reconditioned, repainted as MG 1 and turned over to the general, along with MG 2.

Then he found all was not lost when he obtained permission to have the third of the motor launches raised and reconditioned to be sent north to Yokosuka for his use—yet another personal reward for having won the wrestling match with Fujiwara-san on his arrival in Japan.

General Hopkins threw a big party for thirty-two guests on August 2 in Higgins's honor. It was highly unusual in Japan for the woman of the household to accompany the master of the house to dinners and parties, but Sueno Kotani Yoshida was an exception in many ways. Since the beginning of 1946, she had been the perfect hostess at Higgins's many gatherings, charming the American guests with her beauty and her shy manner, and following perfect protocol with the Japanese guests.

There was a speech praising the commander, and Higgins called the whole event a "good show." As the singing of *Jolly Good Fellow* ended, Sueno decided to sip a beer. When everyone encouraged her to drink some more, the small Japanese woman giggled, had a few more sips, and presently began to sway, even though she was kneeling. She put her glass down and placed both hands on her face, as if to feel if she was blushing, which she was. By the time Sueno

The Good Ship Titanic cruises the Japanese Inland Sea August 1946 with Sueno (in window), American guest, and crew.

had consumed half the glass, she was drunk, but all she did was hide her face and stay in the one spot, gently wobbling from side to side.

Higgins was packed and physically prepared to go, but the next three days brought no news about how he was to actually move. Orders went back and forth until he finally learned he was to wait for LST 308 to arrive from Sasebo. With all but one of his farewell parties over, Higgins had no official duties to occupy his days, so the outgoing military governor could often be seen cruising the Inland Sea around Kure. He said he was looking for the LST from Sasebo that was to take him and his household gear to Yokosuka, but he appeared more fidgety with each passing day. Higgins's boat was kept busy those final weeks in the waters around Hiroshima. Used in the daytime for tours by officers and enlisted men, and he and Sueno used it for moonlight cruises.

He was in no hurry—quite the contrary. He was leaving Higgins Manor with its rich social life, and his well-trained and devoted household staff. Then too, he knew that the minute he stepped ashore in Yokosuka, he would be expected to carry out his job by the book, using methods he had often found ineffective in this recovering country. Most difficult, he was leaving Sueno.

Sueno prayed the rough seas that were preventing the landing ship from navigating between Sasabo and Kure would last forever, so it would not take Higgins away, but on August 26, 1946, it entered the harbor. Higgins's MG relief arrived the same day. "Colonel Snyder appears to be a good Joe—will turn over everything to him," Higgins noted.

The harder Sueno tried to appear normal as she stood watching Higgins's things being carried out of the house, the sadder she actually looked. As his personal gear, including whiskey, was loaded aboard the Titanic, she came and stood beside him. He hadn't noticed she carried two dolls.

"Take this, please." She presented Higgins with Tsukiko, her favorite, and he graciously accepted.

"Also, please take this one," she said, holding out her daughter's gift, a warrior doll.

"Sueno, I can't accept Tae's doll. It's her best one. She loves this doll, and she's still little more than a child."

"Tae says this doll for you."

Higgins knew better than to carry it further as they watched the boat fill with his possessions.

Twenty-two people attended the last farewell party that night, and they managed to polish off the balance of the Japanese liquor that Higgins had won ten months before in his wrestling match with Fujiwara-san.

Later, Higgins slept soundly in his bedroom while Sueno lay awake on her backroom futon, crying quietly until dawn.

All the help from Higgins Manor was at the dock to board the Titanic the next morning. They came alongside the big, blunt-ended LST 308 at 0900. Leaving his launch, Higgins shook hands with each member of his crew and household staff, answered their bows with graceful bows of his own, and climbed aboard the LST.

Tears flowed down Sueno Yoshida's cheeks and she struggled to say, "*Sayonara!*"

But she wasn't alone. From his vantage point on the deck of the launch, Eddie Nakashima noticed that every Japanese servant of the departing commander was crying.

As the LST got underway, the Titanic followed and stayed alongside till both vessels were well out into the Inland Sea. After an hour, the motor launch turned and headed back toward Hiro.

SEVEN

Governing Kanagawa ken

Before Higgins had begun his official duties, Captain Decker let Wally know that he had proposed a change in the Japanese national property law. The change would allow Yokosuka Naval Base to be split up so businesses and civic organizations could use parts of it. The zone had been available only to the Japanese military for hundreds of years, but Decker's proposal would shift ownership from the Imperial Navy to the civilian government.

"I view this project as one of my top MG priorities," Decker had said. "If you've got nothing better to do with your day off before reporting for duty, grab a Jeep and take a drive around the base. It'll help you grasp the importance of the project."

Higgins was awed by the vastness of the base. He found caves in hillsides containing shops and immense warehouses, dry docks larger than anything he had ever seen in America, and an underground hospital with two-thousand beds.

He drove down the coast past Otsu Beach, then swung around the Miura Peninsula that overlooked the entrance to Tokyo Bay, past the giant shipbuilding ways at Uraga, then directly into the mountain to inspect the miles of tunnels.

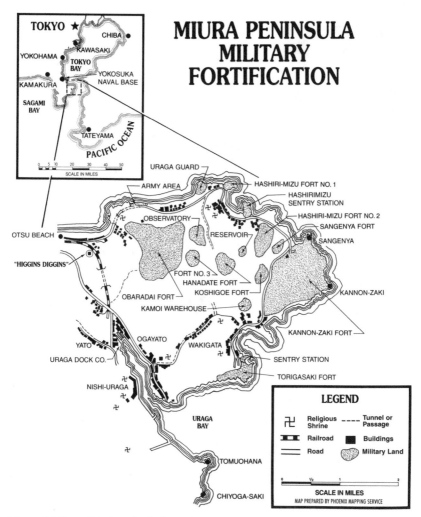

Map of Miura Peninsula defenses

As he examined the tunnels, Higgins found that many contained enormous sixteen- and eighteen-inch guns, in essence cannons, aimed at the mouth of Tokyo Bay—and any foreign fleet that tried to enter. The more he explored, the more Higgins realized that the hills around the Miura Peninsula were honeycombed with defensive caves. "How fortunate the war ended before the Allies attempted a landing!" he thought.

"OK, Governor," he said, as he dropped the ten-inch pile of folders on the empty desk of Commander Higgins, "here's what's got to be done!"

Higgins looked up at his new boss, Commander of Fleet Activities at Yokosuka, Japan, Captain Benton W. Decker.

"Damned if he doesn't look impressive," thought Higgins, "especially in the summer whites. Is he keeping his hand on top of those papers just so I'll notice the four stripes?"

"And by the way, Higgins," the captain added, "welcome aboard."

"Thanks, Benny. Good morning!"

"Sir!" the captain added sharply.

"Good morning, sir!"

Decker went off down the hall.

"That's just hunky-dory," Higgins mused. "The man says he can't get the job done without me, and now that I'm here he treats me like a damn plebe!" For a few moments, as Higgins stared blankly at the pile of work, his mind continued to put his new boss in some kind of perspective. "Did Benny have those jowls under his chin twenty-five years ago at the Academy? I guess he did, but they were more like creases. We're both the same age, and I don't have jowls like that. The stern look of ambition...that's the same as I remember. The SOB's still got a full head of hair...so white, with that little wave. Making rank hasn't come easy for him. Look at all our classmates who've made admiral. I suppose he figures he's regular career and I'm reserve, and he stayed in between wars, and still I only have one stripe less than he does. That must irritate him no end. Even if it doesn't grind him, he probably gets an earful from Edwina about it."

Higgins didn't have much time to think about that, however. On his first full day of work as MG officer at Yokosuka Naval Base, there was hardly time for him to unpack his office gear or organize his desk. The pile of problems to be digested and handled seemed to appear and grow instantly. From that first day, Higgins got a taste for the fast office tempo. He was frequently summoned the short distance down the hall from his cramped space to Decker's office to be given yet another project, or asked to take over and solve some sticky problem with one of Decker's visitors.

One of his first projects was CO Decker's assignment of Higgins to implement his civil management program for the naval district— all of Kanagawa prefecture—the entire area from the middle of Tokyo southward through the industrial and maritime heartland of

Nippon. The program involved close contact with the Japanese Diet and SCAP, and the way Decker envisioned it, would serve as a model for the occupation.

Knowing he was to represent Decker at council meetings, Higgins's mind jumped ahead and predicted the formal language of such gatherings. "I'd better get Eddie Nakashima up here," he thought.

Decker also was trying to bring some of America to Japan. "I've been pushing to get the Thanksgiving holiday made official outside our bases in occupied Japan."

"You mean an official holiday for the Japanese, Captain?" Higgins said. "That'll have to go through the Diet, won't it?"

"Right, and I've got that covered. Mr. Yamamoto, a member of the Diet, is on his way here right now. I'll sponsor the holiday bill and have him introduce it. I want you in my office when he arrives. You're the man I'm delegating to follow through on this baby, Higgins...and all other similar projects."

When Yamamoto arrived they discussed the proposal, and he promised to cooperate. Later in the morning, Higgins had a private meeting with Mr. Sato, chief of the city of Yokosuka. Sato appeared to be the key link to civic organizations in the area, and Higgins was pleased with their first encounter.

"Hey, Higgins, come on!" As Wally was wrapping up his first day's work, Decker leaned into the doorway. "You're invited to the party I'm having for all the dependents."

The two left the building together, stepping off as if on parade, walking in step with decisive strides and swinging arms. Higgins was back on the same team with his Annapolis classmate. But inside, these two were very different.

The Decker Mansion was in its full splendor. At the entrance, koi ogled visitors from their immense aquatic habitat. Edwina showed the many guests through their large home, including the Japanese artwork that occupied the walls. "Benny's etchings," she said for a laugh. As the house tours ended, she led her groups toward the yard, where water-spouting reflectors from Japanese warships sat atop pedestals, forming a fountain. Higgins watched her and admired her hostessing grace and her deft handling of the large gathering. "Adelaide," he mused, "sweet Adelaide would let one group dominate her the whole evening." Then Sueno's image appeared in his mind, and he smiled. "My lovely Sueno...she'd have this bunch wrapped around her little finger with her charm."

Higgins approached Edwina, who was talking to three other wives. "This is what I'd call a real party," he said, and reached into his pocket. "I've been meaning to ask if you'd like to sign my short snorter." Higgins presented the folded money and a pen to the hostess. Edwina squealed as she unfolded three yards of taped-together money and examined the variety of signatures. Higgins's short snorter had grown to include nineteen different issues of paper money. She signed the ten-yen certificate beneath the ideograph of H. Furuichi.

"What in the world is that?" one of the women asked.

"A Navy custom of gathering signatures from people on the currency of their country." Higgins chuckled. "Of course, you have to have a drink or two with the signers."

"Can my husband sign?" a woman asked somewhat timidly. "He's an enlisted man."

"Of course!" answered Higgins.

Decker joined the gathering crowd. "What's all the excitement about?"

Short snorter: Captain Decker's $100 Japanese bill was the sixteenth currency taped to Higgins's short snorter.

"Have you signed Higgins's short snorter yet?" Edwina handed the long string of paper to her husband.

"Hah! I'll go one better. Hold this." Decker handed the strip back to Edwina, pulled a Japanese hundred-dollar bill from his billfold, wrote "B.W. Decker, Capt. R.N." on one end, and handed it to Higgins. "My contribution. Just add it to your strip, Wally." Higgins thanked his boss politely, folded up the short snorter, and put it in his pocket. He'd add eight more bills, but somehow the ice breaker had lost its power of camaraderie for Wally after Decker's addition.

As some of those at the party indicated, American dependents were coming to Japan in large numbers. Depending on their rank, officers' families were assigned a number of Japanese servants, supplied as part of the occupation's reparations. The luxury of having numerous servants spoiled many of the dependents, and a class consciousness was developing. Officers' wives found themselves with only their own group to talk to, since they often snubbed enlisted people and their families. The three wives of the enlisted men who had signed Higgins's short snorter sought him out and seemed to enjoy talking with him about his experiences in Hiroshima. Their genuine interest and friendliness contrasted with the aloof attitudes of most of the officers' wives.

Decker's party lasted till midnight. When Higgins returned to his quarters, the brief contact with the refreshingly unpretentious wives prompted him to make a judgment in his diary:

> Enlisted men's wives are superior to officers' wives, *omoimas* (I think).

Higgins called his administrative assistant, into his office. "Look at this stack of assignments, John. All these folders contain separate projects. Listen..." He thumbed though the folders. "Here's Decker's program to make Thanksgiving a Japanese holiday. Then we've got new laws—in English. You can do some of that, but get help. Here's renovation of the schools, a survey of Yokosuka material needs, a plan for industrialization, changes in national property laws. I've already got a leg up on that one, but it's typical of how much we have to do that involves high-ups in the Diet. Look at this: 'Establish Red Cross.' And here's the paperwork on an orphanage in cooperation with a women's club. The tab on this one is about reorganizing city government. Then we have the sewer system. Here's a doozy: 'Employment of former Jap admirals.'" Higgins looked across the desk at his assistant and got a glazed stare back.

"Don't worry. We can only have so many meetings a day. But in case you get confused about where we're going or who we're going to see, I've made this notebook with one listing on each page. See, the headings are numbered, easy to look up. I've begun to pencil in names, dates, meetings, progress details. When a project is complete I'll just cross it off."

"Or when a new project comes up, you can add a page," John noted wryly. "How many are there?"

"Now? About seventy." Higgins paused a moment.

The two men exchanged a serious look, then laughed.

"You needn't become familiar with this book, John, but I do want you to have some knowledge about the projects. I'd say that out of the rest of the list the most important are...let's see...the study of all Jap companies working in the naval yard, control of VD, sisters of the Sacred Heart, the elections coming up, the reparations program, the police department, democratic education, roads, inspections of jails, hospitals, a dial telephone system, a look at the Social Democratic Party...and there's more, as you can see. The point is, we're going to be very busy."

Requests immediately came across Higgins's desk for appointments with the home minister, the head of the schools, the chamber of commerce, the mayor of Yokosuka, and the finance minister.

A busy week followed, filled with meetings, trips to Yokohama, working luncheons, dinners, and parties. Higgins concentrated on learning as much background as he could on the people he was meeting, their positions and connections. He figured that as Japan struggled to its feet, these same people would gain stature, and the success of these early contacts could prove useful in many ways.

Higgins put Captain Decker's proposal to change the property laws into a letter and hand-delivered it to COM NAV JAP. When he got back to his office, he had visitors.

"A Mr. Tsunoda wishes to see you," said Higgins's secretary.

"What about?" Higgins asked.

"He says he has some plans for industry."

"Where is he from?"

"He is advisor to the Women's Club. And he has a an interpreter with him."

"Show them in."

It took only a few minutes for Higgins to see that Mr. Tsunoda was well qualified to help.

"I went to Shanghai during the war and served the China Aviation Company as advisor on oil. I am a graduate of MIT and married to an American."

"What is your interest now in working with Kanagawa's military government?"

"Ahh...I'm interested in oil, of course. And Japanese naval supply. But I'm also representing three other advisors who were with me at Shanghai."

"They are?"

"Mr. Takehashi, who represents the Women's Club. I am their advisor. I am employed by the chamber of commerce, which Mr. Ichikawa represents. And Mr. Takeuchi wants to run a newspaper. They are waiting outside."

Their proposal included plans for a newspaper, a soda plant, and a textile mill. Higgins quickly made them all designated advisors.

A day later, Mr. Furuichi and his associates from a shipbuilding firm called with a plan to bring new industries to Yokosuka. Higgins told them to work out their plans with Sato and submit a complete report later in September. It was Higgins's plan for Sato and Furuichi to work together under his guidance; they each had the potential to become friends and confidants.

This geographical and military position also brought Higgins in closer contact with General MacArthur's staff. On the Friday of his first week in his new job he met with a delegation from SCAP to discuss idle plant space on a former naval base that could be cleaned up and put to use producing textiles. Higgins relished this kind of project: The Japanese had the necessary know-how, SCAP agreed to make spindles available, the property was in place, and labor was available.

"Money is the only missing requisite," Higgins summed up. "We can all work on that, and get this place up and running." When everyone had left, Higgins stepped outside and took a deep breath. "Another beautiful day!"

As he returned to his desk he noticed the date—Friday, September 13—and it made him pause. "Exactly twenty-seven years ago today I married Adelaide...a long time."

Before he had left Kure, Higgins wrote to Adelaide, asking her if she would like to join him in Japan. She had declined, saying she must stay and take care of her aging parents in New Jersey. "Besides," she had written, "I wouldn't want to be that far from the boys."

Higgins threw himself into his work. Partly by design and partly by good fortune, he had discovered an important method of introducing democratic ways and a free market economy to Japan: face-to-face discussions with Japanese businessmen and personal participation in their social organizations.

He went to information-gathering meetings of organizations, such as the chamber of commerce, where he listened for hours. He questioned the businessmen about current conditions, the mind-set of their fellow Japanese, what they thought of occupation policies, what needed to be done, and how the United States and Japan could cooperate for a speedy recovery. His habit of continually asking for suggestions delighted the Japanese.

Captain Decker enjoys a party on his grounds in Yokosuka.

At the end of that first week, Higgins attended a Saturday night party where he got involved in a songfest. He was pleased that such functions seemed as popular in Yokosuka as they were in Kure.

The workload mounted during the next month, and the sheer quantity of problems and tasks was in itself vexing. One morning he counted thirty-five callers, yet he somehow found time to visit a little girl in a hospital, give out prizes at a school, and see to other humanitarian errands.

But sometimes Higgins also felt hamstrung. The mayor had been in private sessions in Decker's office many times. In mid-September, Higgins interviewed the delegation of Yokosuka city council members in his office.

"What progress are you making on Captain Decker's requests?" Higgins asked.

He got blank stares in return.

"We in the council never heard of Captain Decker's requests," one member finally said.

"Our delegation had wanted to meet Captain Decker and could not do so," another added.

"Why not?"

"The council president has been here. He called on Captain Decker. The president told us we could not see the captain."

"Did not the president of the council tell you what was requested?" Higgins asked. He bit his lip when he discovered that the council president apparently had kept everything to himself.

Meanwhile, Decker's contrasting style was frustrating Higgins. "Decker grabs for the publicity and material things," observed Higgins. "Half the good things in Yokosuka are here. Benny is riding high, sparing nothing for his own home, and living more and more like a millionaire...he preaches democracy and practices autocracy."

Part of it, Higgins felt, was Decker's desperation for two stars, but Wally could wait.

"The only sane way to bring democracy to Japan," Higgins told John in the privacy of his small office, "is by education and persuasion. And if there's one thing I've learned from the Japanese, it's patience!"

On September 18, Higgins looked up from his work and saw a group of callers to Captain Decker's office whom Mr. Sato and Mr.

Tsunoda had described as racketeers. As they were leaving, Decker handed Higgins a list. "See that they get these things, Commander."

When the visitors were gone, Higgins stepped into Decker's office.

"Excuse me, Captain, but did you know who those people are? I heard—"

"I don't care what you heard, Higgins. I know what I'm doing. Now get out!"

Higgins was more concerned than ever. "A racket in prostitution is taking definite shape," he later wrote. "I just cannot outguess him. It is discouraging to try to do a job with all the self-appointed judges and cutters there are around. I am discouraged with efforts to help bring democracy to the Japanese when our senior officers outdo Tojo and Hitler in their attitude!"

But changes were taking place in Japan with remarkable speed. A majority in the Allied Council voted for the home rule bill, then made it unanimous. The Diet passed the political rights bill that made all parties legal, including the communists, who had been banned. General Douglas MacArthur had been accepted by the Japanese as a conquering hero, a god who could do no wrong. For the first year and a half of the Allied occupation, programs suggested by the military government and SCAP were enthusiastically implemented.

Higgins's language lessons with a new instructor suddenly turned productive, his office was moved across the hall into a larger space, and he was further pleased to get a new, efficient secretary, Miss Akinu Valerie Karachi.

Stepping off the train the afternoon of October 5 for a weekend visit to Kure, Higgins found Sueno and Eddie waiting. She looked very sad and much thinner than when he had left Hiroshima ken in August.

"Oh, Higgins-san, it is so good to see you!"

"My little sweetheart."

At Kure Base, on the Jeep ride to Higgins Manor, he found the club had been enlarged and housing was being prepared for the arrival of dependents.

Wally patted Sueno's hand. "You look so thin," he said. "We must go to Shogun's." The couple ate enthusiastically, and Sueno brightened, clinging to Higgins between courses.

In Kure, Commander Higgins and Sueno Yoshida are surrounded by friends at Shogun's.

Later, all the help at Higgins Manor was excited to have him home.

"Eddie," Higgins said, "I need you up north. You can help find me a house. When we get settled Sueno can join us."

Treasuring every minute, Sueno treated Wally like a king, and the short Saturday night and Sunday morning stay in his Hiro house rejuvenated him. Sueno and the rest of the help cried when he left on the noon train.

Back at the office, the work crunch continued. He arrived at Ofuno at 7:00 a.m., was at work at 7:30, and worked until 10:00 p.m.

One day in October, he took a satchel of work and his secretary to the hotel and worked late. The next evening, at dinner with Decker and Edwina, Higgins talked about the workload.

"Yesterday I got so far behind that Karachi and I had to stay and work till eleven."

"Why, that's terrible!" Edwina said, surprised. "Benny, I didn't know your building on the base stayed open that late."

"It doesn't," Decker answered, turning to Higgins.

Higgins sipped from his water glass, then explained, "Oh, we moved over to the hotel at seven and worked until we got hungry." He thought, "I'm getting in hot water over nothing. What would they say if I told them all about the housekeeper I'm bringing up here from Hiro?"

Seeing suspicion on the faces of his hosts, Higgins joked, "Oh, that Miss Karachi—what a form!"

Captain Decker leaned forward and pointed a finger at Higgins. "Commander, I think that what you need is a more stable home life."

"My goodness, Wally," Edwina added, "What would Adelaide think?"

Higgins, who was eagerly awaiting Sueno's arrival, fought to keep from gagging on the water.

For a week after Eddie arrived, Higgins and Eddie searched for housing around Yokosuka. The vast area of Yokosuka, Japan's second-largest naval base, included the fortresses of Miura Peninsula. On the main base and the peninsula there were many barracks and homes formerly occupied by military and shipbuilding officials. The Japanese furnished housing for occupation forces as part of the war reparations program. The military governor had quarters in a barracks on base, but he was also entitled to a house off base. The hunt ended October 18 when Eddie was shown a house that Higgins had picked from a list made available by the Japanese.

Formerly occupied by a top shipyard officer, the large home was exceptional. A one-hundred-year-old homestead without modern toilets or central heat, the house was shielded from the outside world by a wall and steeply rising grounds, yet it was only a few steps from the Otsu rail station. The compound even had a private cave in the mountainside. Conveniently located, it was a brief train or Jeep ride down MacArthur Boulevard to the base, just far enough away from the hustle and bustle.

The date Higgins referred to as his "red letter" day was November 6. It rained when Sueno arrived and for the next two days. The weather just seemed to make those first evenings at their new home all the more pleasant.

When some of the other domestic workers from Hiroshima failed to arrive, Sueno wrote to her cousin to "come work for Higgins-san." The first of what Higgins described as "very pretty" cousins arrived to help keep house.

Entitled to one residence, Higgins was not anxious for his additional new address or its staffing arrangements to be known, especially by Decker or his wife. He was leading a double life, keeping the quarters at Yokosuka Naval Base while maintaining the private Japanese home at 3-52 Otsu cho. Higgins told no one, except John, his administrative assistant.

He continued to sleep on base, but being able to retreat to his private house became necessary for Higgins's sanity, especially when the atmosphere at the base turned foul on November 27. Word came that Magazine Area #31 was going to the Army.

"Those SOBs!" Decker ranted. "That's Navy territory!"

The mood at headquarters was even darker two days later when Decker's meeting with the Navy promotion review board was unsatisfactory and he failed to make admiral. Higgins was very glad to get out of the office.

They had been enjoying the quiet evenings for almost a month when Sueno came to Higgins one evening and knelt beside him, saying nothing. He could tell by the way she had approached that she had something on her mind.

"Yes?"

"Why you not have dinner party and songfest, like at Hiro?" she suggested.

"Why not, indeed."

When Higgins showed his guest list to Sueno and Eddie, they explained that for men in such high positions there was a custom of presenting take-away gifts.

On the secluded grounds at Otsu, Higgins hosted a party for fourteen influential Japanese men, including the mayor, vice mayor, council president and vice president, chamber of commerce president, the chief of police and several prominent businessmen. Also in attendance was Chaplain Rickert, an American. The gathering was a big success, topped off by the delight of the guests with their gifts.

After the last visitor was ushered out the gate, Higgins, Sueno, and Eddie sat down and discussed the party. Their conversation was mostly in Japanese, for Sueno still spoke little English.

"*Enkai tottemo yokatta desu. Arigato,*" Higgins began. ("The party very good. Thank you.")

Sueno and Eddie eagerly agreed that it had been a success and told him how much they had missed entertaining since he left Hiroshima ken.

"I don't know if I should report this or not," Eddie said.

"What is it," Higgins asked.

"You may not like it."

Wally gave him a glance that told Eddie to get on with it.

"I overheard one of the guests call this place 'Higgins Diggins.'"

There was a pause before Wally responded. "I like it," he said.

After awhile Higgins began to talk at home about his troubles at the base. "I just cannot accomplish much with the Japanese at my office. They don't talk much...and many cancel appointments."

Sueno spoke at some length to Eddie.

"Yoshida-san suggests that civilian representatives are afraid. Your office is in a forbidden area. For a hundred years the Yokosuka navy grounds were off limits to all Japanese people except naval officials. Non-naval people could not cross line at gate."

Sueno spoke again and waited for Eddie to translate.

"She suggests that you have Japanese meet with you here in house. They will be more comfortable here, and not afraid to talk."

At a council meeting in December, Higgins listened while Decker was bawled out regarding a court sentencing. Privately, Higgins was pleased. "The people of Yokosuka seem to appreciate what I am doing and lack confidence in Decker's policy—I think they are afraid of me also, but show confidence in my policy," he noted.

For Christmas and the New Year the house at Otsu was decorated, the gardens groomed to perfection, and a carved stone shrine called Inari Jinja was placed in the prettiest corner of the garden. Sueno had discovered a piece of a broken stone fox figurine, which had served as a *jinja*, or shrine, at the spot and persuaded Higgins to have it reproduced and restored. There she prayed for good fortune. Sueno's religious beliefs were a combination of Shinto, Buddhist, Christian, and a deep feeling of respect for ancestors and loved ones that she conveyed by bowing before the Inari Jinja. "The loveliest picture in Japan is Sueno Yoshida-san praying before the shrine," observed Wally.

Winter snow dusts the Inari Jinja and Higgins compound at Otsu.

One bright spot for Higgins was his success in reassembling some of his Hiroshima MG team. Lieutenant Huggins reported for duty at Yokosuka assigned to Internal Affairs. With Huggins, Commander Raleigh, and Lieutenant Commander John Holton, Higgins had a team again—and his favorite singing quartet back together.

Higgins brought the quartet to his secret house for dinners, lunches, drinks, and rehearsals, while Sueno and four of her cousins who had joined the staff helped make the house warm and beautiful.

The long workdays, meetings, parties, visits to his house and then back to base to go to bed were wearing even Higgins, however. "This leading a double life is getting me down—I've never been so tired in my life!" he thought.

But he was making progress. Sueno had been right: The Japanese officials and representatives from the civic organizations of Kanagawa ken responded warmly to the informal meetings at Higgins's Otsu house. Uraga Dock Company assisted generously with supplies. A new "Fountain Of Mirrors" (reflectors salvaged from Japanese warships, as Higgins had seen in the Deckers' yard), installed in the garden, delighted everyone.

Higgins was pleased to be moving ahead with the Japanese, but the effort was soon to be compromised. The first warning came in mid-January. "Lieutenants Heald and Michelet are getting nosy about where I spend my nights," noted Wally. This would not have concerned him were it not for the fact that Michelet was Captain Decker's executive officer. The next day, an order was posted that read "No overnights at Japanese homes."

By Saturday, Michelet had spilled the beans. "Well, it finally happened—Simon Legree Michelet squealed to Captain Decker about Otsu," Wally lamented in his journal. "I wrote a personal letter to Benny stating my case of how the house helps the effectiveness of MG." The following Tuesday, Admiral Dennibrink decided "the job be confined to the base."

Waiting for the wooden cars of the local train to clear Otsu station, Higgins stepped across the tracks and walked briskly up the alley to the gate of Higgins Diggins. He slid the bolt aside, entered the secluded grounds, strode quickly past the pond and sculptured bushes, over the small curved footbridge, then up the stone walk to the main house. The caller had said Sueno was "pretty sick." Wally found her in bed, the prettiest of the cousins hovering over her.

"Hakike ga shimasu." ("I feel nauseous.") After telling Higgins how terrible she felt, she moaned and hid her face in her hands. That night, Higgins took over the nursing chores, kneeling alongside Sueno's futon. "Nuisance!" he taunted her.

"Ugh!" Sueno turned away. She waited a moment, then turned to look at him again.

"Spoiled child!" he teased.

"Ugh!" A longer wail this time, as she covered her face.

"Genki o modoshite—watch for *karada*! *Ima sonouchi genki,"* ("Get well. Take care of yourself! Before long you'll be well,") he taunted.

Higgins disregarded whatever trouble he might bring on himself by staying overnight at Otsu, at the side of his woman as she recuperated. Either because of or in spite of his cajoling, Sueno made a full recovery in a few days.

As quietly as possible, Higgins also continued to hold meetings at Higgins Diggins, the Otsu compound. One such meeting brought doctors from town and the MG team together to deal with the problem of the racketeers' control of prostitution.

"The chamber of commerce could intervene," one doctor said.

"Hai...ah, yes! We could arrange to fool the racketeers," another added.

Before the meeting was over, they had hatched a complete plan.

On Friday, Higgins welcomed two SCAP staffers, Navy Captain Olney and Army Brigadier General Swope to the secluded grounds. Higgins explained his need for a place to conduct face-to-face contacts with Japanese officials, to conduct MG business in a relaxed atmosphere, away from the military base.

"What a grand idea," Swope told him, "and a perfect spot for the purpose."

"Well, it hasn't been all that easy," Higgins said. "The Japs have been all for it, but there is this matter of Captain Decker. He would prefer that all military business be conducted on the base, but the Japanese civil authorities and businessmen haven't been allowed on the base for hundreds of years. We've gone through all kinds of maneuvers getting them there, and once they're on base they're too spooked to talk about anything of substance."

"Hell, Higgins, this place is OK by me," the general said.

"And me too," Olney added. "You've got SCAP backing on it, Commander. MacArthur knows how helpful it is to understand Oriental ways, to respect their need for face. Go ahead, use this place."

But the dispute with Decker only became more intense. The following day at staff meeting the CO's big concern was how important it was that the next Saturday afternoon be regarded as a holiday, which led Higgins to wonder whether Decker understood their real mission. "Three-quarters of the U.S. taxpayer's money is being spent for dependents who contribute nothing to Japan, while all intelligent and sincere effort to rehabilitate is nullified by petty enforcement of rules," he fumed.

During the following week there was an effort to steal John, Higgins's administrative assistant, and critical dispatches concerning labor, food, and fraternization problems were held up. Progress was further fouled because the Japanese typists were not the fastest with English, putting the office fifty letters behind.

By Easter week Higgins vowed to get away by himself and sort things out. He rode the "Army-Navy-Allied" railroad car and noticed there were more civil service than Army or Navy personnel on board.

"Oh well," he thought, "they need a rest. They work three days a week!"

The train ride also showed Higgins how little progress had been made since the war. "After eighteen months there are still no provisions for food or water at the stations," he observed. "It is worse than when we first landed, as then the Japanese hotels were available."

He arrived at the mountain town of Shiba Heights in a snowstorm. After an excellent dinner, he joined a party of GIs and led the singing of *Old Black Joe.* The songfest, which lasted late into the night, was excellent salve for Higgins's irritation.

He had no ski equipment, but Higgins was content to take long morning and afternoon walks, study Japanese, luxuriate in mineral baths, take in a show, dance, sing on the mountaintop, and enjoy the meals.

It was a long trip back on Monday, nearly fifteen hours by Weezel, bus, electric and steam trains to Tokyo and Yokohama, but it gave him additional time to put things in perspective. His thoughts went back to conversations with a neighbor in Mentor, Mrs. Frances P. Bolton, who was a congresswoman from Ohio. She was on the powerful Foreign Affairs Subcommittee, and Higgins decided he would write to her.

Meanwhile, the results of the April Japanese elections brought him joy. "The best possible candidates for mayor and governor elected," he exulted. "It's a tribute to the good judgment of the Japanese. Not a single communist elected in all of Japan!"

Higgins's good spirits were unshaken when Mrs. MacArthur visited Yokosuka, and the Deckers invited only those staff with wives to a party at their house. Or when Huggins and Holton were called in by Decker and told to attend no parties and accept no presents from the Japanese or from Higgins. It seemed to Wally that Decker was only hurting himself by flaunting the custom of gift giving: His staff was sure to insult the Japanese.

Higgins hosted his own luncheon in the garden of the Otsu compound for Chaplain Rickert and his wife, his assistant John, a friend named Oba-san, and his new interpreter, Joe. Eddie was there as a member of the household staff, as Higgins's driver and fill-in interpreter. When they finished the meal, Sueno put a rolled towel at each place.

"Higgins," Mrs. Rickert said, "I'm curious. You've been here far longer than we have. What are your impressions of this land?"

Higgins wiped his face and hands with the hot, wet towel. He got up from the picnic table and paced, gathering his thoughts.

"Let me start with Oba-san's farmhouse." He looked at Oba-san and smiled. "The Japanese farm is like a small-scale American Middle West family farm, with a compound of houses and storehouses. Every inch of ground is utilized, and there is always something growing."

Chaplain Rickert moved down the polished picnic bench and took his wife's hand.

Higgins paused, sat down opposite them, and continued. "Here, children visit their grandparents...they do the same things as our kids in the States. But we have many misconceptions of the Japanese people."

"Like?" Mrs. Rickert asked.

A smile played at the edges of Sueno's mouth as she went about clearing the table.

"The Japanese people are not only skilled and intelligent. There is a large and potentially prosperous middle class. It isn't generally known, but they have had one of our cherished freedoms for many years: free voting." The midday sun reflected off Rickert's collar insignia, catching Higgins's eye, as if to prompt him.

"In the area of morals they are higher than our own. Take integrity, for instance. Not one Nisei was found guilty of disloyalty to America during the war. They are intensely loyal and honest."

Rickert shifted uneasily. "Aren't you forgetting what you told me about the local racketeers?"

"Oh sure, we've taught them the tricks of racketeering, but about the only dishonest thing I've seen in the Japanese system is the custom of bribing prosecutors and police. Nobody has to lock their doors at night, and crime is almost nonexistent."

"*Gomennasai.*" Sueno bowed politely, quietly removed the last plates from the table, and shuffled away, her kimono fluttering in the slight breeze.

"Now," Higgins continued, "the top business talent here has been purged and replaced by less competent men. These third-level managers are following the same policies, but are having a more difficult time. Isn't that right, Joe?" He looked down the table at his Japanese interpreter and staff assistant.

"Yes. And the...ah...the Decker ruling was an unfortunate thing."

"Decker ruling?" asked Rickert.

"Joe's referring to Captain Decker's veto of parties for military government," Higgins explained. "That's a blow to our efforts for cooperation."

"I'm sorry, Commander. Is there anything I can do?"

"No...er, yes, perhaps. I've got a confession, if you will keep it to yourself. I'm going ahead with a party here for city council candidates next Tuesday, at my own expense. Decker can keep his Navy food and booze."

Later, when Higgins and Sueno were alone, he asked, "Why were you smiling when I was giving my thoughts about Japan?"

"Higgins-san very wise about my country. I smile with pride."

Higgins did indeed proceed with his political push. Seventeen city council candidates attended Higgins's party at Otsu, along with the industrialists Ogawa, Tanaka, and Ota. Higgins talked of *Demokurashi*, his concept of how council members could serve the people in the rebuilding of the city. He later called it his most successful party, but when Decker heard about it the next day there was a mini-typhoon in the office.

Higgins's efforts—and spirits—were bolstered, however, when a representative of Nagoya's military government team attended a May 5 meeting on reparations. Afterward, Higgins took the major, Ota, and Tanaka to lunch at his Otsu house, where he unloaded his frustrations. The MG team representative told of his setup in Nagoya, which was similar to Higgins's Otsu home as a meeting place with the Japanese. They continued their talk, and by the time they said goodbye, Higgins told his Nagoya visitor, "I feel much better now. Your visit has been great medicine!"

Higgins planned his May 9 leave to take him south from Yokohama. He would visit military governments at Fukuoka, Nagasaki, Beppu, and Kagoshima, just fifty miles from the southern tip of the southernmost island, Kyushu. Sueno would meet him near Kagoshima. It maddened Higgins that he and Sueno could not travel together.

Though General MacArthur winked at it, MPs were obliged to enforce the nonfraternization policy that required Americans and Japanese to ride in separate cars. Since Higgins had to occupy the "Allied" car while Sueno rode in the Japanese coach, she had gone on ahead.

As if to beg the contrast, he had the company of an American woman from Nagoya to Kyoto. "A not too favorable example of American women," he noted later. "She was all 'gimmmie the leather bag, gimmie the whiskey.'"

At the southern end of the main island of Honshu the train crossed the bridges and the narrow neck of land that joins it to Kyushu. It passed through Kokura, the city whose arsenal was the primary target of the second atomic bomb. Smoke and haze on August 9, 1945, had spared the city and diverted the bomber to its secondary target, Nagasaki.

When the train arrived at Fukuoka, Higgins was met by Lieutenant Colonel Munche, the military governor. Higgins clearly envied the Fukuoka military government. "Here, provost court is being handled by artillery personnel, with cases screened by the legal officer of MG," he wrote. "All MG here live as they please, accept presents, and mingle freely with the Japanese."

"The MG's HQ...Kencho building at Kumamoto is quite adequate, and lined with Japanese books. The enlisted men's compound is in an old castle, with excellent accommodations. The office is in a poor Japanese hotel. The housekeeping is poor both at the office and in the officers' sleeping quarters. Life looks pleasant for MG Governor. Not so much detail or Chicken S—-!"

The little train plunged into and out of thirty tunnels along the southwest coast of Kyushu, past splendid farms, until it reached Kagoshima in the evening. Higgins checked into the hotel, which was situated right on the waterfront. In the distance he could see Katsukazan, the mountain rising from the water.

"But the city is about 90% destroyed—the American bombers that could not find their targets elsewhere in Japan jettisoned remaining bombloads here before returning to their bases to the south," he noted. "The result: near total destruction."

On May 14 Higgins visited Kagoshima's MG quarters and found the prefecture's governor, who reported there was free mixing between Americans and the Japanese and that black-market controls were in place.

Leaving Kagoshima, Higgins could not help but notice that he was all by himself while hundreds were crowded into the other part of the partitioned car. The train took him across the mountains toward the plains of the east coast of Kyushu. It stopped in the hills at the town of Miyakonojo, and when Higgins got off he was met by Makimo-san, a relative of the Kotanis. After much bowing, Higgins allowed his host to carry his small bag. As they walked to the small Japanese house near the station, the American and his Navy uniform caused quite a stir in the small Japanese hill village.

"Higgins-san!" A very excited Sueno ran toward him from the house. Inside the clean, two-bedroom house, Makimo-san introduced Wallace Higgins to his family.

"Five boys," Higgins admitted, "outdoes my four!" He playfully tousled the hair of the youngest. After dinner and some conversation, the American guest and eight Japanese slept soundly on futons on the floor.

The next day was devoted to loafing and a long walk with Sueno. It seemed to Higgins that the more he was with this special person, the more he loved her.

On May 16 Higgins stood on the eastern plain of Japan's southernmost home island, near Miyazaki, and reflected, "Here is the spot where the first Allied troops were scheduled to have landed September 5th, 1945, in the planned invasion of the mainland of Japan...a terrible war that might have been far more terrible had it not been ended by Hiroshima and Nagasaki."

When they left Miyazaki, Higgins managed to get Sueno on the "Allied" car to Oita. He looked at the woman in the seat beside him and marveled at her patience.

"All of my time has been taken by inspections of cattle and jails and factories, offices and parades. Not much time together."

"We have long walk. Very nice walk."

"Ten days leave to enjoy a four-hour walk!"

"We together now," she said.

The day on the northeast end of Kyushu at Oita was no different. While Higgins met with officials at MG headquarters, Sueno waited in the Kameroi hotel. Watanabe-san, a friend who had been Higgins's guest at both Hiro and Otsu, helped out.

"Mr. Makoto Watanabe is in Fukuoka today. Not to worry, I stay with Sueno," Watanabe's wife told Higgins.

Mr. Watanabe, who held the title of chief secretary of the overseas raw materials committee for Japan, called at 8:00 p.m. and offered to take Higgins and Sueno on a tour of the hot springs at Beppu before train time the next morning.

At the train, Higgins said farewell to the Watanabes and had to put Sueno in the coach, while he went to the "Allied" car. When the train stopped at Kokura for a four-hour layover, Higgins went looking for Sueno and could not find her. Frustrated and now worried, he was able to wangle a compartment for a portion of the long trip back to Yokosuka. Sueno had been bumped from the coach at Itozaki, and after standing in a boxcar for twenty-two hours, she arrived two hours after Higgins, totally exhausted.

Upon his return, things at the base eased up for Higgins, and he was feeling better about his work. Michelet had left, and with him went much of Decker's sting. Encouraged, Higgins decided to improve his situation. As Eddie Nakashima drove him out of the base, Higgins told of his plans to obtain a car.

"*Jidosha?* An American car?" Eddie asked.

"A Buick," answered Higgins. "My friend in Ohio has one for sale, and I've written to have her ship it." Old cars were common sights on Japan's streets, their trunk lids removed to make room for wood or charcoal burners. The few prewar autos, imported or domestic, were worn out. There were no cars to be had in 1947 Japan, and Higgins needed an auto for his personal use. He had written to his loyal pen pal in Cleveland to ask her to have the Buick shipped to Japan.

He had thought briefly of asking Adelaide to arrange it. "No use bothering her about it," he decided. "She'd get irritated at even being asked, then she'd start questioning me about coming home."

Unknown to anyone in the family until after the fact, Adelaide had been scrubbing, dusting, and cleaning other people's houses for three months, working long hours as a domestic, to save extra money for her son's wedding.

Although Wally continued to send money home, Wallace Jr. was getting married in June, and, as she explained, "There's not enough for what I want to do for my boys."

"What do you mean, Mom? We don't need anything!"

"You all need nice suits for the wedding. I've saved enough for three men's outfits. Now don't argue with me!"

Three of the Higgins's four sons wore identical blue suits to the wedding. The father of the groom sent a check for the honeymoon.

That same month, Higgins was in Tokyo to attend the war crime trials. His notes betrayed little emotion:

> Koki Hirota—70—Death. Was prime minister in 1936, Finance Minister in 1937—a tool of the army and not guilty of atrocity.
> Hiranima—88 years old—Life. Was prime minister 1938-9, held no cabinet office, a leader of the right wing.
> Gen. Minami—77—Life. Was war minister. Manchurian army.

But when another war veteran was sentenced by SCAP, Higgins found a surprising ally. The Mikasa Memorial, the old battleship that was encased in concrete on the Yokosuka base, was ordered completely demilitarized. Like the USS Constitution and USS Constellation, it had served for years as a memorial to an ancient sea battle.

Higgins stormed into Decker's office to protest, and found his boss as opposed to the order as he. Captain Decker had already protested to General MacArthur. "How could she possibly be a threat, embedded in concrete, her guns inoperable?" he insisted.

"I understand, Captain," MacArthur had answered. "I have protested in vain to the Allied Council. The Russian delegate insists that the Mikasa be destroyed. I am sorry, but it is out of my hands."

Higgins reluctantly signed the order for removal of turrets and stacks.

After a three-day inspection trip to Nagoya, Higgins was greeted at the gate by Sueno.

"Let's go away for the weekend," he said. "We could leave right now."

"Ohh...really?" Reacting more like a teenager than a thirty-four-year-old, Sueno squealed in delight.

"To Shimoda, to the beach resort. I've made all arrangements. Pack your swimsuit!"

"Ohh...I have never seen Shimoda."

Higgins had never seen his pretty Japanese companion so happy. She "oohed" and "aahed" at the scenery as he drove the Jeep south. An hour later they passed through Odawara, then along the coastal road carved into the hillside south of Hakone. After another hour, they stopped for soup and rice at a small roadside inn. A few miles farther south, when they reached the tip of the Hakone peninsula, Higgins steered the Jeep down a steep side street and stopped in front of a beachfront cottage. Wasting very little time, they undressed and lay down on the futon.

"Raku desuka?" ("Comfy?") Sueno asked, as Higgins wrapped his arms around her warm body.

The ocean breeze picked up and made the bamboo window slats hum, then caressed them, as their lovemaking went on and on.

"Anata o aishite imasu." ("I love you.") Her soft lips on his forehead and singsong voice woke the American sometime later. They swam, snapped photos, played in the shallow water, and held each other. They hardly noticed, or didn't seem to care, that it rained all day Saturday and again Sunday.

Nine months later, Higgins would add a double star to his notes of June 28, 1947, a secret, nostalgic code in his diary of the occupation of Japan.

EIGHT

Looking Ahead

Higgins arrived back in Otsu to discover his letter to Congresswoman Bolton had borne unsolicited fruit. Although he would decline a promising offer, he felt compelled to plan for his future.

12 August 1947

The Hon. Mrs. Frances P. Bolton
Room # 458 House Office Building
Washington, D.C., U.S.A.

My Dear Mrs. Bolton:
Many thanks for your letter of March 27th forwarding information on State Department service. Your prompt reply to my previous letter is greatly appreciated. I think, however, it would be unfair for me to seek a connection with the State Department unless I intend to make it a career.

My interests lie more in commerce and industry where my experience can be more fully utilized. I had thought of the possibility of remaining in Military Government work on a Civil Service status until commerce and industry between the United States and Japan becomes reestablished but that may not be necessary.

I am not much of a student of world affairs and certainly no authority but it seems to me that we have an opportunity to develop in the Japanese people a powerful and perhaps much needed ally in our efforts to guarantee the peace of the world.

My work in Military Government has naturally brought me into very close touch with all phases of Japanese life. I am convinced that the Japanese people are the best material on earth to work with and to miss the opportunity of indoctrinating them to true democracy will be sheer stupidity. They are eager for knowledge, intensely human, intelligent and courageous.

It is possible that a very small percentage of the people are secretly resentful and may look forward to the day when they will regain their power. Some of the old "diehards" and bureaucrats are resisting the decentralization of government and the processes set up under the new constitution. They hope to perpetuate the old system as long as possible.

The great mass of people, however, feel that they have gone through a revolution and have been given a new birth of freedom. They are sincere in their desire to adopt our ways. They know that they were misled by false doctrines and are receptive to our teaching. The great danger is that they are also vulnerable to "beating of drums" by radical elements preaching false democracy. There is also great danger of their becoming disillusioned by our preaching of democracy while at the same time imposing an autocratic (military) rule. This is no criticism of the military occupation. An army or navy is of necessity autocratic but it is sometimes confusing to the Japanese to have democratic ideas forced upon them in a manner that must remind them of their former dictator regime.

I think our policies for the occupation of Japan are close to perfect. SCAP has done a marvelous job of setting up a framework but the implementation of the policies in some cases could be improved by a little less military control and a more sympathetic handling by those trained for the purpose.

Please excuse this long discourse and consider this an unofficial expression of personal opinion but I thought you would be interested. Again, many thanks and kind personal regards.

Sincerely yours,

W.L. Higgins

Higgins's feelings about the Japanese and his allegiance to the United States came together on the shore of the Miura Peninsula. There stood a monument honoring the 1853 arrival of American Commodore Matthew C. Perry, a visit that opened feudal Japan to international trade.

In a brief ceremony on Navy Day, October 27, 1947, American Commander Wallace L. Higgins laid a wreath on Perry's monument. Higgins held his salute until the last note of *Taps* trailed away, then continued to look up at Old Glory as it fluttered in the breeze at the edge of Tokyo Bay.

Higgins found the general's offices in the Dai Ichi Building in Tokyo, stepped through the doorway, and was greeted by SCAP's Head of Civil Information and Education, Marine Colonel Donald Nugent, who ushered him into General William Marquat's office. General MacArthur had given Marquat the task of overseeing the economy of Japan during the occupation. As part of that assignment he had set up the Economic and Scientific Section within SCAP, with divisions including Industry and Labor.

Their meeting covered several aspects of the military government, such as reparations, restarting industries, getting the coal mines operational, and the allocation of raw materials.

"We're basically talking about how to get a bankrupt economy going again," General Marquat said.

Higgins agreed and added, "We've got to revise our reparations program to get Japan's economy back on its feet. It's a matter of Japan's survival." When he briefly told the general about some of the projects he had overseen, Marquat showed particular interest in Higgins's grasp of Japan's coal problems.

"Fill me in on your civilian resume."

Higgins recited his business experience, ending with "...and then with Pocahontas Fuel Corporation, Stoker Division, till I left in 1940 to head the War Production Board's Cleveland office."

"You're telling me you worked in the coal industry before the war?" Marquat asked.

"That's correct, sir."

"Interesting. We could use your experience in SCAP, Commander."

"I agree, General. How can I help?"

"Well, let's see. About two weeks from now the United Nations reparations team is going to be here for an inspection. We're to give them a tour of some industries. We'll also need to make a progress report on the recommendations in the Strike Study."

"The survey of Japanese industry by Overseas Consultants."

"Exactly. We kept a number of the engineers that Cliff Strike brought over here on his reparations mission. I've been putting them together with the best American engineering talent available. That's the group you know as 'Overseas Consultants.' They just completed an exhaustive study of Japanese industry which shows that we just can't take reparations if Japan is ever going to become self-supporting again."

"I believe that's a wise recommendation."

"Commander, I'd like you to prepare both the tour and the report."

Marquat accompanied his visitor to the door, returned Higgins's salute, and walked back through the outer office.

"I think we could use that guy in ESS," he said to Colonel Nugent.

"I agree, sir."

The Buick had arrived. Knowing better than to invite Sueno on a potentially frightening tour, Higgins took the big American car for a shakedown cruise to the mountainous area northwest of Tokyo. It was raining when he reached the Itaia Hotel at Nikko, where the innkeeper gave him directions, and a warning.

"Ah so...be very careful drive!"

Higgins navigated up the steep, narrow road, more suitable for mountain goats or Jeeps. He counted forty-seven hairpin turns on the single lane that ran back and forth up the face of the rocky cliff. Most of the turns were too tight for the long car, so Higgins had to stop, turn sharply, back up so the rear end hung over the edge, jockey back and forth while turning, then floor it and make another lunge up the steep grade. At one turn some local hikers came down the road, stopped to watch the rear wheels, and signaled Higgins when the Buick was on the brink of disaster.

When he reached the summit, Higgins stepped out, witnessed a breathtaking panorama, and continued to enjoy it until he realized that there was only one way down. The forty-seven terrifying turns taxed the car's brakes and gears all the way to the bottom.

While still working under Captain Decker's command, Higgins worked long hours for seven days on the reparations report. His words distilled the thinking that had become clear to the occupation: The island nation was in disarray, the original plans to dismantle factories and ship them to victorious Allied countries as reparations would result in a stagnant economy, unemployment, and widespread starvation. Japan was totally dependent on outside aid, putting a crushing burden on American taxpayers. Most aid was in direct grants, U.S. dollars or products, with stipulations on how the gifts were to be used. Higgins argued that aid should have been in loans, as the Japanese requested, to be repaid when the nation recovered.

When the UN team arrived November 17 the introductions went well. Higgins led the group on a tour of industries around Uraga, Yokosuka, Yokohama, and Kawasaki. Brigadier General William K. Harrison's reaction was very favorable, and the reparations delegates were pleased with conditions, but the delegation had no more than left before Decker summoned Higgins to his office.

"Come in, Commander. You'd better sit down for this one!"

As he lowered himself into the chair facing the big desk, Higgins saw the strained look in Decker's eyes. The captain sat Buddha-like, his hands folded over a paper lying on the desk.

"I don't quite know how to say it, Higgins." Decker fumbled with the paper. "This came in this morning." He handed the sheet across the desk. It was dated November 18, 1947.

> From: The Chief of Naval Personnel.
> To: Commander Wallace L. HIGGINS, S, USNR, 144725
> Via: Commander, Fleet Activities, Yokosuka, Japan, Navy #3923
> FPO, San Francisco, Calif.
> Subj: Retention on active duty during the fiscal year 1948; Cancellation of.
> Refs: (a) Your request for retention on active duty during the fiscal year 1948.

1. Your request for retention on active duty during the fiscal year 1948 was tentatively approved. However, recently enacted budgetary legislation has imposed a further personnel limitation which does not permit approval of your offer to remain on active duty.

2. The Chief of Naval Personnel desires to thank you for your loyal service in the past, and it is regretted that your services cannot be utilized on active duty to 30 June 1948. It is sincerely hoped that you will continue your naval career by serving in the Organized or Volunteer Naval Reserve.

3. The Bureau of Naval Personnel will issue your orders and your Commanding Officer is hereby directed to detach you in sufficient time to permit your processing and release to inactive duty prior to 15 December 1947. Copy of separation orders and endorsements should immediately be forwarded to the Bureau of Naval Personnel (attention Pers-311M).

4. Transportation by government air is authorized and directed where necessary.

T. L. SPRAGUE

"'Fifteen December 1947.'" Higgins's face was red and his voice sarcastic. "That's not even thirty days' notice!"

"I know." Decker leaned forward, and for the first time in a year, Higgins saw a look of sympathetic understanding. "I'm sorry, Higgins."

"This doesn't give me much time to get a whole new career figured out."

"What do you think? Will you be going back to Cleveland and pick things up with Adelaide?"

"I just don't know."

Higgins went back to his office feeling like the time a wrestler at the Academy had slammed him to the mat with such force that he could barely catch his breath and get to his feet. At first, he could only see that cancellation of his request for retention on active duty posed a crisis. He was adept at seeing and solving business or Navy problems, but he usually had a partner to help sort through personal decisions. Not this time—he hadn't seen Adelaide in nearly two years. "She wouldn't know how to advise me, anyway," he thought.

"She's thousands of miles away, in more ways than one." He stared straight ahead, still stunned, trying to see his options, trying to think like the logical engineer he was trained to be. "How comforting it would be," he mused, "to lay all this out for Sueno...but it would only frighten her. She's part of the equation. She's as much as said she could be carrying our baby." There was no one in whom he could confide, and for the first time in a very long while, he felt alone. "Maybe I should go back to the States, look for a new job in industry, start over. I wonder if Marquat really has a civil service opening in SCAP. I suppose I could try to stay in MG under civil service. If I leave Japan, I'll waste my knowledge of the language. Lord knows, SCAP needs somebody with experience in industry!"

"Excuse, sir. You need office clean?" Higgins looked up to realize that everyone else had left.

"Sure. Come on in. Clean the whole place out," he said.

When he left, he had examined the advantages and disadvantages of each possible course of action. He came to see a fresh opportunity, where earlier he had seen only disaster.

"I want to stay in Japan where my experience can be put to good use." After letting his decision simmer for three days, Higgins found himself in General Marquat's office.

"That's great, Higgins. I'll make a place for you even though we're overstaffed. We need you."

Higgins left Tokyo and returned to Yokosuka in time for his lunch date with the mayor of Yokosuka. Conversing with Mr. Ota in a mixture of Japanese and English was a helpful distraction. The subject drifted from trade and industry to a discussion of schools.

He was relieved with his decision, yet later, while attending a concert, he sank into his chair and wondered, "What will it be like to be a civilian again...and working for Marquat? And for Mac-Arthur? Since Michelet left, Benny's been easier to get along with, and his programs are pretty good. Well, the die is cast!"

At a Sunday evening party at Wokatsu, Higgins learned that Decker had again failed to make admiral and would have to wait another year for his next promotion review. Decker would not be the only one who was affected by recent changes. Navy friends chatted with Higgins about belt-tightening and staff reductions as orders had been issued to streamline ESS. As of December, all jobs were frozen. It was evident to Higgins that the cost of the occupation must be reduced. "And here I am," he thought, "destined to become a civilian at the very time there's a reduction of civilian employees." It was not SOP to talk shop at an informal gathering, but Higgins decided to ignore the formality.

"Am I out of luck?" Cap in hand, Higgins confronted General Marquat.

"Not exactly, Commander." Marquat beamed a reassuring smile. "I saw the freeze coming and saved one vacancy just for you. I could have filled it a long time ago. It's not what you're qualified for, but it's the only way we can put you on board. The freeze kind of screws up the rating...it's only a P-6."

"I'll take it," Higgins answered.

Higgins's transition from military government of the naval district to SCAP's Economic and Scientific Section took place early in December. He had just moved into Tokyo's Dai Ichi Hotel when a hand-delivered letter reached him.

> Premier's Office
> December 3. 1947
>
> Commander W.L. Higgins
> US Naval Activities,
> Yokosuka
>
> Dear Sir,
> Mr. A. Sasaguchi, member of the Diet concurrently chairman of the Yokosuka District Council of our party, informed me that you will soon be transferred to Tokyo on civilian duty. Availing myself of this opportunity, I would like to express my deepest appreciation for your kind assistance and sincere guidance which you have extended to the Japanese people in general, and particularly members of our party under your jurisdiction.
> Those who have had contact with you have always spoken very highly of you and heartily congratulate you on your new position, but readily express their regret at losing you from the Yokosuka district.

On their behalf I once again express our sincere gratitude for your kindness and hope to be able to continue to have the closest contact with you.
With warmest regards,
Sincerely yours,

Tetsu Katayama

Higgins moved into the annex of the Dai Ichi, a dilapidated, wooden structure, where he was assigned an office marked "Forestry 401." His new title was Industrial Engineer, Chief of the Requirements Unit, Far East Command-GHQ, ESS-Industrial Division, a member of Overseas Consultants, Inc. with a P-6 rating that paid $8,877.75 per year.

On his first day at the new job Higgins had barely figured out where his desk was when he heard the scuttlebutt. The complex was whirring about a world affairs story in the December 1 issue of *Newsweek* titled "A Lawyer's Report on Japan Attacks Plan to Run Occupation...Far to the Left of Anything Now Tolerated in America." James Lee Kauffman, a New York lawyer with considerable Japanese experience, had written the article that included excerpts from the never-published document known as FEC-230.

Higgins read the *Newsweek* story carefully, then tore it out. At dinner with three Overseas Consultants staff members, Higgins passed it around.

"It sure as hell is right on the money," Higgins commented.

"Yeah, 'hell' is exactly what broke loose when MacArthur read it!"

"I hear the edict is to keep *Newsweek* reporters out of Japan."

"Why? MacArthur shouldn't be upset...every word is true," Higgins defended the article. "It's those pinkos from State that created the 'FEC-230' abomination and slipped it down SCAP's throat that should be upset!"

Higgins got a taste of how complex his civilian job would be in a December 10 meeting in General Marquat's office, where there was a single subject on the agenda: coal allocation.

Higgins had read the minutes of the previous meeting, which pointed out that coal was the only natural resource in the home islands, and although it was badly needed, it was not being dug fast enough to meet demand. Since he had experience in U.S. coal mining and knowledge of Japanese coal operations, Higgins was asked for his thoughts.

"If you don't mind me covering some facts that most of you already know, I'll try to summarize the situation. Prior to the surrender, a lot of Japan's mining was done by slave laborers, Chinese and Korean POWs. When the war ended, they walked away from the mines. Now, here we are, a year and a half later, and the mines are still in bad shape. There's a shortage of equipment, a shortage of transport, and there's no incentive for management or the workers to improve. Meanwhile, the price is fixed far below the costs of production. Added to that, we've got union and political problems, mostly of our own making. Unionism has been encouraged by us, by SCAP, and now the leadership of the unions has been infiltrated by communists. As far as production levels, the workers that we refer to as 'emancipated' aren't producing. They aren't producing enough to satisfy SCAP, and I have to throw in that, by any comparison to American coal mining standards, these production levels are ridiculously low. But let's look at what we've told these people. We've told them they now have democracy, and that means that they're supposed to participate in setting their daily quotas. Yet we give no incentives. They are paid, and fed, and housed, regardless of how much coal they mine or don't mine. So, human nature being what it is, they've set goals—the union has set quotas—that are ridiculously low. And the workers have the mistaken belief that democracy means behaving selfishly and being disobedient."

After the meeting, Higgins took the attendees, most of them from Overseas Consultants, to his secluded home at Otsu to meet with leaders of government and local Japanese industrial firms. Sueno, her cousins, and Eddie were busy decorating the Otsu grounds for Christmas. Higgins travelled back and forth between Otsu, Yokosuka, and Tokyo, where he got a gas card and a ration card. On the midway-like Ginza, he also shopped for civilian clothes and Christmas gifts, including toys.

"Is Dad finally going to get home for a Christmas?" Ray Higgins asked his mother as her children arrived home for the holidays.

"No dear, I'm afraid not," Adelaide replied. "He's just taken a job on General MacArthur's staff. Here." She handed him an envelope.

Unfolding the carbon copy page titled "Job Description," he sat down to read.

"Wow!" he exclaimed after a moment, and read aloud to the family. "He's got a lot of areas of responsibility...'the allocation of coal, lignite, paper and all scarce materials and commodities; industrial transportation; Japanese legislation regarding allocations; foreign trade; raw materials import; coal distribution; and supervision of the statistical unit of raw materials.'"

He silently read the tissue-like airmail letter that accompanied the description and handed it to his brother, Bob. Once again, he was attracted to the blistered dish displayed on Adelaide's knick-knack shelf. "What force of heat could melt ceramic that way?" he wondered, as he inspected the dual characteristics of the delicate china.

Except for son Dick, and Wally, the Higgins family was crowded into the small cottage, teasing, laughing, and having a good time. They all felt sorry for the "Old Man," missing still another Christmas in Ohio.

鳥

On December 25 Higgins and Sueno hosted seventy-five Japanese, including many children, at an open house on the Otsu property. That evening, he took Mr. Furuichi home to Tokyo and attended an American Christmas party at the Dai Ichi.

Officially discharged from the Navy on December 26, Higgins was finally able to overtly use his Otsu home as a point of social contact between Japanese and occupation leaders. SCAP even cut an order: "Pursuant to the provisions of circular 116, 8th Army, Commander Higgins is authorized to remain in the home of Mr. Murata in Otsu."

To maintain and strengthen his government ties, Higgins also joined the Tokyo Reserve Officers of the Naval Service Club and was promptly elected its president.

At the foot of the mountain, a few hundred yards inland from the beach at Otsu, just south of Yokosuka Naval Base and across the railroad tracks from the station, Higgins's rambling complex was becoming known as a place where Japanese and Americans could meet informally and get important things done. The layout of the main house with separate servants' quarters, gardens, patio, picnic area, and the large cave was ideal for conducting business and entertaining small groups. Now, too, a sign was attached to the large wooden gate: Higgins Diggins. Visitors ate, drank, talked, and, in lively songfests of popular American and Japanese tunes, sang together, led by host Wallace Higgins.

As 1948 rang in, Higgins read a document with interest. It was James Killern's "Report on Field Trip With Hokkaido Coal Team." Higgins could not believe Part B of the labor chief's paper:

> Communist Influence. 1. Management in several instances blamed low production on the influence of Communists over the workers. Our inquiries on this subject revealed in each case that Communists, according to managements' statements, constituted an infinitesimal percentage of the entire work force.

"Bullshit!" Higgins shouted, to the surprise of everyone in the office. He turned to Meyer, a fellow worker, and continued, "Half the coal miners in this country belong to Zen Sekitan, the communist union."

Meyer nodded in general agreement, not having read the report that Higgins was showing him. The section raised Higgins's hackles so much that he excerpted words from Part B, put them with the tune from a Navy ditty, then had them typed and distributed.

But Higgins discovered how "news" was engineered. What he said in the closed meetings of SCAP's ESS group was not necessarily the story released to the newspapers. One story was headlined: "Coal Mines Praised For Output Increase...Bright Future Pictured For Japan By Spokesmen." The points Higgins had made at the January staff were actually quite different.

"Here we have," he said, pointing to a map, "thirteen companies and forty-four mines. I believe they can reach the present quota of

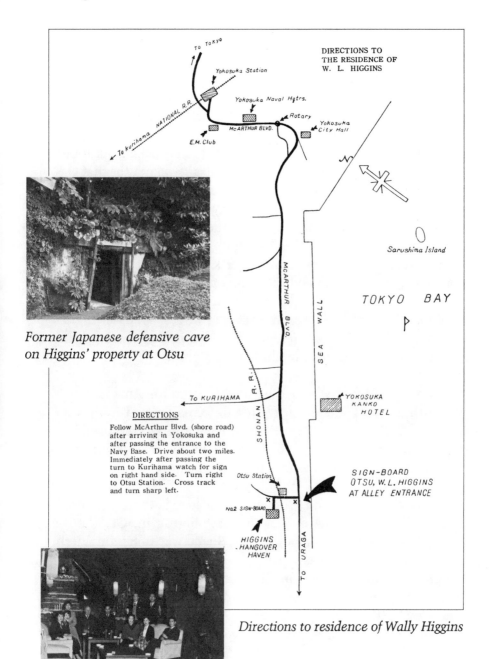

*Former Japanese defensive cave
on Higgins' property at Otsu*

DIRECTIONS TO
THE RESIDENCE OF
W. L. HIGGINS

TO TOKYO

Yokosuka Station

To kurihama NATIONAL R.R.

Yokosuka Naval Hqtrs.

Rotary

McARTHUR BLVD.

Yokosuka
City Hall

E.M. Club

MC ARTHUR BLVD.

SEA WALL

Sarushima Island

TOKYO BAY

SHONAN R.R.

To KURIHAMA

DIRECTIONS

Follow McArthur Blvd. (shore road)
after arriving in Yokosuka and
after passing the entrance to the
Navy Base. Drive about two miles.
Immediately after passing the
turn to Kurihama watch for sign
on right hand side. Turn right
to Otsu Station. Cross track
and turn sharp left.

Otsu Station

YOKOSUKA
KANKO
HOTEL

SIGN-BOARD
OTSU, W.L. HIGGINS
AT ALLEY ENTRANCE

No.2 SIGN-BOARD

HIGGINS
HANGOVER
HAVEN

TO URAGA

Directions to residence of Wally Higgins

*Inside the cave known as Higgins
Hangover Haven, Wally Higgins
entertains guests.*

twenty tons per miner easily. Yet, production per man dropped from fifteen or twenty down to an average of five! Why?"

There was silence in the meeting room.

"And the government mine is the worst!" Higgins compared per-ton mining costs in postwar Japan versus the United States, then added, "I know nothing of production. There are many experts here. Maybe you have the answers, but I just can't help asking questions. Why? Why lower production per man? The answer may be that U.S. mines are automated, but I think it's because our miners get what they earn! Here the mines are losing money because of high labor costs. When the miners reach the day's quota they sit down. And the quota is a ridiculously low figure they have forced management to accept!"

He paused, let the information settle, then said, "The cost of production is 1,620 yen and the selling price of the coal is fixed at six-hundred yen. Now the government of Japan is discussing ownership and operation of the railroads and mines. Well, let me tell you something: If the government wishes to continue, it must justify its existence by a record of production *and* profit!"

For a man of fifty who had been away from his American wife nearly three years, the extensive list of items ordered from Sears Roebuck & Co. in Los Angeles might have appeared strange. The order, dated February 19, included a ninety-five-piece layette, nipples, bottlebrush, and children's handkerchiefs.

Although her sister and two cousins tended to Sueno's every need, by mid-March Higgins was spending more time at the Otsu house. Nearly hidden by her kimono and obi, Sueno was in her final term with their child. Life was not easy for a pregnant woman in the hundred-year-old house. For all its grandeur, it lacked modern indoor plumbing, and the paper walls did little to hold the hibachi-generated heat.

"What will it be like," Higgins wondered, "to have an infant around, this late in life?" On St. Patrick's Day, Higgins took Sueno to nearby Uraga for a stay in the hospital. He returned the following day for a visit and had dinner with her.

On the 19th he attended an ESS meeting on coal, as did General MacArthur. On the 20th, Higgins entertained three cabinet ministers at his home. On the 22nd, Under Secretary of War William H. Draper, Paul Hoffman (a member of the Johnston Mission), and others arrived in Japan and were welcomed to Higgins Diggins. At his first opportunity, the 26th, Higgins prepared his own somewhat different report on the coal situation. He submitted the document, closed up his office, then headed out of Tokyo for what would be a momentous weekend at home and the hospital.

It had been twenty-two years since Wally had fathered his fourth child, and his pretty little Japanese sweetheart was ready to deliver. He stopped at the Yokosuka PX and bought another armful of baby things.

Restless, he attended Easter service in the new Yokosuka base chapel, where a Japanese girls' choir sang Easter songs. He ate dinner in Uraga, then went to the officers club at Yokosuka for a cocktail. Finally, at eight he was back at the Uraga Hospital. At nine o'clock Sueno delivered Victor Katsumi Higgins.

Sueno had written a song for Higgins. After singing *Sueno no uta* (*Sueno's Song/Poem*), from her bed, she handed her lover a copy of the words. Higgins left a copy of the song at the radio station, and it was broadcast the next evening.

Sueno brought the baby home to Otsu April 6, after more than a week in the hospital. Noted Wally: "The baby is a healthy one, with dark hair like his mother but a face that shows a striking resemblance to its American father."

In mid-May, Higgins's son, Dick, visited his father in Yokosuka, and they had a chance to catch up. Higgins chose to have his chats with Dick on two visits to the officers club, and Wally's grown son left Japan after two days, unaware he had a new half-brother at the Otsu house.

Higgins's letters to Adelaide were less frequent, but they were still newsy. Each time one arrived, she copied items of interest into her letters to her four boys. Despite three years of separation, she suspected nothing.

On April 15, 1948, General Marquat ordered Higgins to head up FEC Allocations. Enmeshed in his work for the Supreme Commander at the Dai Ichi through spring 1948, each morning Higgins still had time to watch the appearance of General Douglas MacArthur's elaborate motorcade. "Like the arrival of a king," he mused.

To implement MacArthur's program, Higgins wrestled with the Stockpile Bill, which was to supply Japan with raw materials. He determined what materials were strategic, in what amounts. He decided questions of domestic reserves and exploration, plus development of foreign sources. As each American economic mission visited Japan, he managed to have the principals out to his Otsu home, to be introduced to the leaders of Japan's political and industrial system.

When visitors came to Higgins Diggins the child was kept out of sight in a far corner of the servants' quarters, but Wally's weekends were filled with the joy of sharing time with Sueno and the infant, sunbathing on the lawn, splashing in the fountain of mirrors.

Sueno's English was limited, but Higgins's Japanese continued to improve, and they communicated with remarkable understanding. Not only did Sueno advise him on the nuances of Japanese language and customs, they also developed a very useful technique.

Wally and Sueno splash in the fountain of mirrors at Otsu. They sit on glass searchlight reflectors that had been removed from scuttled Japanese warships.

When Japanese visitors came to the house for business discussions, they usually brought their own interpreters, who sometimes mistranslated. Sueno would sit quietly in the next room, listening carefully. After a visitor left, she slid the paper wall panel aside, stepped into the meeting room, and gave Higgins her version of what was actually said.

At SCAP headquarters in Tokyo in the third week of May, Higgins drove home his observations in yet another meeting. "First," he said, "labor and management are making agreements that are economically unsound in a free economy, and they can only exist by government or artificial subsidies—production quotas that permit leisurely work and promote inefficiency."

The staff listened intently, knowing from experience that when Higgins referred to notes, they would hear substantive comments.

"The output per man is way down, and the solution is not more privilege, or more men, or more hours, or more housing, but more brains, more output per man, lower costs, and more profits. Costs must be reduced, the selling price raised, and railroads must be forced to charge reasonable rates. Next, there's growing evidence of communist activity: strikes, as we've witnessed at the Takenugii Mine. We need countermeasures. In addition, I believe we should support the proposal that many of the strongmen who were purged after the war could be safely returned to responsible positions. I think Japan needs inspiration, and we shouldn't be killing it by banning the singing of company songs or locking up her industrial leaders. The present Japanese government is weak, and it's only being held up with the help of SCAP. To bring about an industrial recovery the government will have to take strong stands, regardless of politics. They need to know they can count on the support of SCAP and the Japanese people. This is a time of crisis; it's not a time for compromise! We've got to create more direct liaisons between Japanese policy makers and our own, on a frank, realistic basis. As things stand right now, there's too little mutual understanding and confidence. There's too much passive resistance and not enough cooperation. We've got to do less reforming and make more of an effort to make the Japanese self-sufficient. The Japanese are confused by our brand of democracy imposed on them by dictatorial and autocratic methods."

Higgins paused a moment and studied his notes, as if considering whether to continue. "Just a couple more points. I've noticed that rubbers are being issued to all personnel going ashore, and they appear on the counters at all the PXs, but the official line is that honest, wholesome love affairs with Japanese girls are a criminal act." Several men in the room shifted in their seats. They knew Higgins was speaking from personal experience. "GIs used to be such good salesmen for America, but due to the stupid non-fraternization policy, the Japanese reaction to us is more and more negative."

Back in the office, Higgins was also working on more pragmatic problems. Three years of seeing the Japanese shiver in unheated buildings prompted him to re-establish contact with a friend at Combustion Engineering Company in New York. He wrote to his friend:

> The prospects for exporting combustion equipment to Japan at the present time are not encouraging. Such exports would have to be purchased with U.S. dollars (which the Japanese do not have) and would have to be approved by SCAP and purchased with SCAP funds. It would seem advisable, therefore, to consider making arrangements with one of the leading "heavy industrial" companies here to manufacture your products under license. It would be necessary to furnish some technical assistance and possibly to invest some money in the company maintaining a representative on the board to protect your interests.
>
> I would like to suggest, therefore, that I return to the States at the expiration of my contract here or early in the year and that I spend several months with your organization for "briefing" on present practice and policy. I can then return to Japan prepared to make a connection with Mitsubishi Heavy Industries or some suitable firm in your name. In the meantime I can accumulate all necessary data and make all necessary preliminary contacts as soon as I receive your reaction to the above.
>
> Sincerely yours,
>
> W.L. Higgins

As the Japanese continued to struggle through deprivation, the luxurious Tokyo Mitsui Club, surrounded by a private park and garden, remained isolated from the hustle and bustle of Tokyo. Vice Admiral C.T. Joy had accepted the October 11 invitation of the president of the Reserve Officers of the Naval Service, Wally Higgins, to accompany Mrs. Joy to the club, which had been taken over by the occupation forces and turned into a GHQ officers club.

Other members of the admiral's staff were already enjoying the cocktail party when Higgins greeted the Joys at the entrance and walked with them up the marble stairs to the reception hall.

"Beautiful place!" Admiral Joy remarked

At the top of the stairs, they stopped before a highly polished sterling silver model of a multilevel temple that rested on an intricately carved table.

"Exquisite," Mrs. Joy commented.

"Did you count the levels on the temple?" Higgins asked her.

"Why? How many levels should there be?"

"One more than you see now. The Japanese require an odd number of levels on their temples. This only has four of the original five. Some stupid American officer liberated one of the stories from the model."

"That's terrible!"

"Who took it?" asked Admiral Joy.

"I don't know, but if I did I'd have 'em shot! It's a religious insult to the Japanese. When we turn this club back to the Mitsui companies, it will likely irritate relations for decades!"

On MacArthur's orders, a team was sent to Washington in November 1948 to advise on the SCAP budget for Japan. The mission included Mr. Wallace L. Higgins, DAC, Ind Engr, P-6, ESS. The long flight from Tokyo to Washington in the piston-powered, propeller-thrusted airliner, chased much of the way by a full moon, required four refuelings.

At his hotel, Higgins called Ohio.

"Wally?" Adelaide answered. "Here...in the States? Washington? Can you see me? Are you crazy? Of course!"

"I just got in, honey," Higgins said. "I don't know when I can get away. Maybe next weekend. I'll call when I know."

Higgins attended what seemed like round-the-clock meetings with Pentagon and State Department people, then it was off to Capitol Hill for budget talks with officials and members of Congress. He visited several headquarters of national professional associations, and after an exhausting week, called his wife to tell her when he would arrive. Adelaide hardly touched the holiday meal she was having with friends.

Wally finished his work the Friday after Thanksgiving and left Washington by train on his first postwar trip to Ohio. Early Saturday morning he transferred to a Greyhound bus and gazed from the window until he saw, at the end of the twenty-mile trip:

MENTOR VILLAGE
Pop. 2,014

As the bus hissed to a stop opposite the town's drugstore, Higgins stepped off, looked around, and spotted Adelaide, sitting at the wheel of the family Oldsmobile. Her blond hair was styled the same, Wally noticed as he walked against the cold wind toward his wife of twenty-eight years. As he neared the car, the thought sped through his brain, "My God, she's fifty years old," followed immediately by, "and so are you!"

He opened the passenger door and leaned in, smiling.

"How are you, Wally?" She looked at him as he put his small black bag on the floor and got in.

"Fine, honey. How have you been?"

"Lonesome! None of the kids made it for the holiday."

They hugged for a moment before Adelaide sat back and started the car. She turned left at Mentor's only traffic light and drove south through the arch of elms that lined both sides of Center Street.

"Hasn't changed much," Higgins said.

Approaching the corner they had lived on, she slowed the car. Higgins turned and stared at the big, yellow house that had been the family's refuge for so many years.

"You know I moved down the street," Adelaide reminded him as she turned right toward the small cottage on Johnnycake Ridge Road. "It's more my size...and the rent's cheaper."

She parked in the drive, and they paused briefly before getting out at the small house surrounded by mature sugar maples and elms. As Adelaide preceded Higgins through the front door, he turned and looked at the farmland and woods from the screened porch that ran across the front of the house. His memory shifted back to prewar days, when he and his sons ran with Brownie, their collie, through the same fields and woods. Without realizing it, he was staring at the random, natural, Midwestern setting and comparing it with the precise ornamental garden at Otsu.

"I wish it were bigger for the boys to come home to."

"Hmm? For the boys to come home to? Yes."

Higgins looked closely at his wife and saw the sadness, and the touch of anger, in the blue eyes he hadn't seen for three-and-a-half-years.

"Well, with all the boys grown, and most of them married, it's probably big enough." Instinctively, he changed the subject. "I'm used to taking off my shoes at the door, but I'm certainly not used to that aroma. Is that apple pie I smell?"

As he made his way through the dining area crowded with the big table and sidepieces, Higgins's eye caught the blistered dish from the ruins of Hiroshima on the small display shelf.

Friends visited Saturday evening, and for awhile Higgins was flung back in time—the same feeling he once had had at a high school reunion.

As his short visit progressed, Higgins couldn't stop making comparisons. Their lovemaking Saturday night was brief and obligatory, so far from the sensual delights to which he had become accustomed.

After a big Sunday meal, Higgins took a long walk, past the big house on the corner, then a mile on the trail through the woods. Everything was so familiar, yet somehow so strange. On Monday after a hearty breakfast, Adelaide drove him to the Cleveland Airport. He had stayed two nights.

They exchanged a hug and kiss at the gate that would indicate to any passerby he might be leaving for a day or two. Then, from some sense of loyalty and duty, Higgins asked, "How would you feel about going to Japan with me?"

She looked at her husband's face carefully, and for an instant her eyes sparkled, remembering something long since dormant.

"I don't think so, dear. I wouldn't want to be that far from my boys."

NINE

Meetings With Influentials

The twin-engined United Air Lines DC-3 touched down at Washington's National Airport just before noon, Monday, November 29, 1948. Higgins hurried to the green Army bus marked "Pentagon."

Most of the day, Higgins attended a meeting where the SCAP mission outlined its fiscal needs to help Japan get back on its feet. The presentation emphasized that the economic condition of Japan was deteriorating, as evidenced by an increase in the issuance of money, an increase in consumer prices, budget imbalance, an increase in wage payments, a lack of improvement in exports, and failure on the part of the Japanese government to stop inflation.

After lunch, Higgins helped outline SCAP's stabilization program and ways to counter problems. The group was discussing the prohibition on importing petroleum and shipping in American bottoms, when Higgins said, "These two policies make it awfully tough for the Japanese economy to recover. Could either of them be changed?"

"The Army has no objection to Japanese importation of crude oil," a general answered. "I think we can change that one."

Then Higgins reported on the availability of Japanese import requirements and their limitations.

"American taxpayer's dollars alone won't buy recovery in Japan," Higgins said at Tuesday's meeting. "We need to look at matters of policy."

Asked to explain, he continued. "I think we need a new policy statement. Present policies are 180 degrees out of phase. We need to remove the brakes to recovery. We need to send more frequent reports from Japan to you here in Washington. And we need to examine a five-year plan. Now, let me list the brakes to recovery." He went to the chalkboard and specified twenty-two areas, including shipping costs, controls on foreign trade, and reparations.

During those first two weeks in Washington, Higgins frequently voiced his concern over U.S. policies in Japan that imposed too much control, and reforms that were too radical. "Leave more of the economy decisions to the Japanese," General MacArthur had told him in Japan.

Yet SCAP economic advisors continued to impose reforms that, to Higgins, were fiscally irresponsible and smacked of socialism. While discussing his concerns with a Republican senator, Higgins was handed a document titled "American Policy Toward Japan."

"This might be of some interest, Mr. Higgins. It was prepared by a group of Governor Dewey's advisors, including Dulles, Hoover, Castle, Grew, and other friends of Japan, as background material for his Japan policy, had he been elected president."

Higgins immediately found a chair and scanned the beginning of the report.

AMERICAN POLICY TOWARD JAPAN
October 15, 1948

SUMMARY

The following contains the record of how American Post-Surrender Policy Toward Japan had been formulated without the knowledge of the general public and often without the knowledge of policy-making officials—by a small group in the government both in Washington and Tokyo. It would not be proper for this paper to pass upon the motives of individuals in this group. It is fair to say, however, that as a group they favored a planned, collectivized economy, the extreme regulation of business that often goes under the guise of "anti-monopoly," a government of men, not laws, and in foreign policy the building of "friendship bridges" to Russia. As applied to Japan, these ideas were calculated to result in:

1. Tearing down the Japanese social structure even though the predictable result was chaos leading to Communism.
2. Depriving the business, managerial career classes— classes traditionally oriented toward the United States— of their influence, wealth and livelihoods through a "purge" by occupational categories.
3. The "deconcentration" of Japanese business into single plant units under the guise of breaking up monopolies.
4. Reducing Japan to a subsistence level at which it could never become self-supporting and the United States would have to continue the relief expenditure of $1,000,000 per day or see Communism overwhelm the country.
5. Transferring power to radical labor and political organizations, including the Communist Party.

Whatever the intent of the group, either individually or collectively, their policy served Russia so well that the Soviet Union has only occasionally and recently (1948) complained about American actions in Japan. Belated and partly successful steps have been taken—mostly by Republicans in the Truman Administration—to change this policy.[1]

Higgins would not only read the report word for word, he so supported the policy that, even after Dewey's loss, he made hundreds of copies and distributed them widely. Little did he realize that his enthusiasm might cost him his SCAP job.

While not in meetings, Higgins was taking full advantage of the resources in the States. Late one afternoon in Washington, Higgins kept an appointment at the Library of Congress. His pursuit and

---

[1]   See Appendix, page 241, "American Policy Toward Japan."

reading of every book he could find bearing on world politics and modern history led him to the treasure of resources in the nation's capital. Mrs. Baker, a librarian, helped him develop a list of recent books that Higgins could obtain from Brentano's bookstore in New York.

By the time Higgins left for New York on Thursday he had a new itinerary: "Combustion Engineering—Herbert Hoover—Bernard White—James Kauffman—*Newsweek*—Klein—bookstores."

Wanting to follow up on the paper that had come into his possession, Higgins carefully reread the document on the train. When he finished, he vowed to have copies made on his return to Japan for distribution to key SCAP people.

In New York, Higgins met with his old friend, Joe Santry, at Combustion Engineering Corporation. They discussed the need for combustion equipment in Japan, and Higgins told Santry he had signed on for another year with SCAP.

Next, Higgins kept an appointment with Herbert Hoover. He found the apartment of the former president in the Waldorf Towers, and for two hours they discussed the Japanese economy, occupation problems, and foreign aid.

Higgins also met James Kauffman, the man who had uncovered the offensive "FEC-230 Directive" that had been imposed on SCAP and revealed in a *Newsweek* story the previous year. Then he had a long chat with the foreign affairs editor of *Newsweek*, and shared with the editor his own endorsement of the Dewey paper, "American Policy Toward Japan."

By the end of his New York visit, Higgins had also called on Gulf Oil, Atlantic, and the National Coal Bureau. He was cultivating contacts with companies that might do oil, coal, and boiler business with Japan.

Higgins devoted another two weeks to SCAP mission work in the Pentagon, and on the Hill he visited Ohio Congresswoman Frances Bolton. He promised to write to her frequently from Japan.

"Having completed temporary duty with Civil Affairs Division on or about 15 December 1948, you will proceed to your proper station..."

"Adelaide?"

"Wally?"

"Sweetheart, I'm afraid this isn't the best of news."

"They're sending you back over there, aren't they?"

"Well, I knew I'd be going back..." The phone was heavy in his hand.

"Really? You didn't make that crystal clear when you were here." She paused a moment. "Will we have a chance to see each other again before you have to go back?"

"They have me down for an immediate flight."

"Couldn't you tell them you've only spent two days out of the last three-and-a-half years with your wife?"

Higgins said nothing.

"Wally...?"

"Yes?"

"Take care of yourself."

"I will. I..."

She waited for him to complete his sentence, but when he didn't, she gently laid the phone in its cradle.

On the plane, he shuffled the snapshots and stared at them again. They were all taken in his Japanese home or garden, all of an Oriental woman and baby.

By late December, the new duplicating machine in Higgins's SCAP office was turning out copies of the policy paper that were subsequently distributed to influential SCAP personnel. The nine points of SCAP's stabilization program that the mission team had worked so hard on at the Pentagon were formally brought to MacArthur's attention, and the allocations work that Higgins plunged back into had taken on added importance, as described in the directive from the Department of Army:

> Improve the effectiveness of present allocations and eliminate
> black market.

December 31, 1948

My dear Mr. Higgins:

I am just in receipt of yours of December 24th and am deeply grateful for it. I am going to try to get to some of the people who might have a way in to those who are formulating policies and getting them carried out.

If you have anything on the Communists I would deeply appreciate it. I have been Chairman for two years of the Subcommittee on National and International Movements of the House Committee on Foreign Affairs, and we have just recently finished a study of the situation in China. I am forwarding a copy to you.

I would like so much to have some accurate information about what has been going on in Japan. If you will continue to write at the above address I shall be grateful, and assure you there will be no delays. I am back at my desk and anticipating the coming months with considerable interest.

Wishing you all good things in the New Year, I am
Very sincerely yours,

Frances P. Bolton

Word reached Higgins in January that other ESS divisions were proposing to take over the role of Allocations. He submitted a paper to the chief of the Industry Division, maintaining that the nine-point directive to General MacArthur had focused new importance on Allocations, and Higgins accused "certain empire builders who see an opportunity to expand the scope of their activities and to justify their present high ratings." He pointed out that "the present plan is functioning smoothly with all industries operating within reasonable balance consistent with availability."

"It is rumored," he concluded, "that a new plan of allocation is in preparation by individuals in SCAP who seem to consider themselves qualified to operate outside their assigned activities and who seem determined to make a difficult task out of a simple operation. Those directly concerned with the problem including the Chief of the Requirements Unit are not consulted in this planning. It is difficult for one who is interested in minimizing the burden on the American taxpayers to understand the reasoning behind these increased controls superimposed on controls." He attached a list of 172 commodities, products, and industries the Requirements Unit was currently reviewing.

Throughout 1949 there were differences of opinion within SCAP. At a meeting on textiles, the discussion centered on prices. The local price was higher than export prices, and this could bring charges of dumping.

"What would happen," Higgins asked, "if controls were removed and the free market were allowed to operate?"

"Chaos! Why, the local price would go up five times!" answered Sherwood Fine.

"Oh?" As an economist on Marquat's staff in the labor division of ESS, Fine had Higgins's attention.

"In the U.S., supply and demand works OK," Fine explained, "but in Japan it doesn't work. They've always had controls and subsidies."

"Wouldn't costs bring about fair prices?" Higgins asked.

"Costs don't mean anything in Japan," Fine argued. "They form no basis for setting selling prices."

For all the gravity of the SCAP squabbles, Wally had the talent to get the important participants together at his Otsu hideaway and make suggestions until they put their differences in perspective. It was during such a retreat to Higgins Diggins that the H-H-H-R quartet (Higgins, Holton, Huggins, and Raleigh) came up with a new song.

> We're the boys of ESS.
>   Marquat's boys are we.
> We are here to bungle up
>   Japan's economy *Banzai*!
> *Ohio Gozaimas Konichiwa*
>   *Ikaga Deska Genki Des*
> *Sayonara Kudasae*,
>   ESS is SCAP's Creation
> to stabilize Japan.
>   With shorter hours, higher wages
> we don't give a damn,
>   ESS knows all the answers
> So we do so *des*
>   If we put our heads together
> *Nippon Dance Des!*

The H-H-H-R quartet warms up to Japan's top recording star by singing new words to Ohio's fight song.

In a more serious moment, Higgins wrote to Herbert Hoover, reporting on Japanese economic and population problems.

ESS/IND, GHQ, SCA
APO 500, c/o P.M.
San Francisco, Calif.
18 August 1949

Hon Herbert H. Hoover
Waldorf Towers
New York City

Dear Mr. Hoover:
    You may recall our discussion of Japanese economic and occupation problems in your apartment last December. Since then many changes have been made to improve the situation and many more are in the making. The Japanese budget has been balanced, the political situation has become stabilized under Mr. Yoshida, the communist advance has been checked, an exchange rate set, and controls relaxed. There are definite signs of progress in spite of the temporary economic

set back due to export surpluses and removal of some of the artificial props.

The "Dodge policy" of balanced budget and rationalization, while vigorously, and, I think, honestly supported by Mr. Yoshida and his cabinet is being opposed by certain groups on lower echelons of the Japanese Government and in SCAP. This was to be expected but I am hoping that the line will be held and that rationalization of industry and government, including SCAP, will be carried out in the interest of the future of the Japanese people and the American taxpayer.

One of the great problems remaining is that of overpopulation. I am enclosing a suggestion from Mr. Ishizuka, formerly president of the Japan Steel Company and now an industrial purgee. This indicates the thinking of some of the more responsible Japanese who are greatly concerned over the problem.

Other areas, such as Borneo, could be suggested for development but it would seem advisable for Japan to first develop fully her own sparsely settled and undeveloped Hokkaido. This has been neglected since the war for lack of capital before the war because there were too many "greener pastures" in the Far East.

Allow me to add my belated congratulations to those of the rest of the world on your 75th birthday. Thank you again for your courteous attention on the occasion of my visit last December. I suspect that you have had some influence on the changes taking place.

Sincerely yours,

W. L. Higgins

1 Enc.
    A proposal Concerning
    the Japanese Immigration
    Problem, by Kumejiro
    Ishizuka

P.S. I would consider it a personal favor if you would send me
      a copy of your recent address at Ohio Wesleyan U. and also
      at Stanford University. I heard portions of both addresses
      over the radio here in Tokyo and they were so inspiring,
      I think every American should know them by heart.

A friend and confidant at the American Embassy gave Higgins a rough draft of yet another report on the occupation. The paper, "The Occupation of Japan: An Appraisal," was accompanied by a note asking that Higgins review it and add his comments.[2]

Meanwhile, Higgins's own path also was shifting. Following a policy created a year earlier to hold personnel in the Far East Theater, Higgins signed a reemployment leave agreement at 0900 on September 23 that would have him serve SCAP on MacArthur's staff two more years. There was a provision for a forty-five-day leave upon signing the two-year contract, but at 1000 the same day, he was declared "surplus" and handed notice of termination. The explanation was "Job abolished and mandatory reduction in force of Industry Division."

"Just thirty days ago I received an efficiency rating of 'excellent'!" he protested.

"Nothing I can do," said the head of the Industry Division.

Higgins's last official ESS business had been a week's trip through Hokkaido, after which he had reported his concern over the advance of communism there. Remembering, he shrugged, for he was not the first to be pushed out of SCAP for telling the truth. Joe Reday, chief of SCAP's Industry Division in 1946 and 1947, had been banished from Japan by MacArthur because he wrote the truth about the occupation in an article that appeared in *Fortune*.

As an American who had chosen the Japanese manner of living for the past four years, Higgins thought in both languages. "*Shikata ga nai,*" he now said to the ocean. ("It cannot be helped.")

While Higgins was being terminated at ESS, news of Decker's promotion to rear admiral had reached him. Before he left Japan, Higgins had visited his old classmate and former boss in Yokosuka and offered his sincere congratulations.

Three days later, new arrivals took jobs in the same office where drastic cuts were being made. The *Stars and Stripes* announced that reemployment leaves would be discontinued. Probably because of his conservative views, Higgins was included in the 1949 staff

---

2   See Appendix, page 255, "The Occupation of Japan: An Appraisal," and suggestions by W.L. Higgins.

reduction. He wryly observed that many young and inexperienced advisors were being brought to Japan at the same time the veterans were being released.

Despite the termination, he updated the status of Japan policy periodically, frequently writing to his home state's representative in Congress. In 1951 he wrote that during the two-and-a-half years since his "summary" of October 15, 1948, many changes had taken place:

> The communists reached the peak of their power during the spring and summer of 1949 at which time they planned to stage a bloody revolution in October, provided their "August offensive" proved successful.
>
> SCAP immediately took cognizance of the situation and issued a statement denouncing communism. For the first time the man on the street learned that the occupation did not favor communism.
>
> It is now generally believed that the danger of communism from within Japan has passed, but we must be careful not to recreate the danger or to allow the pendulum to swing too far in the other direction causing a revival of imperialism.
>
> The things we must realize as basic are that the Japanese are not unlike us; they do not want "something for nothing" but they insist on equal opportunity for survival. As long as we permit 50 percent of Japan's steel capacity to lie idle while we increase our own 20 or more percent, as long as we bar her from our markets and close her sources of supply, as long as our business men are selfish and demand high tariffs and subsidies to block competition; we cannot look to Japan for wholehearted cooperation.
>
> "Self preservation is the first law of Nature." There is too much vitality and courage and ambition in the Japanese people to submit to slow economic extermination.

With his views being sought in Washington, Higgins returned to America in December 1949 as a private citizen with three goals: He wanted to represent the Combustion Engineering Corporation in Japan, he was positioned to advise on American policy toward Japan, and he wanted a divorce.

TEN

Family

Wearing his black commander's uniform, Higgins paced the deck of the USS Randall, pondering the changes sweeping through his life. On December 8, 1949, two days out of Yokosuka, headed for San Francisco, Higgins was returning to America to arrange a divorce from his spouse of twenty-nine years, to explain his decision to his sons, Dick, Ray, and Bob, and to try for the support of Adelaide's father. He also was determined to find a new job representing an American company in Japan in the coal, oil, or boiler business, and to report to his Washington and New York contacts his impressions regarding Japanese-American relations and the defeat of communism.

Events of the past few months had been swift and dramatic. Love for his Japanese sweetheart and their twenty-month-old baby had prompted him to write to Adelaide and disclose the facts. In response, he promptly received an angry letter. Then no sooner did he decide to stay in Japan than he lost his job at SCAP.

As a reservist, Higgins had served two weeks' active duty in October aboard the USS Manchester. While at sea, he had written to Congresswoman Bolton and received a reply that made it all the more imperative that he return to America. On the deck of the Randall, Higgins stopped, pulled out the congresswoman's letter, and read it again.

November 7, 1949

Commander W.L. Higgins, USN
ESS-IND-SCAP
APO 500, c/o Postmaster
San Francisco, Calif.

My dear Commander Higgins:

It was a surprise to get a letter from you from the sea. Needless to say I was intensely interested in what you wrote. The whole horrible mess is so tragic that I find myself seeing all the colors of the rainbow whenever I think of it. We could not have played into the Soviet hands more perfectly.

When will you be back in our part of the world again? I hope not before too long as there is so much to discuss which cannot be put on paper. I am expecting to be in Cleveland from now until the first of the year when Congress reopens. With kind regards,

Sincerely yours,

Frances P. Bolton, M.C.

Higgins leaned on the ship's rail and watched the sea move by. After a few minutes, he put away Mrs. Bolton's letter and took out a folded paper, his agenda. It read:

Adelaide
$100/mo. plus more when able for boys—1/2 bonds if still intact—she pay expense—life insurance to continue until I remarry.

He underlined the word "bonds" and gazed out to sea, lost in thought about how Adelaide would react to his plans.

"Ah yes, Adelaide." Moving away from the rail to get out of the wind, Higgins found a place to sit and write. The previous night he had sung with the officers of the Randall, and the words to a long-forgotten song that reminded him of his situation had come back to him. He turned his attention back to the piece of paper:

I'm going back to where I come from
where the honeysuckle smells so sweet it dern near
   makes you sick.
I used to think my life was humdrum
but I sure have learned a lesson that is bound to stick.

Having filled the panel of paper, he turned it over and wrote the ending words to a railroad ditty he knew by heart:

Now come on you ladies you must take warning
from this sad story and learn
Never speak harsh words to your loving husband
He may leave and never return!

The wind grabbed at the paper, revealing the scribbles on the back. Higgins smiled as he recognized Sueno's attempts to write in English:

Hig Hig Higgin Higgins This is a pen There's to bed and to
rise Home, Home Their Finest Hour

"Four years together and she still avoids English!" He shook his head at the slow progress of his Japanese partner. But somehow Sueno had learned to understand his feelings and temperament without the help of formal language. Her responses were unlike anything he had experienced in three decades of marriage to his American wife.

The tender care that Sueno had given him was now also extended to their child. Her care went beyond affection; she was totally devoted. During the two years he worked for MacArthur in Tokyo, she had accepted his need to stay at the Dai Ichi. She never even murmured about his hard work at SCAP or the long hours of volunteer work for Japanese organizations. She always helped by graciously social-izing and by steering Higgins in the many nuances of Japanese customs. She seemed to fully support his strenuous work schedule by always being sympathetic and never complaining, and she seemed to condone his need to be away in America these next three months. Through Sueno, Higgins had acquired a deep understanding of the character of the Japanese people. If communication meant an ex-change of feelings, then Wally and Sueno had often achieved it.

"Perhaps love, or a feeling for others," thought Higgins, "exchanged by what people *do* for one another, could be the universal language that bridges differences."

He remembered the look in her eyes, and Sueno's last words to him: *"Sayonara, Otohsama."*

After the Randall steamed under the Golden Gate Bridge and into San Francisco Bay the morning of December 20, Higgins spent three days phoning, meeting businessmen, and shopping for Sueno. He bought blouses, a dress, and a coat in Oakland; wool and satin yardage in San Francisco; shoes, slacks, and six pairs of nylon stockings in Los Angeles.

Higgins was in Los Angeles for Christmas with his mother, his sister, Ruth Lindsay, and her husband, Herb. Ruth was an exceptional cook, and Higgins found it difficult to push away from the dining table of his sister's American-style food. Higgins and Lindsay got on so well that Herb decided to drive his brother-in-law as far east as Las Vegas. They sang all the way across the desert, then the pair made their way through all the Vegas clubs.

Higgins stayed at the Cleveland Athletic Club for ten days, then, New Year's Day, 1950, he drove to Mentor. His son Ray and daughter-in-law June were at the house on winter break from their university studies. Wally, in his uniform, stayed in the bedroom with Adelaide during most of his visit, talking. Harsh words did not make their way into the rest of the house, but when Wally left, Adelaide could not hide her tears.

"What's the matter, Mom?" Ray asked.

"Oh, nothing. Your father's decided to stay in Japan—with *that woman!*"

"What woman?"

Adelaide repeated Wally's shocking story and his plans.

Their efforts at sympathy were resisted, and June and Ray returned to Columbus the next day knowing little about the divorce.

Higgins next travelled to his hometown of Trenton, New Jersey, to obtain his birth certificate, marriage license, and other family records. He also called on his father-in-law in Elizabeth,

New Jersey. As a boy of thirteen, Detmer D. "Dick" Petersen had come to America from Germany, worked hard, married Ella Pike, and produced only one offspring, Adelaide, whom they admittedly had spoiled. Petersen listened with understanding as Higgins explained his situation. Dick Petersen loved his adopted America and was as proud of Wally as if he were his own son. The Petersens had grown fond of their son-in-law and their grandchildren.

"Pop, I'm between a rock and a hard place!"

Petersen studied the man in the commander's uniform sitting before him. "Don't worry, Wally. I'll see to it that Adelaide cooperates in setting you free. If you can send her monthly support, I'll supplement it and see that she manages."

During the three months Higgins was in the United States, he made two more short trips to Cleveland for hearings, culminating in a divorce decree based on incompatibility. From then on, whenever her family visited, any mention of Higgins was avoided. And Adelaide continued to refer to Sueno as "that woman."

Higgins's four sons from his first family were grown, married, and living away from home, so he was free to turn his full attention to his second family in Japan, and to a new job and career. Indeed, when he returned to Japan in March, Wally Higgins was an employee of Combustion Engineering.

⛩

By mid-April, the government had granted Higgins permission to engage in business activity in Japan. He was authorized to serve as special representative of Combustion Engineering-Superheater, Inc., while also being retained to represent Japan Steel Works, Ltd., Uraga Dock Co., Ltd., and Japan Mining Co.

Higgins also received licenses for two marriages. A traditional Shinto ceremony was arranged through Japanese friends and Sueno's family. In a black kimono, he stood before a priest with his stunningly dressed and coiffured Sueno and flawlessly performed his role in the Oriental ritual. Immediately thereafter, he changed into his commander's uniform for a Christian wedding, conducted by a Navy chaplain.

The reception at Higgins Diggins included much of the Kotani family, some of whom had journeyed from Hiroshima, and some of whom were already servants in the Higgins household.

Higgins was moved, at this turning point in his life, to consider the nature of the woman he had met at Hiroshima five years earlier and now had taken as his second wife. He never seemed to tire of appreciating her outward beauty, of watching her move about, of watching her face, her eyes, as they talked.

"She's so beautiful—on the inside," he mused.

The spell she cast over Americans extended to Higgins's friends, as evidenced by an excerpt from a letter to Higgins from a Navy friend who had last been with Wally at Kure in 1946:

> Please give my love to Yoshida [Sueno]...and I do mean "love." She, Takahashi [Higgins's interpreter], and Sato did so much for us at Hiro and were always so happy and considerate of us that it is impossible to think of either of them without affectionate regard that is more like the love of members of a family for each other than like a friendship. I am happy to see that she looks younger and more attractive than ever and the "little girl" [Tae] has truly become a beauty...
>
> You sure brought up memories by your reference to the Good Ship Titanic and I can still hear your voice telling the sad story or singing *Moshi, Moshi, Annane.*
>
> All in all, I frankly envy you your present situation. Maybe I'm just becoming too God damned old to appreciate what we do have here [in the United States] and prefer to live in the past. Say, that's a good idea. Let's go back to our little Hiro shack with our purloined electric stove, a bowl of Mandarin oranges on the table, assorted bottles of Kirwin's (?) beer and Suntory "kamikaze" whiskey (complete with vitamins, yet) and our Rube Goldberg showerbath.
>
> It sure would be pleasant and I shall continue to hold the hope that I will again see you at some future date and that in the meanwhile you will let me hear from you occasionally.
>
> With my deepest personal regards for you and the other charming members of your family but, again, with "love" to Yoshida, I am as ever,
>
> George Barrows

Wally was pleased to even further cement his family, and Sueno was ecstatic when Miss Shigeko "Tae" Kotani, a young lady of fourteen, was adopted by Higgins and took the name Shigeko Kotani Higgins.

Too, Ernest Makoto Higgins was delivered at the Higgins home in Otsu on August 16, 1951, assisted by a neighbor as midwife. Higgins assembled his family a week later and snapped their picture: Victor Katsumi, his hair combed forward and cut straight over his eyes in the style of a Japanese three-year-old, Tae Higgins, dark-haired and as tall as her mother, and Sueno, dressed in kimono, holding Makoto, as Ernest was called.

Higgins's Otsu family kept expanding. Sueno's cousin had suggested that several relatives would like to come work as gardeners, housekeepers, and such. They, in turn, suggested others who would like to "come visit." Everyone stayed. One day, Higgins finally asked when a particular person was going to go home and was dismayed

Wallace L. Higgins and his second family in Otsu.

to learn that, honoring the custom of lifetime employment, he had hired one of Sueno's distant relatives for life.

Higgins employed a young man named as typist, translator, and personal secretary. After proving his value, Noboru-san asked Higgins if he would sponsor him and help further his education. Wally consented, bringing his total staff to nineteen. Obviously, the servants quarters were expanded, and the gardens, barbeque area, and cave, with its bar and dance floor, also were brought to perfection.

In addition to directly supporting individual Japanese, he also supported Japanese institutions, like education. When he discovered the degree to which girls were being shortchanged by the education system, Higgins not only saw to it that Tae got good schooling, but initiated and sponsored many programs in public and private schools. His efforts proved timely because the occupation had begun emancipating women, forcing curriculum improvements in girls' schools. In addition, Higgins encouraged Rotary and local governments to back educational film programs.

Recognizing his vigorous efforts to establish education through motion pictures, Yokosuka's Mayor Ohta requested that Higgins kick off the first session. A large audience of children, parents, and local dignitaries attended the meeting in the city's assembly hall. After being introduced by the mayor, Higgins waited for the applause to subside, then spoke in carefully phrased Japanese, followed by English for the benefit of the Americans:

> The purpose of this meeting is to inaugurate a program of education through motion pictures. It is our understanding that the program will provide educational films for children primarily, but there will be films for grown-ups, also.
>
> The motion picture can be a powerful force for good because of the lasting impression made on the mind through pictures. The educational authorities sponsoring this effort will exercise good judgment in providing pictures that will portray the truth without distortion and lead the Japanese along the road of true democracy and right thinking.
>
> Man is not what he thinks he is, but *what he thinks—he is*. A nation is a collection of individuals—its character is shaped by the thinking and the acts of its people. To become big, Japan must think big—to become honest, Japan must think honest.

The habits and thoughts of centuries must be changed if Japan is to become a true democracy. Adopting the democratic way of life does not mean forsaking everything that is Japanese. There are many admirable things in the Japanese customs. Retain the good and reject the bad. Accept the good features of democracy and adopt them to your own way of life and Japan will again become one of the respected nations of the world.

One of the most encouraging signs in Japan today is the eagerness for learning on the part of its children. It is hoped that this program will make it possible for all of the children in Yokosuka to broaden their knowledge of world affairs and the Christian way of life. Thank you.

During the twenty-six years he was in Japan, Higgins labored to improve life for the Japanese people. Although he spent as much time with his civic contributions as his professional pursuits, they, too, met with occasional resistance. In 1953, an eye doctor on the Yokosuka Navy base asked him to find a manufacturer who would build typewriters for Japanese blind people without profit. Higgins enthusiastically communicated with the Lions Club of America and got permission to distribute the machines in Japan through Rotary. Angry at Higgins's initiative, the eye doctor tried to have Wally's base privileges revoked and a Japanese Rotarian suggested that Higgins, the only foreign member in Japan Rotary and vice president of the Yokosuka club, be dismissed.

Higgins was, however, more than just a member of Rotary. He had helped revive Rotary in Japan, joined the Yokosuka club, established democratic processes in the conduct of Japan Rotary meetings and had a twelve-year record of 100 percent attendance. By the time *The Rotarian* published an article of his in 1962, there were 360 Rotary clubs in Japan with a membership of nearly fifteen thousand. Higgins also was a frequent speaker at Rotary meetings. He revealed much of his motivation for these efforts in a letter to the local Rotary president defending his actions after the eye doctor's attack:

During the entire eight and one half years I have been in Japan I have conscientiously worked for the good of Japan. I have always tried to help at all levels of society, business, and government, first as a Naval officer, later as an official of SCAP and later as a businessman. I would like to point out my reason for joining your club. I knew before joining it would be difficult for me because of my ignorance of the language. I did not anticipate ever receiving any business or material advantage from my membership. I was hopeful however, that I would be able to help your club as a foreigner, in handling matters of an international nature. I still think I can be helpful. If I did not think so I would not want to be a member.

Higgins later helped Japan host the 1961 Rotary International Convention and personally hosted hundreds of the delegates.

When Higgins's mother died in 1953, he wrote to his sister, Ruth, in Pasadena, California. "I am in the process of writing my own will as one never knows what may happen after passing the halfway mark. My case will be even much more difficult unless I spell out my desires carefully ahead of time. The big problem is to provide for the future of my new family. My first family is already taken care of. I may not live long enough to see the result but my earnest hope is for my two 'mixed blood' boys to become a credit to

Although he was the only foreign member of the Yokosuka Rotary club, Wallace Higgins was elected its vice president, then president.

the countries of both parents and a factor in promoting international understanding."

By 1961, little Tae had become a young woman. Higgins and Sueno had seen to it that she had received the best of schooling and was trained in traditional skills, like tea pouring, so that, as Sueno expressed it, "she will qualify for a husband." One day she came to her parents and said, "I am ready. I want a husband. Will you arrange to find one?"

Because of the family's status, the arranger insisted, "Only a man in the professions will do as husband. He must be one of the class made up of doctors and other professionals."

Higgins was polite when the first prospect, a young doctor, called.

"You want me to marry your daughter..." the optimistic physician began. "OK, here my conditions." He proceeded to list demands that included a house, property, and an exorbitant amount of yen.

"Get out!" Higgins responded.

The next prospect was Yutaka Wakabayashi, the assistant superintendent at Yokohama's mental hospital. He was a doctor, thirty-two-years-old, and he made no demands. Higgins asked about his family.

"My father is Dr. Shozo Wakabayashi, a general practitioner of medicine in Tokyo. My mother is Chieko, a housewife. I have three brothers and two sisters."

Higgins liked him instantly. Yutaka spoke excellent English, but Higgins purposely spoke in Japanese. Sueno listened to the discussion, and when the candidate had left, she told her husband that she approved. The long process of the traditional arranged marriage was complete, and Tae was married to Yutaka Wakabayashi in traditional Japanese style November 25, 1961.

Each year at Christmastime, Higgins mailed a personalized greeting to his growing list of friends. The card was a picture of the Otsu garden home, plus a montage photo of his Japanese family and the families of each of his four American boys. The caption read: "FROM THE INTERNATIONAL HIGGINS FAMILY."

There were two years when Richard and his wife lived in Japan with his father and Sueno. With that exception, Higgins spent no Christmases with the rest of his stateside family between 1941 and

1971. Although Higgins made brief trips to the United States every four or five years, his heart was in Japan. It wasn't until years later that family members realized the trips were required so that Higgins could retain his U.S. citizenship. During those thirty years his American family hardly knew their father.

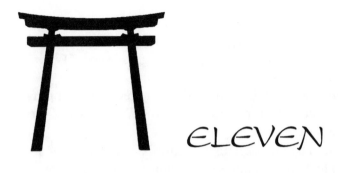

ELEVEN

U.S. Technology Goes to Japan

To understand how Japan's economy grew from total postwar prostration to a leading position in the world, it helps to recall the emperor's words as he closed his August 15, 1945, surrender broadcast:

> Unite your total strength to be devoted to the construction of the future. Cultivate the ways of rectitude; foster nobility of spirit; and work with resolution so you may enhance the innate glory of the Imperial State and keep pace with the progress of the world.

The drive toward *ichiban* was underway. One reason Higgins stayed in Japan and helped in peaceful reconstruction was his admiration for the strong work ethic of the Japanese people.

With the purchase of property at Atsugi Heights and the construction of a second, more modern, home there, Wally further displayed his commitment to his own second home, Japan. For several years the Higginses occupied both homes before moving permanently to the Atsugi property before his son Ray finally visited Japan in 1965.

Ray saw a motivated nation, and he could feel the spirit in the way they worked. After touring Japan for a week, Ray returned to his father's new house at Atsugi, where Higgins asked, "What are your impressions, Ray?"

Ray's answer was doubtless affected by the repetitive tapping of carpenter's hammers in the neighborhood. "Work, work, work. They sure are a busy people!"

"It's *ichiban*," Higgins explained. "Number one! The Japanese are determined to be number one in the world. They just may do it, too. I'm telling you, Ray, America's workers better get off their asses, or they'll be left in Japan's dust!"

Higgins saw the national policy and intense motivation of *ichiban* as a part of the incredible recovery equation. Then there was the financial and technical aid from the United States, an America that also bore most of the enormous cost of defending postwar Japan. In the dark, early years of her recovery, the United States sent food, grants-in-aid, raw materials, plus some of America's best business brainpower and industrial know-how to Japan.

Like others, Higgins, recognized some of America's "help" as highhanded and inappropriate. He pointed to some measures that hobbled the rebuilding process: reparations, the purge of business and industrial leaders; banning patriotic and company songs; the dictatorial rule of young SCAP advisors who often failed to ask the opinions of the Japanese; and the socialistic policies of Americans like Owen Lattimore, whose activities led to strikes and labor strife.

The Japanese themselves prolonged and compounded problems, he admitted, because of their surplus of labor, protection of small and inefficient shops, their coupon economy and detailed controls, poor roads, lack of housing, a perceptible inferiority complex, underpricing of goods, their nonexistent sales efforts, labor unrest, and government resistance to foreign capital investment.

By 1949, the fourth year of the Allied occupation, major problems with the Japanese economy had grown. To assist General Mac-Arthur, Washington sent an American financial expert to make recommendations for improving the country's economy. Joseph M. Dodge was a Detroit banker and former president of the American Bankers Association. Dodge made an intensive study and described the problems to SCAP as

Too many people,
Too high a birthrate,
Too little land,
Too few natural resources.

Swelled by repatriates, dramatic increases in life expectancy, and an increased birthrate, the population of Japan exploded from seventy-two million in 1945 to eighty-four million by 1950. Domestic food production could not feed all the people, unused industry lay in ruins, Japan's merchant fleet—destroyed in the war—was virtually nonexistent, and just as industries began to recover in early 1949, a worldwide slowdown and labor strife devastated her economy.

On several occasions, Higgins hosted the visiting banker at his Otsu home, always with some of Japan's ablest leaders in attendance. Discussions were held on the need to curb inflation and put the unbounded energy of the Japanese people back to work.

During this period, Higgins presented a speech he called "A Look At Japan At The End of 1949" on several occasions. His notes indicate the points he hit hardest. He began by stating that commu-

Japanese leaders participate in open discussion of economic problems with members of the Dodge Commission on the lawn of Higgins Diggins.

nism had been checked, that militarists had been crushed and stood no chance of regaining power except through the Communist Party. He said that MacArthur was still respected, but not worshipped, and "The emperor is still emperor."

He believed that the evils of the occupation had about balanced out its benefits, in the form of relief funds. "The people are regaining some initiative but have little to hope for," he observed. Higgins's view was that labor had too much power, and industrial efficiency was falling off. "Japan," he said, "must utilize its resources or die." He urged that labor be held "within bounds," that it trade directly, using its own funds. "If it does these things, and ships in Japanese bottoms, Japan *can be* self supporting."

In Joseph Dodge, Higgins found confirmation of his own conservative views about Japan's economic needs. Since Higgins knew many of the top managers of major Japanese companies, he steered the visiting consultant to them. Dodge's principal recommendations for recovery were to realign production to favor export, reduce costs, and embrace sound monetary controls with curbs on borrowing and

Joseph M. Dodge, leader of a mission to advise General Mac-Arthur on stabilizing Japan's economy, is welcomed to Higgins's Otsu home.

spending. An economic stabilization program was established that eliminated detailed coupon-type controls.

A few months after Higgins returned to Japan in 1950, the Korean War broke out, and Japan became the staging base for American troops and supplies. In addition to enterprises like reconditioning WWII Jeeps, the war boom floated Japan's economy largely on "the three Bs" of beer halls, brothels, and black markets.

Still, the economy struggled. One group of Japanese and Americans worked together to solve its problems. At first in contacts arranged by ESS, then in small informal groups, and socially in businessmens' clubs and organizations, as consultants and client companies, they gathered to speak the common language of business.

Higgins was especially active. He contributed ten-thousand yen to reactivate the America-Japan Society in 1950 and hosted an all-day party at Otsu for the group in 1951. He joined the Yokosuka lodge of the Grand Lodge of Free and Accepted Masons of the Philippines, the American Club of Tokyo, and Japan Rotary.

With Higgins's encouragement and to his delight, General MacArthur and SCAP accepted—and the Japanese government adopted—the Dodge Commission's recommendations. Inflation was stopped in its tracks, and Japan was nudged toward a free-market economy.

Higgins was also contributing in his analysis of power capabilities. Higgins's study "Hydro-Electric Capacity of Japan," made for SCAP in 1949, pointed out the potential to greatly expand this type of power generation by building dams and reservoirs. But such development had one killing drawback: In a land where even steep hillsides were terraced and cultivated, space for agriculture was too valuable to be flooded. As a consequence, Japan desperately needed electricity generated from steam power.

For the next five years, Higgins put equipment designed by Combustion Engineering and manufactured by three Mitsubishi Heavy Industry companies into hundreds of Japanese companies and power stations, making, as he said, their boilers "No. 1 in Japan." When Combustion Engineering royalties for these sales rose into millions of dollars, the American company decided to raise Higgins's retainer instead of paying a commission.

Higgins had other successes as well. Responding to the needs of American servicemen for auto insurance, Higgins founded Capital

Insurance Company. He was also always "prospecting." In a letter to the American ambassador, Douglas MacArthur II, General Douglas MacArthur's nephew, Higgins offered his services to members of the ambassador's staff, based on his contacts with a broad segment of Japanese industry. And those he had. In addition to his successes for Combustion Engineering, he had become the sole representative for Gulf Oil in Japan and his Japanese clients included the Uraga Dock Company, the Japan Steel Works, and the Showa Aircraft Company. "In order to assist in maintaining contact and be of all round service," he wrote to the ambassador, "I hold membership in Stateside Engineering Societies including the ASME, S.N.A.& M.E. and in the Rotary International, American Japan Society, American Club & Press Club."

It was, as Higgins's letters pointed out, a critical time in the history Japan-United States relations. A January 2, 1955, letter to Congresswoman Bolton read in part:

> My dear Mrs. Bolton:
>
> It has been a long time since I have written you to bring you up to date on what has been happening in my Japanese world....
>
> Conditions in Japan have been very difficult and uncertain right up to the close of the year. Several of my Japanese clients have had a hard time remaining in business but with the recent change in government a new air of confidence seems to be generating....
>
> There is one matter that I would like to call to your attention for possible action. You may recall my conversations with you when I was in Washington on a budget mission for SCAP in 1948 and again in 1950. At that time I was very much concerned over the "empire building" in all agencies in SCAP to say nothing of the Communistic line followed by many of the top SCAP officials.
>
> At the time I suggested that the Civil Service personnel in SCAP could be reduced 80% without reducing the effectiveness of our efforts to guide the Japanese along the road to Democracy and a stable economy. When, subsequently the order finally came through almost a year later to reduce 10%, I was number one on the list for dismissal. This I was prepared for and did not protest as I felt that SCAP had run its course and would phase out with ratification of the Peace Treaty.

Empire builders and parasites die hard. When the Peace Treaty was finally ratified and there was no longer any need for the kind of guidance enforced by SCAP, a brand new Empire was created known as J-5. Many of the "hangers-on" from SCAP gravitated to J-5 and are still in Tokyo assigned to space in FEC headquarters. No one seems to know what they are supposed to do except to occupy space and continue to be a burden on the U.S. taxpayer.

Many of these people are friends of mine and I would not like to see them lose their jobs but surely there must be some place in our Government Service where their talents can be used to the benefit of the government and for the good of the individuals. A more demoralized group of people could not be found anywhere. When I have occasion to visit anyone in J-5 I come away depressed and bewildered. Fortunately these people are hidden away where they have few contacts or the facts might become a scandal.

It is my opinion that in the interest of the American taxpayer and of good public relations—inquiry should be made of the justification for an activity of this kind.

My Japanese family is growing fast. Katsumi age 6½ is finishing his first year in school and Makoto age 3½ is just what a 3½ year old ball of fire should be. Everyone has been quite well but Mrs. Higgins and I are both badly in need of a vacation which we plan to take in a few days. The American President Lines run a holiday Cruise of 2 weeks from Yokohama to Manila and Hong Kong and return. We leave the day after tomorrow. It will be my first vacation in many years and our first long trip together.

Again Congratulations on your latest victory. Kindest personal regards and a Happy and Glorious New Year.
Respectfully yours,

W.L. Higgins

Following the habit acquired when he became fluent in Japanese, Higgins was browsing through his *Bungei Shunju* newspaper on March 31, 1955, when the headline "Blue-Eyed Executives in Japanese Companies" caught his attention. "The Japanese economy is under the control of blue-eyed company executives," the article insisted. "How is American capital with its 'streamlined imperialism' undermining the Japanese economy, nay, Japan itself? We must know the 'how.' EVEN AMERICAN-MADE HUMAN BEINGS FOUND HERE." The long, blistering article focused on Americans infiltrating Japanese companies and ripping off Japan with expensive license fees.

Higgins discussed the newspaper article with Sueno, had it translated and copied. Then he wrote an American's response to the editor.

BLUE-EYED EXECUTIVES IN JAPANESE COMPANIES

I recently had the pleasure of reading an article by Yoshio Tsujimoto, a reporter of *Yomiuri*. The article appeared in *Bungei Shunju* and was entitled "Blue-Eyed Executives in Japanese Companies." The article deals with the subject of how American capital and its "streamlined imperialism" is undermining the Japanese economy and begins by describing how the daughter of a friend of the author suddenly discovered that blue-eyed executives, whom she previously thought to be customers, were actually working in the company which employed her. While she knew she should quit her job, if she did so she would find herself in economic distress. The question presented by the article was whether the Japanese should resign her employment and what effect the introduction of American capital and techniques would have upon the Japanese economy. The author of the article is inclined to the view that a further introduction of blue-eyed executives into Japanese business should be resisted because it will be harmful to the Japanese people and workers.

To help the Japanese people obtain an answer to this problem, it has occurred to me that they would be interested in knowing what effect the blue-eyed executives have had on business in the United States and the American people. If the wish for profit, which the blue-eyed executives have, has been bad for the American people, the Japanese people may well conclude that it will be equally bad for the Japanese nation. If, on the other hand, it has resulted in raising the standard of living of the American people, put more money in the pocket of the American worker, and enabled him and his family to live more comfortably, it might be well for the Japanese people to encourage their own businessmen to obtain the help and assistance of blue-eyed executives so that the Japanese nation can become strong economically and again take its position as the outstanding industrial country in the Far East.

Fortunately, these matters do not have to be left to conjecture. For five years a study of this subject has been made by a staff of 25 experts in the United States by the Twentieth Century Fund. The result of this study has recently been published in a book entitled "America's Needs and Resources."

This study shows that because of the capital investments which the blue-eyed executives have at their disposal, they have been able to improve American productive facilities and techniques here. While they have been paid for doing this by the American companies which employ them, the result has been an aggregate income for the 160,000,000 Americans in the United States which exceeds the combined income of the 600,000,000 people living in Europe and Russia. It far surpasses the total income of more than one billion inhabitants of Asia.

The study further shows that under the guidance of these blue-eyed executives, the productivity of American business is increasing so rapidly that the income of the average American family had increased in 1954 to the astronomical figure of $5,330 for each family, and by 1960 it is estimated that it will be further increased to $6,000 per year.

During this period of time in which the worker and his family have been able to improve their standard of living, American companies and the blue-eyed executives who have acted as officers and directors of these companies, have been subject to the most rigid Government control. If they conspire to raise prices and increase the cost of living, they are subject to severe penalties and criminal prosecution. If they treat their workers unfairly, they will be punished. If they deal unfairly with even one stockholder they are subject to suit and personal liability. They must be open, and not secretive, in dealing with the public, and the affairs of their companies are subject to audit by independent certified public accountants each year.

Many of these blue-eyed executives are foreigners or of foreign ancestry but their skill and talents have been welcome by American business because American business has realized the importance of their skillful management.

While some of them head the companies which employ them, they are not only subject to the Government regulation described above but they are in fact really employees and servants of the companies which are owned by the shareholders, large and small. Only recently the head of one of the most prominent companies in the United States was removed by the shareholders because they did not approve the policies which he had been following.

After the war there have been some American business men in Japan who have tried to take unfair advantage of the Japanese people. These are inferior persons and should be dealt with severely. None of them, however, have been the blue-eyed executives of the reputable American companies which Mr. Tsujimoto has described in his article.

These companies have invested billions of dollars in the development of production techniques and machinery. We, in the United States, have seen what benefit has been derived by the American worker and his family from the introduction of these techniques and machinery into American business. Poverty and suffering have been almost eliminated. For those who wish to work there are good jobs available. Students, graduating from schools in the United States, find ready employment, and their help is eagerly sought by American companies. Is this true in Japan so that the Japanese people do not need the help of the blue-eyed executives?

Just as the United States is a great industrial power in the West, so is Japan a great industrial power in the East, but, as Mr. Tsujimoto himself has pointed out, because of the tragedy of war, Japan has been unable to keep abreast of the latest technology in business affairs. The blue-eyed executives in the United States are willing to help Japan in these matters and introduce the latest techniques into Japan since they realize that a strong Japan is essential to the stability of the world. The Free World now looks to Japan to assume her place as a peaceful leader among the nations of the Far East, now torn by war and bloodshed and suffering.

Will Japan fail to heed this call and withdraw within herself?

Should the Japanese girl mentioned at the beginning of this article resign her position or should she stay and help to make Japan a great, strong country dedicated to the cause of peace and happiness for her people?

Should the Japanese people be deprived of what the latest techniques can produce, or must they continue to pay high prices for inferior products?

We here in America are anxiously awaiting the answer. We should like to share with the Japanese people some of the things that we have obtained through the blue-eyed executives. We are asking them to give the Japanese companies the same help they have given to American companies so that the Japanese people too may prosper.

The American companies who have developed the latest techniques are not only willing to offer them to Japan but they are willing to subject themselves to the same kind of regulation and control by the Japanese Government as the Government control they are subject to in the United States to insure that their affairs will be conducted in Japan in the best interests of the Japanese nation. They have much to offer to the Japanese people—workers and business men alike. It is hoped that those who sneer will not be permitted to deprive the Japanese people of the right to work and enjoy the benefits of their labor in the same way that we in the United States are able to do.

The initial blue-eyed executives article in the *Bungei Shunju* had destroyed much of the goodwill between the two countries and touched off efforts by Japan to keep out American investment. Higgins's response was printed in some Japanese publications, but fighting such propaganda was difficult. Higgins had copies made of his response and sent them to Americans and Japanese who might be influential in restoring good faith between industrialists of both countries.

Higgins also found problems aplenty dealing with his own countrymen. Navy personnel looking for off-base housing convinced Higgins that he should spearhead local private development of housing. The mayor of Yokosuka asked him to serve as a consultant on this and other matters. With Japanese interest and financing, Higgins began to put together land acquisition plans and blueprints for an apartment complex near the base.

As an American taxpayer, the buildup of Army, Navy, and Air Force personnel and the rush to bring their families to Japan at taxpayer expense bothered Higgins. He prepared the rough draft of a letter to Senator Harry Byrd, a budget watchdog in Washington, and sent a copy to his trusted friend at the American Embassy in Tokyo, "Duke" Diehl.

The next morning, Higgins learned from a friend at the Navy base that the point was moot. "The Navy no longer needs the off-base housing," exclaimed Higgins's friend. "We just got fifteen million bucks approved for new government quarters!"

The action by Washington infuriated Higgins on several levels. On March 25, Higgins wrote to Diehl:

> In further reference to my letter of yesterday and draft to Senator Byrd, I learned today that the Navy has received virtual assurance that their request for some $15,000,000 for Government quarters in Japan will be approved. They are therefore no longer interested in the meager [$]1.5 million they were hoping to receive from the Japanese because of the limitations placed on price of houses.

Diehl offered some minor modifications of the draft and Higgins mailed his letter to Senator Byrd April 11, 1955[1]. Its tone was clear. "My close observation of the situation here in Japan has led me to the conclusion that the United States taxpayer's money is not only being spent recklessly but in such fashion as to build ill will and alienate a country that could and should be one of our strongest allies," Higgins wrote.

Enclosing a copy of his Byrd letter, Higgins wrote to General Maxwell Taylor, the commanding general of the Far East Command, the following day. He outlined the housing situation, his position, and asked to discuss it with a member of Taylor's command.[2]

Higgins wrote to other influential Americans, including Joe Dodge, with the result that the huge project was scaled back. It was

---

[1]   See Appendix, page 268, for complete text of Higgins's April 11, 1955, letter to Senator Byrd.

[2]   See Appendix, page 270, for complete text of April 12, 1955, letter to General Taylor.

determined that so much elaborate housing was not needed. This was just one of many battles. Sometimes his own entrepreneurial interests were involved; just as often his interest was protection of the American taxpayer.

Problems came from the Japanese as well. The history of Japan's economic recovery revealed some subsidizing of select products. Higgins's correspondence traced both sides of the issue.[3]

Higgins also urged Japanese manufacturers to concentrate on producing top-quality goods and charging top prices for them. He found an ally in the president of the Political Federation of Japanese Small Business and argued his quality philosophy at Japanese Rotary, MITI, with his clients and business contacts.

Higgins had become, in fact, a Japanese patriot. Soon after his election to the presidency of the Yokosuka Rotary Club, he had members lustily singing Rotary and patriotic songs. On October 13, 1955, Higgins noticed a story on Japanese naval history in the newspaper *Mainichi* about the gradual destruction of the memorial on Yokosuka Naval Base. He wrote the next day to his good friend, the mayor of Yokosuka, and enclosed a personal check for ten-thousand yen.[4]

As the war receded in importance, however, Higgins and other critics felt their muzzles loosen. Much was written about General MacArthur and his closest aides in Japan. Some of the writers used memoirs and SCAP press releases to create their own versions of history, but very few had gotten to really know the supreme commander. Higgins believed MacArthur was a brilliant military man, but saw flaws in the occupation. Others who had also seen, and written about the flaws, were promptly banished from Japan. But when the occupation ended, freedom of the press returned. Privately, Higgins and his friends talked and corresponded about the facts of Japan's occupation.[5]

---

3 See Appendix, page 272, for correspondence regarding subsidies.

4 See Appendix, page 275, for letter to Mayor Umezu and Mr. Mitsugi Ohkura.

5 See Appendix, page 278, for complete text of August 27, 1955, letter to W.W. Diehl.

鳥

As the 1960s began, the winds of change stormed Japan. President Dwight D. Eisenhower announced that his visit to Japan on June 19, 1960, would coincide with the date when the Revised Security Pact was to automatically become effective.

Higgins saw a calamity in the making. The Japanese communists were planning massive demonstrations to embarrass the American president and bring down the unpopular government of Mr. Kishi. Higgins wrote to his friend, Frank J. Lausche, in the U.S. Senate:

> Even should violence and bloodshed be avoided Mr. Eisenhower would have no opportunity to "meet the Japanese people" which is the announced purpose of his visit. He would be kept insulated from the people by a force of over 20,000 police now being mobilized for the purpose. Should violence break out, and the chances are more than even that it will, Mr. Eisenhower would be blamed personally as he was by Krushchev at Paris. It would break his heart and do great harm to our position in Japan and the Far East. He can accomplish no good by coming at this time and he runs a great risk of doing much harm.[6]

The "Haggerty incident" validated Higgins's alarm. Arriving in Japan in advance of Eisenhower's visit, Press Secretary James Haggerty apparently saw an opportunity to avoid the crowds and ordered his car to be driven away from the airport. Police were deployed at the main building to protect Mr. Haggerty during his brief interview at the airport. There, the main body of the Zengakuren—Japan's communist-dominated labor movement—waited to present a petition to him. The extremists became angry at Haggerty's attempt to "escape" and stormed his car. Police were taken by surprise and had no time to redeploy.

---

6   See Appendix, page 280, for complete text of June 8, 1960, letter to Senator Lausche.

Relations between the nations were set back when American and Japanese television carried scenes of rioting Japanese attacking the American limousine. After the attack, others besides Higgins saw the need to delay the president's visit.

Higgins found it confounding that Washington did not understand the powder keg it could detonate by an Eisenhower visit. On June 16 he wrote again to Senator Lausche, saying the announcement had just been made over the radio that Mr. Kishi has requested that Mr. Eisenhower's visit to Japan be postponed because of the bloody riots held outside the Diet building the previous night. "It must be difficult," he wrote, "for the people of the United States to understand the political situation here, and the conditions that will permit a group of juvenile delinquents and labor hoodlums to defy law and order and get away with it on a grand scale." Higgins further explained that the Japanese were politically immature and not ready for the U.S. brand of democracy thrust upon them by SCAP, that they readily accepted the freedoms and privileges, but not the responsibilities of democratic citizenship.

"The communists," Wally reported, "have seized upon this fertile opportunity to provide the leadership, organization and 'causes.' It seems to make little difference whether they shift from anti-Kishi to anti-Security Pact or anti-Americanism or some other anti."

In Higgins's view, the United States could not escape the responsibility for introducing communism. The United States had flown Japan's foremost communist, Mr. Nozuka, to Japan from Manchuria in 1945 and made him an advisor to SCAP. SCAP had built up the Communist Party with the hope it would serve as an opposition party, thereby preventing a return of the rightist element. SCAP's efforts were so successful that, in 1949, the Communist Party held thirty-six seats in the Diet. The tactic had succeeded far too well, and General MacArthur had to outlaw the party.

The mistake of introducing communism in Japan was second only to the way in which the United States destroyed faith in the emperor, the Japanese form of religion, and their respect for all authority, Higgins believed. "It will take years of patient endeavor to restore the traditional Japanese respect for law and order," he lamented in his letter to Lausche.

Higgins enumerated these factors, saying it wasn't difficult to understand how the situation had developed "in a country comprised of hard working, intelligent, moral and God-fearing people":

1. By nature and tradition the Japanese people are passive and shun responsibility. They have been known to stand by and witness robbery or even murder and do nothing as private citizens to interfere.
2. The old leaders they had followed before the war were purged, stripped of authority, and discredited.
3. The police were made a laughing stock under the occupation and the only authority respected was the U.S. Military.
4. The Communist party was encouraged by the U.S. Occupation and built up as a recognized political party with the backing of SCAP.
5. Ultra progressive labor and other laws were forced upon a reluctant interim government.
6. Due to inexperience the bad features of our democratic way of doing things were embraced and many of the important advantages left alone.
7. The Japanese Government has failed to keep the public completely informed of its policies and to explain the reasons for the New Security Pact and other matters. The people in general do not know the new pact is better for Japan than the old one.

Higgins concluded the letter by stating, "We must not condemn too hastily. It is difficult to admit our mistakes but I think history will record that we made our full share, however well intentioned, in dealing with Japan."[7]

In an August 8, 1960, letter to Lausche, however, Higgins reported a "turn for the better" and describes the mood of the Japanese voter.[8]

---

7   See Appendix, page 283, for Higgins's comments on reaction to the communists in his July 3, 1960, letter to Senator Lausche.

8   See Appendix, page 286, for complete text of August 8, 1960, letter to Senator Lausche.

By 1960, the Japanese auto industry had also begun showing signs of its success to come. In a letter to the American admiral commanding the naval forces in Japan, Higgins revealed how the unbalance started, stating in part:

> American businessmen in Japan have been wrestling with a problem for the past several years; a problem that has caused a great amount of ill-feeling, e.g., the importation of American Automobiles.
>
> Under the Occupation no Japanese was permitted to own an automobile that was less than 10 years old. It may be partly for that reason, the Japanese Government seems determined that Americans will not ride around in a late model car unless, of course, it is Japanese.
>
> The latest "liberalization" of the rules provided for the import of about 1000 new foreign cars a year but during the past year only 5 cars have been *approved* for import by American businessmen *through legitimate channels*. The rules are made so ridiculous that it is impossible for me for instance, to import an American car after paying for it with my money and paying 100% duty. I must show a net worth of 30 million dollars to do so. Representatives of General Electric, Westinghouse and similar large companies having the capacity to import a car in the company name have been trying in vain to get approvals for over a year.
>
> Meanwhile a minimum of 2000 American automobiles are dumped on the Japanese market through the "grey market" channel of the U.S. forces and U.S. Embassy.
>
> Yes, these sales are legal but the Japanese take a very "dim view" of the obvious racket worked by nearly every Embassy employee and nearly every officer and many enlisted men of our armed forces who bring a new car at U.S. Government expense with the express purpose of selling it at a big profit (enough profit to buy a new car Stateside) when leaving Japan.
>
> This is not a complaint as I am perfectly satisfied with my Japanese car but I thought I would pass the information along for what it may be worth.

During the same year, Higgins further trumpeted his concerns in an article titled "The Truth About Japanese Wages":

A Japanese automobile which costs $3,000 in Japan retails in the U.S. for $1,950 and the estimated *cost of production* is around $1,600. Obviously the export market in this case is being subsidized by the domestic market. This may explain the low export prices of other items which are manufactured with relatively high cost materials or where the productivity rate has not yet been raised sufficiently to offset other disadvantages.

In the same article Higgins showed that the Japanese laborer received a total compensation—when all the fringe benefits were included—comparable to that of American workers.

More and more, Higgins found himself speaking and writing about conditions in Japan. When the chief of training and development of the U.S. Army in Japan asked Higgins to speak to a group of American managers on the subject of "Employee Motivation," Higgins replied, "If you are willing to tolerate my deficiencies I shall be happy to be of service."

The speech was so well received that Higgins was persuaded to write an article later published in the October 1961 issue of *Challenge* magazine.[9] In summary, he stated:

Productivity in the U.S. is increasing at a 2% rate annually whereas wages are being boosted at a 3½% rate. A continuation of this ratio can result only in inflation and non-competitive prices. In Japan the cost of production is decreasing year by year as a result of productivity increases averaging 9% and wage increases averaging only 5%. In the final analysis the basic law of economics will operate. I predict for Japan a gradual merger of the old and new employment systems and for America a slow down in the rate of wage increases but an increase in fringe benefits and closer employee-employer relations. In the end, the two competitive economies will not be so far apart in their labor relations as they now appear to be.

---

9   See Appendix, page 288, for complete text of article.

Higgins knew that the only way the American management of Combustion Engineering would get a grasp of matters such as patents and the huge potential of Japanese partners was to have them see for themselves.[10] In 1959, he talked Don Walker into coming to Japan.

Higgins prepared Walker by pointing out that service at hotels, clubs, and stores was still incredibly good, but that some foreign families had spoiled their own help to the point where no Japanese family that could afford a maid would hire people who had worked for a foreigner. "It is a great joy to travel Japan off the beaten path," Wally reported, "and get millionaire service at little cost. Tipping is taboo with the Japanese, and they resent foreign tourists and business-men who play 'big shot' by tipping. A 10% fee is generally added to the bill and help is forbidden to take tips." He ended by telling Walker that Japan was a wonderful place to live, a retired man's paradise, a tourist's paradise, but a poor place for a foreigner to make a living.

Other recent visitors had views of the Japanese social influence on American GIs that Higgins, by now a longtime resident, felt were inappropriate. A young Navy chaplain, Lieutenant W.M. Moore counted the number of bars, clip joints, and brothels around U.S. military bases in Japan. His comments were critical of the way Japanese were "'contaminating' young American servicemen" and advised his troops to "not do in Rome as Romans do." Because the chaplain was so widely quoted in the Japanese press, Higgins responded in a letter dated October 1, 1961, in which he wrote that, based on his sixteen years of experience in Japan, he could not lend support to the lieutenant's views. "On the contrary," Wally stated, "I have found Japanese morals to be superior in some ways to American morals. Over a period of many years I have found that 'sin is where you find it.'"

Since Lieutenant Moore had focused on Japanese morals, Higgins asked how many bars and cabarets he figured there were in Atsugi or Tachikawa, or Yokosuka, or Tokyo before the U.S. occupation. "How many prostitutes on the streets? What was the incidence of

---

10   See Appendix, page 292, for Higgins's comments on Japanese use of
       American patents. Both the *Challenge* article and 1955 correspondence
       with D.F. Walker shed light on the subject.

crime, of fraud, of theft, of rape, of VD and of murder as compared with today? Who taught the Japanese punks the art of procuring and racketeering? Who introduced the clip joints?"

Meanwhile, Japanese industry had grown to a strong competitive position, and Higgins noted that the *zaibatsu*, the giant combines that had been broken up in the early days of occupation, had re-appeared, while new *zaibatsu*, like Hitachi, also had emerged.[11] "By force of circumstance," Higgins said, "Japan must be a processing nation. If American businessmen recognize the great potential of a cooperative effort with Japanese industry through mutually profitable processing agreements, Japan's tremendous resources of energy and talent can be beneficial to both nations. If they fail to do so, and if they follow a policy of containment, the dam will burst and the waters will flow into other channels."

Gripped by the need to spread the true story of what was going on in Japan in 1960, Higgins sent copies of his correspondence with Senator Lausche to several influential people: Japanese and American clients, heads of associations, company presidents, friends, military commanders, White House staff, Joe Dodge, Herbert Hoover, Victor Riesel, and other columnists.

Encouraged by his writer friend, Ray Josephs, of New York, Higgins also prepared an article he titled "What Is Japan?"[12] In the article, Higgins described Japan as "a land of cherry blossoms and 'honey buckets,' of tea ceremony and suicide, of jets and oxcarts, of courtesy and rudeness, of kabuki and jazz. One need only to turn a corner...and step backward one hundred years." He told how the Japanese embraced the new, while tenaciously holding on to old traditions. "One can say that its economy is sound or that it is bankrupt, that its politicians and statesmen are immature or that they are the smartest in the world. Abundant evidence can be found to support any view pro or con."

Higgins also wrote about how, before the war, the Japanese were perhaps the most honest and law abiding in the world, about how

---

11   See Appendix, page 296, for Higgins's additional remarks on *zaibatsu*.

12   See Appendix, page 298, for complete text of Higgins's article "What Is Japan?"

theft, rape and major crimes were almost unknown. "The Yen was the second or third strongest currency in the world, indicating a stable and prosperous economy. There was no unemployment and no poverty. Employers took care of their workers as if members of the family. Young people traditionally took care of their elders. There was security from the cradle to the grave—perhaps the greatest 'social security system' the world has ever known..."

Wally observed that after fifteen years of occupation, citizens had taken to locking their houses at night, and theft and sex crimes were common. "The whole nation seems to be pleasure mad. Forces of law and order are openly defied and reverence for Emperor, church and family seem to have been cast aside."

Noting that war damage was mostly repaired, that the people had plenty of life's necessities, Higgins wondered what was responsible for the change, and again outlined the efforts of the Americans, both pro and con. In less than a century, Higgins wrote, Japan

> emerged from a feudal clan to the position of one of the great powers. The brains, energy and determination responsible for that progress is now beginning to "put the show back on the road." One of the wisest of Japan's statesmen said to me during the early days of the occupation that "Japan regards the occupation only as an interlude, a pause in her forward progress."
>
> I predict that great progress will be made during the next few years. Japan, like the rest of the world, is turning to the younger generation. Business leaders have appeared in abundance. The economy is "bursting out all over." Nothing will stop them. We Americans may have to get out of our easy chairs again to meet the competition!
>
> In all fairness I must point out our efforts to bring Democracy to Japan have not been in vain. Some of the reforms have been beneficial and others will work out in time. When Japan has recovered from her bad case of indigestion from swallowing too much in one gulp, she will emerge as a strong Democratic country and a valuable asset to the free world.

TWELVE

Karma

Wally and Sueno found their seats on the plane. Excited and nervous, she stroked her fur cape before removing it and handing it to him to place in the overhead rack. On this 20th day of April, 1964, they were leaving Haneda for an around-the-world vacation.

Following a boat trip and a visit to Amsterdam's tulip gardens, they flew to Houston, Texas, and Higgins began showing his Japanese wife the vastness of America. After El Paso, they visited Deming and Albuquerque, New Mexico, where Higgins bought some desert lots. They moved on to Tucson, Arizona; Hollywood, California; New Orleans, Louisiana; Tampa, Miami, and Key West, Florida; and, on May 9, landed in Washington, D.C. At the forty-fifth reunion of his Naval Academy Class at Annapolis, Sueno was "a big hit" with Wally's classmates, much to his delight. Higgins and Sueno then stopped in Pittsburgh, Pennsylvania; Cleveland, Ohio; and Chicago, Illinois, to visit each of Higgins's American-born sons.

At Chicago's Midway Airport, Ray met his father and step-mother, who, in a formal kimono, resembled a large Japanese doll. Ray took them to their room at the Palmer House in downtown Chicago and then on to the apartment in nearby Evanston that was home to Ray, his wife, and son. After eleven-year-old Raymond Jr. had shown his Japanese grandmother his room, his goldfish, and

Jane Mansfield poses with Sueno Higgins in Hollywood.

his shell collection, he could hold his curiosity no longer and quizzed her about her obi, the sash around her waist. Unsure of her English, Sueno left nearly all the talking to Wally.

"Ray," Wally said before they left, "you, June, and young Raymond have got to come vacation with us in Japan!"

"We will," Ray assured him.

As soon as Higgins and Sueno were gone, Ray Jr. turned to his mother and asked, "Mom, how come I have three grandmothers when most kids only have two?"

Higgins and Sueno Higgins arrived in Toronto June 9 to visit Dr. Yutaka Wakabayashi, Tae, and their son, Yoshi. Yutaka was in Canada beginning the second of two years in a psychiatry course at the University of Toronto. Sueno and Higgins had missed all three of them, and had especially missed watching their grandchild grow up.

While discussing their return to Japan, Higgins had an idea. "Yutaka, you will need a house for your family when you get back to Japan," he said. "We've moved to Atsugi Heights, and the house next door is for sale. Sueno and I will buy it for you as a belated wedding present."

They next flew to New York and were met by Higgins's son, Dick. Ten days were filled with drives to Philadelphia and Trenton, where Higgins showed Sueno his "boyhood stamping grounds." They attended the musical *My Fair Lady*, the New York World's Fair, and had time for visits with friends and dinners with Dick. Higgins's lawyer also revised his will, reflecting the changes in his life, and Higgins signed it.

They went to West Point, Niagara Falls, returned to Toronto, toured the St. Lawrence Seaway, then were off to Montreal, Amsterdam, London on the 14th, then Paris, Amsterdam again, and Oslo. In Stockholm, Higgins and Sueno attended Rotary at the Grand Hotel, where they met Russian Premier Nikita Khrushchev.

In Europe, the whirlwind tour did not slow. In Berlin, Higgins compared the still war-damaged city to the rebuilt cities of Japan and described its slow recovery as "unbelievable!" They also enjoyed *Madam Butterfly* at the Vienna Opera House. Higgins attended Rotary meetings at each stop in Zurich, Geneva, Milan, Venice, Rome. In Madrid, Higgins was disappointed to learn there was no Rotary in all of Spain.

Their swing through southern Europe was made more memorable when Higgins got sick from the water in Rome and shy Sueno

Wally and Sueno met Nikita Khrushchev in Stockholm. Khrushchev was persuaded to step out on the balcony for a photo.

was pinched in a crowd of Italian men. In Cairo on July 22, Higgins had a private conference with President Gamal Abdel Nasser. After stopping at Karachi and Bangkok, they returned to Japan July 29, in time for Higgins to attend Japanese Rotary. He would share a speech about his trip with several Japanese Rotary clubs.

Meanwhile, Ray and his family planned a trip to Japan in the summer of 1965. When Adelaide found out, she phoned and asked, "You're not going to stay with *that woman*, are you?"

Ray assured her it was "merely a vacation trip."

Angrily, Adelaide extinguished her half-smoked cigarette in the blistered dish from Hiroshima, which was now serving as an ashtray.

Past Yokohama and the Yokosuka Naval Base, down MacArthur Boulevard and a stretch of beach at the small rail station marked "Otsu," Higgins pulled into the alley and stopped outside their former home. The Higgins Diggins sign was no longer on the wooden gate. Higgins turned to look at Sueno, June, and Ray Jr., now thirteen, in the back seat.

"We've given this place up since moving to Atsugi Heights. Lived here nineteen years without central heating or modern plumbing," he declared.

Ray rolled down the window and looked up at the small, rugged mountain that rose from the grounds beyond the stone wall. Over the wall to the left, he could see the tops of carefully manicured bushes, and to the right, tile roofs of several buildings inside the secluded compound.

"It was a grand old place," Higgins said. "Can't go in because there's new owners." He started the car and slowly backed out.

Wally drove them around the Miura Peninsula, including the underground tunnels with elaborate gun emplacements. "Here, in this side tunnel we found eighteen-inch guns," Wally explained. "The Japs could have blown our fleet right out of Tokyo Bay."

Arriving at Uraga, the shipbuilding port near the entrance to Tokyo Bay, the occupants of the car found themselves staring upward. One end of a ship rose above them like a skyscraper, so large they could not see the entire vessel. Higgins drove to a spot a quarter mile away, on the other side of the dry dock, where they could see the giant from end to end.

"Supertanker," Higgins explained. "One-hundred-thousand-ton displacement. We're building them for merchant marines of all nations."

Higgins then drove westward past Kamakura to the coast of Sagami Bay and slowed as they went along the beach area opposite the island of Enoshima.

"That's the Miami Beach of Japan," Higgins said. There were few people on the sand, however, and one woman held a parasol.

"Notice all the tents and awnings and umbrellas on the beach?" Higgins asked his curious American audience. "Japanese try to avoid tanning. They don't want dark skins."

The next day they visited a farm that was similar to an American tree nursery, where Higgins had purchased nursery stock and become friends with the farmer. The farmer showed them how they trained trees in artistic shapes using bamboo splints, careful pruning, and patience. They were invited into the farmer's house for refreshments and sat on the padded floor before a low table.

"Ocha wa ikaga desu ka?"

"He wants to know if you want a cup of tea," Higgins translated.

After Sueno, Higgins, and the farmer had bantered for a moment, Wally said, "This isn't what it sounds like. They have a very popular soft drink you might like. It's like a citrus Seven-Up, but the Japanese name is pronounced in a way that sounds like 'cow piss.' He asks if you would like that?"

Raymond Jr. and his father laughed, then both said, "I'll have some cow piss!"

Higgins, Sueno, and Ray's family checked into Tokyo's Imperial Hotel, the structure designed by Frank Lloyd Wright. Alongside, there was a tall, modern, high-rise hotel attached to the original stone building by an underground passageway. Ray left his family at the Imperial and accompanied his father to the headquarters of the Mitsui Company.

At noon they were whisked by limousine to the secluded grounds of the Mitsui Club, where Wally, Ray, and Wally's longtime friend Mr. Nii toured the gardens and snapped pictures in the light rain. They finally entered the marble building. Higgins pointed out that the model of a temple at the top of the stairs was pure silver.

In the large, private dining room, the trio was served by six waiters.

"Do you like sushi?" Higgins asked his son.

"I'll try anything!" Ray answered.

Nineteen rather small, colorful, exotic, and generally tasty courses later, Mr. Nii revealed what Ray had consumed: "Seaweed, octopus, oysters, jellyfish, clams, raw fish, fish eggs, pheasant eggs, asparagus, rose petals, and chicken."

A week later, at the Fujiya Hotel in the Hakone mountains, Higgins and Ray decided to take advantage of the swimming pool. They had the pool to themselves. As Ray stood in the shallow end, Higgins slipped into the water, naked.

"Ever see a eunuch before?" His voice reverberated off the tile walls of the enclosure.

He swam to the end of the pool, flipped and stroked effortlessly past Ray, who noticed that Higgins was missing part of his anatomy. They swam side by side for many laps before they both stopped and hung onto the side of the pool.

"When did you have the operation?" Ray asked.

"Last year, shortly after getting back from our trip. I got sick in Italy and felt worse in Spain."

"What was it?"

"Cancer of the colon. But in addition to taking a six-inch section of intestine, they removed the testicles as a precaution. I feel pretty good now, Ray."

With twenty years to catch up on, they talked for more than an hour. When the conversation turned to cultural differences, Wally observed, "One thing I've learned from the Japanese is patience. They seem to take forever to reach a decision. They'll stall and procrastinate and study it again. They discuss a problem all up and down the organization...share it with everyone who could be affected." His hand wiped a few drops of water from the top of his bald head, and he continued. "It's frustrating. I used to get upset, but I learned to wait."

"Sounds like Reilly's advice, to 'use a delayed response.'"

"Funny thing is, the Japanese do get problems solved; they get it done. The result is usually better than I expected. I think Americans could learn a lot about decision-making from them. I think most Americans make their minds up pretty quick."

"Too quick, maybe," Ray agreed.

"Indeed," said Higgins. "Maybe there's a reason. We've got to remember the conditioning of the Japanese. They've been crowded together on these small islands for thousands of years and have developed a culture of group cooperation."

The following week, the family was settled back into Wally and Sueno's Atsugi home. The western portion of their house included a sunroom, with comfortable upholstered wicker furniture, Higgins's extensive library, a bar, and a coffee table.

Wearing a short, white, Western-style dress, Sueno sat in the chair near to Higgins and Ray. They were joined by June, Raymond Jr., and Ernest Makoto, who sat on the floor. Having fixed everyone a soft drink, Higgins returned to his seat and lifted his glass in a toast.

"To a pleasant final two days of your visit!"

"It's been great so far, Dad," Ray said. "Couldn't have been planned better."

"Well, I wish you were going to be here longer. Two weeks isn't long enough to see Japan. I would have sent you down to Hiroshima and the southern island of Kyushu if there was more time."

"Didn't you two meet at Hiroshima?"

"Kure. Sueno's family home is at Hiroshima."

Sueno nodded and smiled her affirmation. They had been with Sueno off and on during the past two weeks, and she had been quiet most of the time.

Ray hesitated before asking. "Did you see the Hiroshima bomb when it exploded?"

"*Hai!* Yes, I saw it."

"Can you tell us about it?"

"Oooh, sooo bright. Like sun! *Pika don,* brighter than the sun." Sueno raised her hands over her eyes. "Oooh."

She and Higgins spoke a few phrases in Japanese, then he explained. "Sueno says she was watching the B-29 in the sky until it disappeared. She was protected by the mountain between Hiroshima and their farm. She lived twenty kilometers from the center of the blast. Had the two bombs not ended the war," Higgins added, "there would have been a bloodbath. I've seen the defenses on these islands, and an invasion would have made the slaughter on Okinawa look like a Sunday school picnic!"

When Higgins finished, Sueno said in English, "I think now bomb good thing. Save so many lives!"

Ray didn't know what awakened him. Perhaps the mere presence of someone in the guest house, the creak of the wicker chair, the sound of her breathing, or the sudden silence from the cessation of rain. He opened his eyes and saw Sueno sitting forward in a chair only a few feet away.

"Ohayohgozaimasu." ("Good morning.")

"Good morning." He looked at his watch. "I'm not sure if I was awake or asleep," Ray explained. "I've been relaxing here on the floor for an hour, and it seems like just a moment. It's very restful and peaceful here."

His father entered the room.

In the Japanese guest house, author Ray Higgins explores the concept of karma with Sueno.

"I was telling Sueno," Ray continued, "that I've been experiencing wonderful feelings of serenity."

"Sounds like you've found your karma." In their conversations, Wally had introduced his son to the concept of karma, and Ray had begun an exploration of questions about life, meaning, and death. "Why do I exist?" he mused. "What is my purpose in life? What's going to happen, and does it matter? What is the ultimate destination?" In his attempts to find out what karma meant, he heard many replies, but whatever karma was, Ray decided, his father must have had personal knowledge of its meaning. Wally had, after all, alluded to his belief that the real meaning was in the journey, the doing, the attitude, not the destination.

When Ray Higgins and his family stopped in Hawaii for the final week of their vacation, they were greeted by his brother, Dick, who was working in Honolulu, and by Dick's wife and daughter, who was the same age as young Raymond. Dick took them to the far side of the island and showed them the house Wally had bought for retirement.

Although he had been planning to retire and settle with Sueno and the two younger boys in Hawaii, Wally still was not ready to relax. In fact, his activities had increased. From 1966 through 1971 he was busier than ever with consulting and business projects. In Okinawa there was a reclamation of land project. In Guam, Vietnam, and Japan, he sold power equipment. His Capital Insurance business grew, and he studied the feasibility of opening an insurance office on Guam.

As he made plans for them to move there, and unaware that she had other plans, Wally and Sueno vacationed in Hawaii. Secretly, Sueno arranged with her family and gardener to create what she called a "Hawaiian Garden" on the Atsugi property. When she and Wally returned to their home in Japan, he was surprised to find it transformed: It was Japanese on one side and Hawaiian on the other. Sueno was persuasive and convinced him to remain in Japan.

Wally nonetheless plunged into more work: Combustion Engineering sales; Japan Steel projects; Gulf Oil activities; housing projects; tourism projects; Rotary; the America-Japan Society; International Public Relations, Ltd.; Overseas Consultants; his mentoring of Noboru-san, the young man he had sponsored; contacts with the American Embassy and his legislative friends in Washington.

When friends from America visited Higgins and Sueno in 1970, they took snapshots of Higgins and Sueno in their garden. Ray was shocked when he saw the photo of his father. Higgins had undergone another operation for cancer and looked truly old.

Still, from Wally's perspective, life in the summer of 1971 was sweet. Feeling refreshed from a swim at the Atsugi Naval Air Base, he took a late afternoon stroll through the garden with his beautiful Sueno. Grandchild Yoshi, Tae's son, joined them at the curved, red bridge near the fishpond.

His karma was clear.

THIRTEEN

Wa-ree

*E*nlarged and glowing red, the August sun touched the horizon, rendering the slope of distant Mount Fuji amber. In close formation, two military aircraft took off from the Naval Air Base at Atsugi. The jet planes climbed steeply, then turned toward the suburban hilly area known as Atsugi Heights, forty-five miles south-west of Tokyo.

It was August 15, 1971, twenty-six years to the day since propeller-driven Japanese kamikaze planes last used the same runway to take off for suicidal attacks on advancing Allied forces. Two weeks later in 1945, General MacArthur's plane landed on that same runway.

Practicing the final takeoff and landing of the day, the American Navy pilot waved to his wingman, a Japan Self Defense Force pilot. One by one, lights came on in the windows of tiny homes on narrow, curved streets that wrapped around the Atsugi hillside, following the terraces of former farmland. Three-quarters of the way up the hill a dark spot of garden green identified the Higgins home, which was larger than the others. The village of small, brightly-lighted shops was a short distance above their home, each store decorated with colorful signs, lanterns, and pennants, each throwing patches of light onto the street.

Western eyes perceived such panoramas as though in miniature: narrow roads with small cars; small, box-like, tightly-spaced houses;

little stores; miniature trees—even the people appeared small. A compact, black 1970 Toyota turned off the main road at the grocery store near the top of the hill and bounced down the tree-lined lane toward the dark spot on the hillside. Its headlights barely increased the twilight's illumination of the low wall ahead.

There were three people in the garden. The man, dressed in a white, short-sleeved shirt, gray slacks, and leather thongs, was called "Higgins-san" by his many Japanese friends. His ruddy face was clean-shaven. Blue-gray eyes were separated by a straight, slightly large nose, and the gray in the hair on the sides of his bald head seemed appropriate for his seventy-two years. The woman who stood alongside him near the sculptured, small evergreen bush was Sueno Kotani Yoshida Higgins. Only the wrinkles at the corners of her eyes and her silver-streaked hair, tied back in a double knot, hinted at her fifty-eight years. Her smooth, white skin and doll-like face suggested a younger woman. She was an even five feet tall, weighed 100 pounds and was dressed in a dark silk kimono. In his school uniform of white shirt, blue shorts, and blue knee-high socks, eight-year-old Yoshi sat on the small, curved footbridge and played in the water that ran under the bridge.

The two adults stood on the high path of the garden, examining a recent planting. The noise from the two jet fighters faded, and only the sound of water cascading over the rocks and into the fishpond could be heard. The lush and seemingly isolated garden was smaller than it appeared; the entire property of house and gardens occupied less than half an acre.

Sueno discovered a full, creamy white bloom on the gardenia bush, reached out and picked it. She held out the blossom to show her husband.

"Wahhh...Kore wa tottemo kirei desu ne! Sooo pretty!"

"Soh, totemo kirei ne!" ("Yes, very beautiful!") Higgins agreed.

She inhaled deeply as Higgins bent to look at the plantings. It had been only a month since the *uekiya-san*, or gardener, finished extensive replanting, and already new growth was showing. Higgins reached beyond the recent plantings to the clump of bamboo he had planted seven years before, pointing out the thickness of the mature stems.

"Yada wa!" ("No!") "Ooh," she said. She bent her body away and shielded her eyes with the palm of one hand. Her forehead wrinkled

Sueno Higgins stands before a torii. Traditionally a gateway to a Japanese temple, it also identifies sacred locations.

as she searched for the words in her husband's language. "Bamboo...too much like spear." She did not have to explain. How long had it been? Twenty-five, twenty-six years, since the expected landing?

Higgins looked at her: She had added maybe five or ten pounds...a streak of gray in her hair...a bit more mature...but just as pretty as the skinny little girl called "Yoshida-san" he had met at Hiroshima. He gently took the flower from her hand, slipped it into her hair, and gave her a glance of understanding.

Tell her of the recent chest pains? He dare not. His first cancer operation, twenty years after leading the inspection of Hiroshima's bomb damage, had taken its toll. Tell her of his love? His body language substituted for words of either language. Their eyes met with expressions of devotion far stronger than most young lovers.

Though Higgins's cancer had not reappeared, he experienced increasingly frequent heart pains and made arrangements for the Wakabayashis to take care of Sueno if anything should happen to him. The Hiroshima house was now in Sueno's name, and his will was written.

This was one of the days he felt better. Following his morning swim at the Naval Air Station and an afternoon of rest, Wally was at peace with his world, and his words flowed softly.

"*Yatto niwa mo watashi ga omotte ita tohri ni natta!*" ("Finally, the garden is just like I always wanted it to be!")

"*Wa?...karma?*"

"Finally, karma...ahh, yes, my sweetheart," the American whispered. "This is what I've always wanted. I suppose you could say my karma, my destiny."

The boy on the footbridge sat up as the car passed the garden. He looked at Higgins and asked, "*Otohsan?*"

"*Otohsan!*" Higgins confirmed.

As Higgins answered, the youngster exploded like a firecracker. Higgins's eyes followed Yoshi as he ran across the lawn, jumped the low stone wall, and managed to get to the Toyota in time to open the door for the driver, his father.

Dr. Yutaka Wakabayashi stepped out from the right side of the car and smiled at his son. Forty-two-year-old Yutaka tousled the boy's hair and stretched his slight, five-foot-four frame. The front door of the neighboring house opened, and Tae Wakabayashi hurried out to greet her husband. Looking pretty at thirty-five, Tae, in a white cotton dress, carried a two-year-old child on her hip. The courtesies, smiles, and chatter of the four Wakabayashis made it apparent that family was all-important to them. This Saturday evening, Yutaka was home from his office in Tokyo, where he practiced psychiatry.

Higgins took Sueno's hand. "Sweetheart, let's go meet Yutaka. I want to talk to him." The funeral for Yutaka's father had occurred only two weeks earlier, and Higgins had done much planning of his own affairs during those two weeks. In a gesture unseen in public in the Japan of that day, Higgins put his hand around his wife's waist as they crossed the bridge, strolled out of the garden, and through the gate.

A few minutes later, Higgins and Yutaka walked into the sunroom of the big house. Tae and Sueno were with the children in the Wakabayashi home. The American had just received a new music tape from the States, a recording that was a favorite of Yutaka's when he trained in Toronto. As the music started, the two men touched drink glasses and sat on the wicker sofa.

"Did you make the arrangements for the girls?" Higgins asked.

"Yes, the Labor Day surprise is all arranged, just as you planned. I'm sure they will enjoy the outing. How are you feeling today?"

"Had a great swim at the base. Pulse is up from yesterday to sixty-five."

"That's encouraging. You must be careful not to overdo yourself, Higgins-san."

"I know. I'm already cutting back. This week I've only been to Tokyo twice...Matsushita, Toyota, Japan Steel, M.S.K....oh, and the America-Japan Society luncheon." Higgins sipped his drink, then leaned forward as he put it down.

"Yutaka, I want your opinion on something. You know Mr. Takahata of Japan Steel?"

"Hai."

"He came up with the 'Idea of the Week,' to hire new men while also keeping the older men. He suggests buying land in Hawaii for a company house, as an incentive in recruiting junior executives. Do you think the promise of company-paid vacations in Hawaii would appeal to young executives?"

"Hai! Ah, yes, great appeal."

"I told Mister Takahata I would develop a mail campaign, describing a week in Hawaii each year, to send to executives of medium-sized firms. Any ideas?"

They conversed until bedtime, when Sueno returned from "girl talk" with her daughter. The lights of Atsugi Heights flickered off, as families stretched out on their futons. Wally and Sueno climbed into their American-style bed. He pulled the sheet up over her shoulder, kissed his sweetheart goodnight, and switched off the light.

Soon, the only sounds were of a frog croaking in the fishpond and Higgins's gentle snoring.

"Ahh! Ahhh!! *Itai! Itai!"* A woman's loud scream pierced the night. "No...no!" Sueno shouted.

Higgins was jolted out of a deep sleep. Sueno was sitting bolt upright, clutching her forehead, her body writhing in great pain.

"Ohhhh, oooh!" She fell sideways into his arms.

"Sweetheart, what's wrong? *Doko ga itamimasuka?*" Higgins held her with his left arm and reached for the bedside light. "Where does it hurt?"

"*Atama*...my head, my head...oooh, it pains, sooo much!" She screamed loudly again. "Ahhh!"

Sueno continued to hold her head, squeezing it between both palms, as her eyes stared upward.

Higgins leapt from the bed and raced barefoot out of the house. He vaulted the low stone wall, ran across the lane, and pounded on the Wakabayashi's door.

"*Yutaka!* Yutaka! *Tasukete!* Wake up, damn it!"

Bedroom lights came on at several neighboring houses. A surprised Dr. Wakabayashi opened his door.

"Something is terribly wrong with Sueno!" Higgins shouted. In their nightclothes, the two men ran to Higgins's house.

"Cerebral hemorrhage." His fingers on Sueno's forehead, Yutaka was sure. "We must get her to the hospital quickly!"

"*Moshi moshi!*" Higgins spoke into the phone to his driver, Yanagi-kun. Yanagi had the car ready in the lane in minutes.

At Zama Hospital, the unconscious patient was examined, then wheeled to intensive care. She had indeed suffered a cerebral hemorrhage and lay in a deep coma.

Sobbing, Higgins sat at her bedside, rubbing her hand. When dawn arrived, he was still there. And he was there when the sun set.

"Commander," Dr. Wilson said, "you'd better get yourself something to eat, and get some sleep. You don't look so good, yourself. There's not much we can do until she comes out of this coma."

Higgins kept vigil at the bedside for two days. Then, on Tuesday, August 17, Yanagi drove him to the Tokyo office of Dr. Morton, Higgins's personal physician, for a regular health checkup.

The doctor was shocked by what he discovered. Higgins's cancer had become life-threatening.

"I'm ordering you into the hospital immediately. We'll probably have to operate. It's a good thing you've got your driver here."

The ride to Zama Hospital was as hurried and wild as the one two nights previous. Higgins barely made it alive. At 7 p.m. he was placed in the same room where Sueno lay in a coma.

Two days of transfusions and rest prepared Higgins for the removal of the cancer on Thursday afternoon. Meanwhile, Sueno slept on.

After Dr. Morton operated on him, Higgins was sent to recovery, then returned to the room he shared with Sueno. She stirred when his bed was brought in.

"*Otohsama.*" At first, Sueno spoke in just a whisper, but her voice grew stronger as the coma wore off. She was coming out of it! "*Otohsama.*"

Her husband heard her.

"Sueno...Sueno, my sweetheart!" he answered.

"Wa-ree!" With great effort, Higgins turned his head toward the sound. Never before had Sueno attempted to call him "Wally."

"Sueno!"

Two attending nurses looked at each other.

"Did you hear that? They're calling for each other."

"Are you thinking what I'm thinking?"

Together, they dropped the side rails, rearranged tubes, and brought the beds together. The patients' hands reached out, each searching for the other, touched, then clasped. As the nurses left the room, one snatched a tissue from the box on the bedstand and dabbed the corners of her eyes.

Friday afternoon and most of Saturday, Higgins and Sueno lay in each other's arms. Late Saturday afternoon, Higgins moved the covers over Sueno's shoulder. She felt cold.

"Sueno?"

There was no answer.

Ignoring the tube in his own arm, Higgins turned and sat up.

"Sweetheart!"

She did not move. His eyes widened in panic.

"Oh, God, no! Doctor!"

Standing at the joined beds, the doctor searched for vital signs. "She's gone," he said.

"No, not my sweetheart." Higgins wrapped his arm around her body and began to sob, gently at first, then uncontrollably. "Oh, no!"

"Morphine," ordered the doctor.

On November 1, 1971, Ray's brother, Bob, phoned him. "Hey, if you expect to see Mom alive, you'd better come and visit her. She's at the Cleveland Clinic."

Bob was there when Ray arrived at her bedside. Adelaide was hooked up to tubes and looked terrible. She was asleep, and they stepped out into the corridor.

"Doc thinks it's her kidneys," Bob said.

"Gee," Ray replied. "I expected it to be her heart, or lungs, since she smoked so much!"

"They don't really know," Bob added. "I had her transferred here to the Cleveland Clinic from Lake Erie Hospital two days ago."

They talked awhile, then went back into their mother's room and sat in wooden chairs on opposite sides of her bed. Without waking her, Ray slipped his hands around his mother's left hand.

Bob left an hour later, leaving Ray alone with Adelaide. As he gazed at her frail face, he thought about how much his mother had loved her boys. Even after they were grown and married, they were always welcome to come "home" to her small apartment. It seemed to Ray that after his father had returned to the United States to request a divorce, Adelaide had "lived for the boys." She never dated after Wally left.

Adelaide's hand twitched and she opened her eyes.

"Ohhh...I'm so glad you came, Ray!"

"June and I will drive back later this week to visit longer. How do you feel?"

"Not so good, honey. I'm not going to last very much longer. Oh, it's so good to see you. I thought you'd forgotten me!"

They talked only a short time before she dozed off again, but she wouldn't let go of his hand. Twice more she awoke, squeezed Ray's hand, and talked briefly about the fun times she remembered of "my family."

When Bob returned in the evening, Ray left the hospital and caught the last plane back to Chicago. The next morning, when their brother Bud arrived at her hospital room, the bed was empty, the bedding gone, the mattress rolled up.

The letter from Higgins's doctor had arrived two months previous. When Ray and June returned from Adelaide's funeral to their home in Wilmette, there was a telegram in the mailbox from Japan. The communications caused Ray to make plans to travel again to Japan in November 1971. Higgins's wire asked Ray to "come bring the Old Man back to my native land." Ray's mission was to bring his father to America for radiation treatment.

It took several weeks to make all the passport, visa, plane reservation, and inoculation arrangements. Ray made reservations on Northwest Airlines to arrive in Tokyo on Sunday, November 21.

Leaving the country just a few days before Thanksgiving meant that Ray Jr. would miss coming home from college for their traditional holiday weekend.

"Why are you going?" June protested. "Why, you hardly knew your father!"

Ray worried about leaving his wife; she had broken down on a previous occasion when left alone. As the plane took off from Chicago's O'Hare Airport, he looked back at the receding city with torn loyalties. After all these years of so little contact, it had fallen to him to "bring the Old Man home."

Ray was tired when his plane landed at Haneda near Tokyo. After going through customs, his eyes searched the Oriental faces of those waiting outside. Would he recognize Tae or Yutaka Wakabayashi? What would he do in this strange land if they didn't meet him?

"Wait." Ray spotted a youngster. "That child's face. I recognize it!"

It was Yoshi, six years older than the little boy Ray remembered from his previous visit. The boy's face was unmistakable! Then he recognized the Japanese parents standing with him, the mother holding a much younger child. Dressed in a red kimono, Tae recognized Ray and waved. Ray was struck by Tae's resemblance to her late mother.

On their way out of the airport, Ray had a moment of panic as Yutaka pulled into traffic on what seemed to be the wrong side of the street. Then he recalled, "This is Japan, where cars keep to the left."

There were many more autos on the highway than he remembered from his 1965 trip. Modern buildings and factories occupied places where he remembered shanties and rice paddies. He was also thankful that Yutaka spoke excellent English, and that he did not have to drive or find the way to Atsugi.

"How is Dad?" he asked.

"Much better." But the pained expression on Tae's face told Ray not to expect much.

When the car turned into the narrow lane near the top of the hill, Ray recognized the surroundings and knew that 1543 Terao, Ayase Machi, was just ahead. On the corner, its storefront covered with pennants and signs, he saw the small Japanese food store. As the Toyota bounced down the narrow alley, they passed two familiar Western-style houses, and he realized they were almost there. The car stopped at the low wall next to the gate. In the twilight, Ray saw that the garden had matured, with bamboo trees twice as tall as he remembered, so tall they hid the house higher on the hillside.

Dressed in a gray kimono and far thinner than Ray had ever seen him, Wally opened the door and came to greet them. His usual ruddy complexion was white, even to the top of his head. For the first time in Ray's memory, he and his father wrapped their arms around each other and hugged for a long time.

Recalling the custom, Ray removed his shoes and slipped his feet into a pair of slippers on the stoop. Inside, the house was much as he had remembered. Half the house was Western-style, with hardwood floors. The side nearest the garden was Japanese-style, containing the guest house and bath. On the low wall between the living room and dining area rested an intricate wood carving, with tiny figures at a feudal castle. The large figurine of an emperor for celebrating Boys' Day that had stood in front of the fireplace was missing, however.

"Victor Katsumi took it back to the States with him," Wally explained.

"How are you feeling, Dad?"

"Rotten, but what could you expect from an anemic eunuch like me?" Wally paused, then added, "You know, Ray, I can't remember a thing about the two months after my sweetheart died. I just stayed in bed or moped around the house."

"When did you decide to go back to the States?"

"Well, one morning I woke up and realized I was still alive. God must have some reason for it! That's when I sent the wire to come help me get back. Now, tell me about your mother's funeral. I heard she died on the second?"

Ray told Wally about Adelaide, then briefed him on the rest of the stateside family. When he finished, Wally led him to a small bedroom in the Japanese part of the house and showed him Sueno's shrine. Wally explained how the Japanese honored the recently departed. All the things she liked surrounded a large portrait of Sueno on the dresser. There was a bowl of fruit, some candy, mangoes, a glass of water, a pack of her favorite brand of cigarettes, a candle, and incense sticks.

"For forty days the ashes of the departed are kept on the shrine," he said. "Sueno's ashes were removed and taken to the cemetery at Kamakura in October, but her spirit is still here on the shrine." Wally moved closer to Sueno's picture. "When I got word you were coming, I moved the shrine here. We originally had it set up as a shrine in the Japanese guest room, but I thought you might want to sleep there." He put his hands together and bowed to Sueno's picture.

"Where do you want me to put my suitcase?" Ray asked.

"Where would you be most comfortable? On the floor of the Japanese guest house or in our Western-style bed?"

Ray thought about the pleasant guest house, flanked by garden on three sides, with its soft rice straw matting, and the feelings he had experienced there in 1965. But he decided to avoid the effort of getting out the bedding.

"Gee, Dad, I'm so bushed from being up for twenty-two hours, I think I'd prefer the bed. Jet lag has gotten to me!"

"Fine. You can have our room. I moved into Vic's room last month. Wanted to be closer to the kitchen."

As Ray turned to leave Sueno's shrine, Wally said, "Oh, about the water. When you get up in the mornings here, don't turn on the water faucet. The first water from the tap is for Sueno, so if you're up any morning before me, just draw a fresh glassful and use it to replace the glass on her shrine."

In Wally's room, Ray opened his suitcase and hung a few clothes in the shallow closet. The master bedroom was furnished with only a bed and a dresser. To conserve space, drawers and a closet were built into the walls. A very delicate, very old-looking Oriental painting in a vertical frame hung on one wall.

As he finished putting his shaving gear in the bathroom, Ray heard voices from the kitchen and went to find his father there with Tae. She had come next door and prepared them each a large bowl of soup. She served the men and left immediately.

As soon as Tae was gone, Ray looked up. "She seems so sad!" he commented.

"I guess so. She's been like that ever since I told the Wakabayashis I wanted to go back to America."

"How have you managed here alone?"

"Tae comes over several times a day and looks in on me. She's been pretty good about fixing the meals. And I manage to get my own breakfast. Then I also have a cleaning woman come in twice a week. She feeds me on those days."

At Wally's urging, Ray gave him more news about the family and about how Adelaide had managed the past few years.

"When I went back to the States the first time after three years in Japan, I might have stayed—if your mother had changed. But she hadn't. Adelaide was a wonderful mother and cook. But Ray, she was not much of a wife."

"She was awfully good to us boys and our families."

"I'm sure she was. Yes, she was the world's best mother...and if only Sueno could have baked pies like Adelaide! One thing for sure, Ray—Japanese women really know how to treat their men."

They talked for hours and then prepared for bed.

Wally leaned in the doorway of Ray's room. "My driver will be here in the morning to take me to Zama Hospital for a blood transfusion. You sleep as long as you want to in the morning. Good night, son."

As Ray climbed into bed, he heard his father moving about in the next room. Because the walls were so thin, Ray could tell Wally was pacing. Finally Ray heard him stop and then the springs squeak as Wally sat on the bed. Ray could hear his father sobbing, stopping only to exclaim, "Oh God! Why did you take her first? She was so beautiful. So beautiful on the inside. Why didn't you take this old bastard instead!"

Ray started to get out of bed, but hesitated, for the weeping had subsided. From all the years he had lived in the same house with his father before the war, Ray could not picture the hard-boiled man actually crying. His head sank back into the pillow and he fell into a deep sleep until 11:00 the next morning.

When he awoke, the house was quiet. All Ray heard were typical neighborhood noises: a dog barking, the steady rhythm of a carpenter hammering. He dressed, ate a small helping of cereal, and explored the guest house. Connected to the main house by a walkway and the Japanese bath, the square structure was built without a single nail. He slid the paper door back and forth and admired the workmanship. He stepped onto the *tatami*-mat floor and remembered how comfortable it was to stretch out on. In an alcove on one side was the family shrine, on another side, a cedar box to store bedding. The wicker chairs still looked inviting.

The sound of splashing water in the garden startled him. Ray turned to look, and as he stepped out the sliding door onto the porch, he saw the back of a woman in a black kimono standing by the fishpond. For an instant he thought, "Am I seeing the ghost of Sueno?"

He slipped his feet into a pair of thongs on the porch. Tae was feeding the koi and turned as he approached. A large white and orange carp broke the surface and darted away with a morsel. Another, white and black with billowing red fins gave chase.

"*Ohayohgozaimasu!*" Ray tried to use proper inflection.

"*Ohayohgozaimasu*, good morning," Tae replied. She continued in her halting English. "*Otohsama*...go early this morning. He told me...ask you...if you like me make lunch."

Still hungry from such a small breakfast, he said, "Oh, yes, Tae. I would enjoy a real Japanese meal...if you don't mind."

Tae bowed, hurried into the kitchen, retrieved some money from a jar in the cupboard and excused herself to walk to the corner market. Refrigerators in Japan were much smaller than those in America, and the custom was to go to the store every day, often to get food for a single meal. As she disappeared up the lane, Ray began to explore the neighborhood in the opposite direction. What had been terraced farmland below the house in 1965 was covered by suburban homes in 1971. Each home was on a tiny lot, twenty-by-twenty feet. The houses were built to within inches of their property lines, and all were two or three stories high to obtain maximum living space from minimum land.

Higgins's lane ended at a low wall by a gate, so Ray stepped over the wall and scooted down the stone embankment to the street below. He began to circle the block that surrounded his father's place. "My God," he realized, "the Old Man's place would hold nine of these Japanese houses!" Wally was practically giving his home to the Wakabayashis.

Ray passed several children playing in the street, and they exchanged smiles. By the time he had climbed the hill to the main road, turned left at the corner, and arrived at the small food store, Tae was coming out with her purchases. His offer to help carry the packages was met with resistance that meant it was not the customary thing for the man to do.

On reaching the house, Tae went into the kitchen. Ray waited out on the sun porch. And waited. Forty minutes later, his stepsister announced, with apologies, that lunch was ready. She placed a bowl of soup before him. Nearby sat a colorful plate of *sashimi*, vegetables, rice, and, in the center of the table, things she refused to identify. He ate everything.

Wally arrived home shortly after Ray finished eating.

"Come with me, Ray, I want to show you my Capital Insurance Company office." His driver was waiting. On the ride into Atsugi, Wally explained his plans to turn the business over to Emoto, Nagashima, Mrs. Shimamori, and the other employees. Higgins had started Capital Insurance-Yokosuka when he saw the need for Americans stationed in Japan to have insurance protection.

"The company was operated from offices in Atsugi and Yokosuka," he told his son. "Last year we attempted to consolidate the company and shrink its size. I quickly found out you just don't lay employees off in Japan! You can't just fire someone you no longer need."

"What did you do?" Ray asked.

"Well, I eventually arranged to cut our surplus staff some, but it cost a hell of a lot through early retirements and separation payments. What I really want to do now is give the company to the great staff that have been running it for years. Three of them have been with me nearly twenty years."

"Can they run the company without you?"

"A damn sight better than I can! I've already discussed it with Mrs. Shimamori and the others."

The car stopped in front of a modest storefront bearing the name "Capital Insurance Company" in English. The atmosphere brightened considerably when the half-dozen workers saw Wally enter. Greetings were exchanged in both languages, and Ray was introduced to Mrs. Sugizawa, and Messrs. Emoto and Nagashima. The four went into a glass-enclosed office and talked. As Wally and Ray left, each worker in the office stood by the door, shook hands, and bowed. Tears ran down the cheeks of the women. Wally had announced he was leaving Japan for good.

Back at the house, Wally wanted to start the packing with his business papers. A converted den in one corner of the house had served as his office. The small room contained a large desk, a four-drawer file, a safe, and several small tables on which were piled various folders. At his request, Ray carried in two large Army footlockers and placed them in the middle of the *tatami*-mat floor. Wally sat at his desk while Ray kneeled on the floor beside a footlocker. Wally began by reaching into a file drawer and pulling out a folder. "No use for this now," and threw it in the wastebasket.

Ray, noting it was marked "Communism" said, "Wait a minute. That might be interesting. Mind if I see it?"

While Wally sat pulling papers from the drawer and stacking them on the desk, Ray skimmed the discarded folder. It was full of typed reports and letters from 1945 through the 1950s and told a chilling story of communist attempts to take over Japan. Ray was shocked by what it revealed. Up to that moment in 1971 he had never heard of infighting on MacArthur's staff, or of Japan's number one Communist being flown back to Japan from Manchuria in 1946 at American taxpayers' expense to head up the Japanese labor movement.

"Hey, Dad, this tells stuff that has never been made public! It could be valuable historically!"

"If you want it, you can keep it. Just put it in the footlocker, and we'll ship it to Bud's house in the States."

The next folder was marked "Politics." It contained a detailed account of politics in Japan from the beginning of the occupation up to the election of 1960. Ray placed the whole file in the footlocker for shipment.

Wally next handed Ray a folder with his military orders, and another with SCAP policy papers. Then he handed over several folders with newspaper clippings of projects he had been involved in when working for MacArthur as head of the FEC Allocations Committee. There were reports on Higgins's analyses of Japan's hydroelectric power potential, and of the troubles at the coal mines in northern Japan. Meanwhile, Wally was busy sorting out things he would need to continue his business from the States. Weak from his exertions, he decided to go lie down.

"Pack things of historical interest to ship," he told Ray, "and throw out the rest."

Ray worked through the day, finding everything exciting and worth keeping. The papers told how Japan had returned to her feet, and an amazing story of one patriotic American who devoted twenty-six years to helping her do it.

Next Ray tackled the safe as his father had instructed. Ray sat on the floor in front of the small safe and reached in. The top shelf was packed solid with bundles, each containing about thirty sheets of paper, some bound by rubber bands, others tied with string or ribbon. Ray removed the string from one bundle and unfolded the top sheet. Higgins's handwriting appeared across each strip. Turning it over, he discovered brittle paper containing Higgins's travel orders from the Presidio to Sixth Army Headquarters in the Philippines. The other sheets were folded into strips on which to keep a diary. By writing very small he had an immense amount of information on each strip. The first bundle covered each day from August 19, 1945, to July 1, 1946.

After the safe, Wally asked Ray to check a crawl space over the den.

"I stored a few things in it. I want to take inventory."

Following his instructions, Ray found a ladder, climbed up, opened the door and looked in. Wally handed him a flashlight. Close to the opening, Ray counted five cartons labeled "Fine Scotch Whiskey." There was nothing else in the storage space.

"Pull one down," Higgins told him.

They opened the sealed carton. The labels were accurate.

"I bought some at the PX several years ago and almost forgot about it," Higgins said. "We'll take some of this with us when we go into Tokyo to have lunch with Mr. Tanaka. It will serve as going-away gifts. The Japanese love good Scotch, and they can't buy it." While Ray fixed lunch, Wally went to his bedroom and gift-wrapped each of the bottles from one case.

On Thursday, November 25, 1971, father and son were up early to take the train into Tokyo. It was Thanksgiving Day in America, but outside U.S. bases it was just another work day in Japan. Wally had it figured they should take the train a short time after the early commuter rush. They stood during the first part of the ride, but managed to get seats after transferring to the main line. It was not nearly as luxurious as the 125-mile-an-hour ride in the nose of the Bullet Train Ray remembered from his 1965 visit.

Ray was amazed at the stamina of his seventy-three-year-old guide. The fresh blood seemed to have helped. They walked and took taxis between their many stops. Tokyo was booming. New office buildings and skyscrapers were going up everywhere.

"*Ichiban!*" commented Wally. "They are determined to become number one."

They met with Dr. Morton, the man who had written home about Sueno's death and suggested that one of Wally's stateside sons come to Japan. He gave Wally his medical folders, prescriptions for his use in the United States, and talked about the arrangements for Wally's hospitalization. Because he was no longer on active duty, he could not be treated at Bethesda Naval Hospital, as he desired. But there was a bed waiting for him at Washington's veteran's hospital.

They entered the Mitsui Building. Higgins wanted to show his son the office he was giving up at Japan Steel. They left the elevator and passed through glass doors that opened onto an office area that nearly occupied the entire floor. A lone enclosed office stood in the center of the vast bullpen.

"This is it!" Wally said as he opened the door. "Space is so valuable that very few executives have an enclosed office space. Japan Steel has been most generous in allowing me to use this when I've been in the city."

As he retrieved a file from the desk, a young man entered, spoke in Japanese with Wally, then told them, "Mr. Tanaka is ready to have lunch with you. Ahh, you are really going? Back to America? *Hai!* Ohhh, we will miss you."

Wally introduced Ray and retrieved one of the gift-wrapped packages from his satchel. Wally's protege thanked him profusely and bowed, then led them to the largest of several private offices on the perimeter of the floor. Wally greeted Mr. Tanaka, a top manager, and introduced Ray as "my number three son." Again, a package was presented and reluctantly accepted with profuse *arigatos*.

Higgins was taken to Zama for yet another blood transfusion to get his blood count up for the long trip. Ray recalled that all through World War II his father had faithfully donated blood to the Red Cross every month. Now he was getting some of it back.

Back at the house, Ray began packing clothes in the bedroom that Wally and Sueno had used for about eight years. Figuring it would be easier to unload the drawers on the bed, Ray pulled on one, and by tilting the drawer off its tracks, removed it entirely. Something shone from the emptied cabinet when the light hit it. Ray peered in and saw a sword. He reached in and removed the ancient weapon from its hiding place. The ten-inch blade was sharp as a razor, and the handle was inlaid. Ray took it to his father, who studied it a few moments.

"I'll be damned!" Wally rubbed his thumb across the blade. "Why, that's a samurai sword, used to commit *seppuku*, or *hárikari*. I'll bet it's Sueno's. She must have had it hidden in there all these years." He was quiet a moment. "If she had ever been disgraced...if I had ever turned against her...she would most likely have used it to end her life."

Later, opening a bathroom cabinet, Ray found several cases of Doctor Scholl's Athletes Foot Powder.

"Why twenty-four cans of this?" he asked his dad.

Wally laughed when he saw it. "When I landed in Japan I had the worst case of athlete's foot you ever saw...been troubled with it all my life. So I brought cases of powder with me. Ha, funny thing! As soon as I started to live Japanese style, it went away. For twenty-six years I've taken my shoes off at the door to walk on the *tatami* mats. Just leave it there, Ray. Let Yutaka throw it away."

When Yutaka came to the house, Wally showed him where the Scotch was stored and gave him an inventory of household contents. They walked through, Wally showing Yutaka what was to stay, and what was to be shipped to Ohio. Then they all went into the den, where Wally and Ray explained how Yutaka should ship the cartons and trunks.

"Where is Tae?" Higgins asked.

"Ah, she's over at our house tidying up," Yutaka answered. "She's not feeling well."

"Why, she hasn't been over here in two days!" Wally was visibly upset. "I'm leaving this evening, and she hasn't said 'boo' about my going. I thought she'd want to spend some time with her Old Man!"

"It's hard to explain." Yutaka was embarrassed. "She's feeling terrible." He turned to leave. "I will tell her that you want to see her."

Answering a knock at the door, Ray opened it to find an immense Japanese woman who wanted to see Higgins-san. Wally came into the living room and greeted her warmly. Their rapid-fire Japanese conversation was full of emotion. Wiping away a tear, she pulled out a package. He, in turn, retrieved a package from the bedroom and gave it to her. As they talked, and as she wiped more tears from her eyes, an insistent tone came into her voice. She pointed to the back of the house.

"This lady is my masseuse," Wally explained to his baffled son. "She stopped by to say goodbye and wish me a safe trip. Now she is insisting that I need one last rubdown before I travel."

"Go ahead!" Ray advised. Soon after they retreated to the bedroom, he heard hands slapping skin.

When the masseuse was gone, Wally elaborated. "She runs a massage parlor in Yokosuka. Been giving me rubdowns for twenty-five years. Whenever I felt worn out, I stopped by her shop. Funny thing is, when we first arrived here in Yokosuka, a bunch of us went to her parlor. The younger guys all went for the girls, but I really wanted a good massage, so I requested the fat woman who owned the parlor. There just aren't many really good masseuses in Japan. She's one of the best."

Wally answered the next knock at the door. A Japanese man and two women removed their shoes and stepped in. Again, there was an emotional discussion in Japanese, an exchange of gifts, and tears

"Part of the crew from the Yokosuka office," Wally explained. "Called to wish the Old Man their best."

Yutaka returned. "I'll be taking you to the airport about six o'clock." Wally gave maintenance tips as the two walked the property, then sat down and reviewed some papers.

Another caller came to the door, a man who had been Wally's driver and protege for many years. When he left, Wally told Ray the visitor was the young kamikaze pilot Higgins had taken in, then sponsored through college.

Their next visitor was the cleaning woman and her sister. They had come to not only say goodbye, but had brought supper. Yutaka stayed and ate with them.

When it was time to leave, Yutaka had the car ready and helped Ray carry out the luggage. They could hear Wally at Sueno's shrine, crying.

Yutaka and Ray waited at the car. Wally came out the door, sat on the stoop, and put on his shoes. As he approached the car, his eyes were red.

"Where the hell is Tae?" he snarled.

"She's coming," answered Yutaka.

She hurried across the lane, dressed in her prettiest kimono, her eyes even redder than Wally's. His words seemed to hit her as she started to get into the car.

"During my last few days in Japan, I expected you to come see the Old Man!"

Tae buried her head in her hands.

"Damn it, I raised you from a little girl! Is this the thanks I get?"

As Tae raised her head, her red eyes looked pleadingly into his. "House sooo sad!" she whispered.

The departure from the airport seemed to deflate most of Wally's anger. At customs, Tae clung to him and wept unashamedly.

Wally Higgins and Ray boarded their Northwest Airlines flight. As they strapped their seatbelts on, Ray explained his interpretation of Tae's reluctance to come to the house. "First her mother was taken from her, and now you, a kind man who came to Hiroshima and was so good to her, now you're leaving her as well. She meant no disrespect by not coming over. Remember her words? 'House sooo sad.'"

"Maybe so, Ray." He paused, then added, "But, though I treated her like a daughter from the time she was nine, she never really included me when she brought her young friends to the house. I don't honestly feel that any foreigner will ever be accepted as a true member of the family in Japan."

Wally hung on to life for a year after returning to America. He leased an apartment in Cleveland and often went to the VA hospital for chemotherapy. The end came November 27, 1972.

Following a memorial service with full military honors at Mentor, Ohio, the body of the former military governor of Hiroshima, American patriot, and friend of Japan, was cremated. His son, Victor Katsumi Higgins, took an urn with his father's ashes to the crypt in Kamakura, Japan, and placed it alongside Higgins's sweetheart. They had both come from Hiroshima—with love.

Appendix

Chapter 9, page 165

This document allegedly was prepared by Governor Thomas Dewey's advisors, including John Foster Dulles, Herbert Hoover, Joseph C. Grew, and other friends of Japan, as background material for what would have been his Japan policy had he been elected president. Despite Dewey's loss, Wally Higgins supported the policy vociferously, making hundreds of copies and distributing them widely. He also did anything he could to achieve the aims, a goal that may well have cost him his SCAP job. Many of the points in this paper also appeared in Robert H. Welch Jr.'s 1952 book *May God Forgive Us*.

AMERICAN POLICY TOWARD JAPAN
October 15, 1948

SUMMARY

The following pages contain the record of how American post-surrender policy toward Japan had been formulated—without the knowledge of the general public and often without the knowledge of policy-making officials—by a small group in the government both in Washington and Tokyo. It would not be proper for this paper to pass upon the motives of individuals in this group. It is fair to say, however, that as a group they favored a planned, collectivized economy, the extreme regulation of business that often goes under the guise of anti-monopoly, a government of men, not laws, and in foreign policy the building of "friendship bridges" to Russia. As applied to Japan, these ideas were calculated to result in:

1. Tearing down the Japanese social structure even though the predictable result was chaos leading to Communism.
2. Depriving the business, managerial and governmental career classes—classes traditionally oriented toward the United States—of their influence, wealth and livelihoods through a "purge" by occupational categories.
3. The "deconcentration" of Japanese businesses into single-plant units under the guise of breaking up monopolies.
4. Reducing Japan to a subsistence level at which it could never become self-supporting and the United States would have to continue the relief expenditure of $1,000,000 per day or see Communism overwhelm the country.
5. Transferring power to radical labor and political organizations, including the Communist Party.

Whatever the intent of the group, either individually or collectively, their policy served Russia so well that the Soviet Union has only occasionally and recently complained about American actions in Japan. Belated and partly successful steps have been taken—mostly by Republicans in the Truman Administration—to change this policy.

INITIAL POST-SURRENDER POLICY

In Feb. 1945, the Far East Sub-Committee of the State-War-Navy Coordinating Committee (SWNCC) was set up with Eugene H. Dooman, assistant to Under Secretary of State Joseph C. Grew, as its chairman. The Committee's function was to prepare a "statement of general initial policy relating to Japan." Most of the social, political and economic policies embodied in the statement were worked out by a State Department group known as the Far East Area Committee. A major role in preparing policy toward Japan and presenting it before the Post-War Committee of the State Department was played by Joseph W. Ballantine, Director of the office of Far Eastern Affairs.

Grew, Dooman and Ballantine, with long experience in Japan, were convinced that the Emperor system in some form had to be recognized, because otherwise the Japanese would never surrender (this conclusion has been verified by nearly every competent observer in Japan since the end of the war). Furthermore, they knew that the Emperor system—good or bad—was the cement that held together the Japanese social structure and that without it, Japan might be impossible to govern during the occupation. They also felt that the Japanese business class on the whole had formed the strongest opposition to the militarist clique which precipitated the war.

A group which had by this time infiltrated the State Department along with other government agencies violently opposed these views both from within the State Department and by a campaign of vilification against Grew in left wing New York City newspapers and magazines. The leaders of this group were Owen Lattimore; former Deputy Director, Pacific Operations of the OWI; John Carter Vincent, chief of the China Division of the State Department; and Lauchlin Currie of the Board of Economic Warfare. It was suspected that through Currie confidential information was leaked to the press and used in the attacks against Grew. Vincent and Lattimore had accompanied Henry Wallace on his 1943 flight to China and Siberia. The group's Bible was Lattimore's then newly published book, *Solution in Asia*, which recommended the abolition of the Japanese monarchy, the banishment for life to China of all members of the Imperial Family, the dissolution of Japanese big business and the purge of business executives. The group's chief protector was Assistant Secretary of State Dean Acheson. To what extent Acheson was aware of where their policies were bound to lead is unknown.

The group's immediate objective was to remove Grew, Dooman and Ballantine. After the broadcast of the Potsdam Declaration, the Japanese—as predicted—refused to surrender until they received assurances regarding the status of the Emperor. These were contained in the final message sent by Secretary Byrnes which the Japanese interpreted, rightly or wrongly, as a tacit recognition of the Emperor's position. Byrnes, the new Secretary of State, had asked Grew to continue as Under Secretary until Byrnes's return from Potsdam.

Grew then submitted his resignation and Byrnes accepted it and appointed Acheson as Under Secretary. Grew did not feel that he could accept Byrnes's suggestion that he go to Tokyo as Political Advisor to General MacArthur. Dooman also resigned at this time. Acheson immediately appointed Vincent in Dooman's place as chairman of the Far East Sub-Committee. Ballantine asked to be relieved of his post and was replaced by Vincent.

As these changes took place, the post-surrender policy evolved under Grew was officially adopted on Aug. 29, at the last SWNCC meeting attended by Dooman. The substance of the policy was cabled to General MacArthur in Tokyo that day. The document was then sent to him on Sept. 6. But the version sent to MacArthur on Sept. 6 contained several highly important insertions that had not been in the document adopted at the Aug. 29 SWNCC meeting.

The key additional clauses read:

> Policies shall be favored which permit the wide distribution of income and of the ownership of the means of production and trade.
>
> To this end it shall be the policy of the Supreme Commander:
>   a. To prohibit the retention in or selection for places of importance in the economic field of individuals who do not direct future Japanese economic effort solely toward peaceful ends;
>   b. To favor a program for the dissolution of the large industrial and banking combinations which have exercised control of a large part of Japan's trade and industry.

In the Initial Post-Surrender directive—an elaboration on the policy statement—these clauses were expanded to read:

> 23. You will prohibit the retention in or selection for positions of important responsibility or influence in industry, finance, commerce or agriculture of all persons who have been active exponents of militant nationalism and aggression, of those who have actively participated in the organizations

enumerated in paragraph 5 (g) (Page 8((35)), Part I, General and Political) of this directive, and of any who do not direct future Japanese economic effort solely towards peaceful ends. (In the absence of evidence, satisfactory to you, to the contrary, you will assume that any persons who have held key positions of high responsibility since 1937, in industry, finance, commerce or agriculture have been active exponents of militant nationalism and aggression).

25. (b) (1) Require the Japanese to establish a public agency responsible for reorganizing Japanese Business in accordance with the military and economic objectives of your government. You will require this agency to submit, for approval by you, plans for dissolving large Japanese industrial and banking combines or other large concentrations of private business control.

WASHINGTON AND SCAP

The Lattimore-Currie-Vincent group thus put themselves in a position to control the formulation of policy in Washington. Whether by accident or design, individuals who shared their views quickly infiltrated the agencies in SCAP in Tokyo which were charged with executing Washington's directives. The late George Acheson, who had also served in China with Vincent, became MacArthur's diplomatic advisor. Edward D. Welsh, an OPA economist, became chief of the Anti-Trust and Cartels Division. Dr. S.M. Fine, another economist, became economic advisor to General Marquat, head of the Economic and Scientific Section. Colonel C.L. Kades, a Treasury Department lawyer, became deputy chief of the Government Section. Theodore Cohen, a State Department employee, became head of the SCAP labor division and is an economic advisor to General Marquat.

SCAP lent itself readily to shadow control by such groups. It was organized along Army lines and the titular heads of most divisions were officers unacquainted with economic affairs who were glad to have advisors. These advisors to a considerable extent were drawn from the OPA and other New Deal agencies and appeared in Tokyo as War Department

civilian employees. General MacArthur has frequently complained—off the record—to visitors about the "boatloads" of
New Dealers sent to Tokyo. About three months ago, he
informed an intimate friend that in his opinion, economic
affairs should be turned over to the Japanese and the United
States Army confined to a military role.

From 1947 on, policy-making for Japan was increasingly
taken over by the Army, particularly by Under Secretary of
War Peterson and his successor Under Secretary Draper. They
sent a number of missions of business men to Japan and used
the reports of these missions as the basis for changing the
radical policies in force in Japan. However, they met and are
meeting resistance on many levels in Tokyo. An effort by
Peterson to dispatch five leading American executives to
Tokyo to serve as a sort of economic cabinet failed when in
early 1947, General MacArthur refused to accept them except
as part of his Army organization. Since it was obvious that
the executives would not and could not work under these
conditions, Peterson dropped his plan.

REPARATIONS

The basic reparations policy toward Japan is contained in
the Potsdam Declaration: "Japan shall be permitted to maintain such industries as will assist her economy and permit the
exaction of just reparations in kind, but not those which
would enable her to rearm for war." Before reparations in kind
were removed from Japan, the experience of the Russians in
Germany had demonstrated the almost complete futility of
this approach. In an off-the-record press conference after his
return from the 1947 Moscow Conference, Secretary Marshall estimated that 90 percent of the reparations removed
from Germany by the Russians represented a complete loss.
Bomb damage, obsolescence and the virtual impossibility of
integrating Japanese plants with other industrial installations
in the rest of the Far East would make Japanese reparations
in kind almost worthless. Former Under Secretary Peterson
once remarked that what the Chinese wanted was not Japanese machinery, but the crates in which it would be packed.

The first reparations mission to Japan was headed by
Reparations Commissioner Edwin Pauley. Pauley was accompanied by Owen Lattimore as technical advisor. Pauley's

report was largely written by Lattimore and his recommendations followed those in *Solution in Asia*. The Pauley report recommended the removal of 95 percent of the Japanese pig iron capacity, 88 percent of its steel ingot capacity, the reduction of thermal power plants by 50 percent, restriction of the chemical industry to manufacturing fertilizer, and the complete removal of the aluminim, magnesium, synthetic oil, nickel smelting and synthetic rubber industries. Pauley's recommendations were made public on Nov. 28, 1946.

The Pauley recommendations were demonstrably unworkable and Under Secretary Peterson sent Clifford S. Strike, president of the engineering firm of F.H. McGraw and Co., to Japan at the head of another reparations mission. Its first report in February, 1946 substantially modified the removals suggested by Pauley. Thirty Strike Mission engineers remained in Japan, and Strike was authorized to form an organization known as Overseas Consultants. Utilizing the best American engineering talent available, Overseas Consultants made a tremendously detailed survey of Japanese industry. They concluded: 1) That practically no reparations could be taken from Japan if the country was ever to be self-supporting. 2) The reparations would be virtually useless to other Far Eastern countries. 3) That the existing plants if left in Japan could, however, make a great contribution to the overall recovery of the Far East. Overseas Consultants, furthermore concluded, that even if virtually no reparations were taken from Japan, its merchant fleet rebuilt, and its steel capacity increased to above the prewar level, the country would have only a bare chance of becoming self-supporting by 1953. The Overseas Consultants report was published in March 1948. In April, Under Secretary Draper took another mission (now called the Johnston Mission) to Japan. This mission cut even the small reparations recommended by Overseas Consultants. Its conclusions are now supposed to be a subject of an American proposal before the Far Eastern Commission.

Herbert Hoover, who visited Japan in May 1946, anticipated the conclusions reached by Overseas Consultants and the Johnston Mission in a letter to Secretary of War Patterson dated May 7, 1947. Hoover remarked:

I am convinced that there must be a revolutionary change in the whole concept of "levels of industry," "plant removal" for reparations, and destruction of peace industry plants, if the Japanese people are to produce enough exports with which to pay for their food and other necessary imports, or become a stable and peaceable state. That drastic change is necessary must be evident by now from the fact that the American taxpayer is called upon to furnish upwards of $400,000,000 in the next fiscal year to keep the people barely alive; and unless there are revolutionary changes, it will continue indefinitely.

DECONCENTRATION

The first step toward effectuating the recommendations of the Post-Surrender Directive regarding the break up of Japanese business was the appointment of Corwin Edwards to head a mission to Japan. Edwards is now the director of the Bureau of Industrial Economics of the Federal Trade Commission. His mission presented a voluminous report in March 1946 (State Department document No. 26 28).

This report was given to State Department economists under the direction of Edwin Martin, director of economic affairs in occupied areas. On May 12, 1947, it was submitted to the Far Eastern Commission as an American policy directive called: FEC 230. It was also sent to General MacArthur with the notation that it incorporated "measures which already have been or are being implemented...with the approval of SCAP." FEC 230 was classified as confidential and therefore withheld from the American public.

On the innocent-sounding clause in the Sept. 6 policy statement recommending a "wide distribution" of income and ownership, State Department economists had reared FEC 230. FEC commanded the immediate dissolution of excessive private concentrations of economic power. It defined these concentrations as: "Any private enterprise or combination operated for profit is an excessive concentration of economic power if its asset value is very large; or if its working force...is very large; or if, though somewhat smaller in assets or working force, it is engaged in business in various unrelated fields, or if it controls substantial financial institutions and/or substantial industrial or commercial ones; or if it controls a substantial number of other corporate enterprises; or if it produces, sells, or distributes a large proportion of the total supply of the product of a major industry..."

Creditors, stockholders, managers or any individuals who have "exercised controlling power" in any excessive concentrations would have: 1) All their holdings taken away, 2) be ejected from all positions of responsibility and, 3) be forbidden to purchase new holdings or acquire new positions during the next ten years. FEC 230 carefully stated that no effort would be made to obtain a fair price for their holdings:

> The overriding objective should be to dispose of all the holdings in question as rapidly as possible to desirable purchasers; the objective should be achieved even if it requires that holdings be disposed of at a fraction of their real value.
>
> Furthermore, a decided purchase preference, and the technical and financial aid necessary to take advantage of that preference, should be furnished to such persons as small or medium entrepreneurs and investors and to such groups as agricultural or consumer cooperatives and trade unions.... All possible technical and financial assistance should be furnished the trade unions concerned.
>
> Finally, FEC 230 applied to the interests in Japan of American and other United Nations business. These interests were to have special consideration only "insofar as this can be accomplished without limiting the effectiveness of these measures.

A copy of FEC 230 was obtained in Tokyo in September 1947 by James L. Kauffman, a New York lawyer with long experience in Japan. Kauffman wrote a private report on FEC 230 and similar measures which were being imposed on Japan by the occupation authorities. After his return to the United States, a copy of this report was taken to Washington by John D. Biggers, President of the Libbe-Owens-Ford Glass Company. Biggers showed Kauffman's report to Secretary Forrestal, Secretary Harriman and a representative of the State Department. Forrestal was impressed and seriously concerned and indicated that he would check with Under Secretary Draper, who was then in Japan. Draper later confirmed Kauffman's report of the measures being taken in Japan. (The measures included an anti-trust law that went considerably beyond American legislation). In its issue of December 1, *Newsweek* published pertinent excerpts from the document and thus made it public for the first time. Senator Knowland of California denounced it on the floor of the Senate several times. FEC 230 was finally withdrawn for "redrafting" and now rests in limbo. Nevertheless, many of its provisions are still being enforced.

Meanwhile, Welsh's Anti-Trust and Cartels Division in Tokyo had gone ahead with drafting an economic deconcentration law based on FEC 230. Changes in the bill were ordered by Draper as it was pending before the Diet. On December 10, in its last session before adjournment, the Diet passed the law, but only after observers from the Government Section of SCAP were sent to the Diet Building to insist upon its passage by methods which were described as "extraordinary pressures."

Welsh had also drawn up a set of standards governing the application of the law. Their objective was to reduce Japanese business wherever possible to a single plant standard. These standards were communicated to the Japanese Government but were later modified, presumably on Washington's orders. A Deconcentration Review Board with limited powers composed of five American executives was sent to Tokyo to supervise the working of the deconcentration law. Welsh's agency remains as the executive agency.

The members of the Johnston Mission reacted strongly against Welsh's ideas. Paul Hoffman, a member of the mission, pointed out to Welsh that the reorganization of a big corporation, as he knew from experience, was a difficult and complicated undertaking and some of the Japanese companies scheduled for deconcentration were among the biggest in the world. Hoffman thought that Welsh's staff would be lucky if they managed to reorganize two or three companies instead of the 325 scheduled (later reduced to 131).

Two examples will show the effect of the deconcentration law on American business interests in Japan:

1. The Nippon Sheet Glass Company in which Libbe-Owens-Ford owns a 27 percent interest was ordered to split into two companies to provide competition. This would mean operating two furnaces in different locations

while the company has only enough fuel to operate one, and a glass furnace cannot be operated part time.

2. As late as April 1948, the International Standard Electric Corporation was forced to protest to General MacArthur directly to halt the sale of holdings by the Nippon Electric Company, Ltd. in the Nippon Communication Industrial Company, Ltd. International Standard owned the largest single block of stock in Nippon Electric. Nippon Electric's share in Nippon Communication represented an original investment of $1,000,000 and was to be sold largely to employees of the Nippon Communication for about $15,000.

THE PURGE

Instructions in the Post-Surrender Directive were first implemented by forbidding some 200,000 Japanese Army and Navy officers from holding positions of private or public responsibility and cutting off their pensions. This categorical purge included such officers as the late Admirals Yonai and Suzuki whose vital role in overcoming military opposition to the 1945 surrender was recognized by the occupation. The occupation thus lost the services of Japanese of the highest character.

During 1946, the purge was extended to politicians and to some industrialists and publishers. The Japanese soon began to use it as a political weapon—one group presenting trumped up charges against another. Officers in the Government Section of the occupation were cultivated by Japanese in order to influence decisions on the purge. This has deeply involved the occupation in Japanese partisan politics to the detriment of its prestige.

General MacArthur states that a directive from Washington directing the purge of business men had been sent him in 1946, but that he had pigeonholed it until the pressure became too heavy. It is impossible to check the existence of this directive in the State Department. In any case, on Jan. 4, 1947, one Cabinet and Home Ministry and four Imperial ordinances were promulgated greatly widening the purge and extending it to about 8,000 top executives in all Japanese business. Nearly every executive in every company came under this purge by occupational categories. For example, in the case of newspapers there were listed all chairmen, vice chairmen, presidents, vice presidents, directors, auditors, chiefs of compilation bureaus, editors in chief, chiefs of research bureaus, managing editors, chiefs of editorial staffs and news editors.

The result was a sweep of Japanese business talent which has seriously affected the efficiency of what is left of Japanese corporations. The way was open for Communists and radicals to infiltrate into Japanese business organizations, especially newspapers. The dossier in the G-2 Section of SCAP notes that Yoshio Shiga, the number three Japanese Communist, was frequently consulted by the Government Section regarding the purge. American Communists received positions in the Government Section.

Purgees' relatives to the third degree were also banned from holding positions of responsibility for ten years. The purge committees operated in secret without any rules of evidence. The purge was supposed to be run by the Japanese, but on numerous occasions the Government Section has overruled the Japanese and ordered the purge of those it deemed objectionable. The most notorious case of this kind was the purging in May 1947 of Tanzan Ishibashi after he had served as Finance Minister in the Yoshida cabinet with SCAP's approval for about a year. In this case, the Government Section overruled the Japanese Central Screening Committee which had twice exonerated Ishibashi.

The purge has produced a dangerous psychological reaction. The conservative and business classes who looked upon themselves as the natural supporters of United States policy have been alienated to a considerable extent and even driven to consider Communism as an alternative.

In a significant and foreboding statement on his purge, Ishibashi recently wrote: "Many Japanese are coming to entertain great doubt as to American democracy, the reaction therefrom already leading some of the more intelligent classes to turn to Communism. Among those well acquainted with what is happening, suspicion is being entertained as to whether or not General Headquarters is following such undemocratic policies for the purpose of forcing Japan to embrace Communism."

LABOR AND COMMUNISM

Deconcentration and the purge (plus various other kinds of economic "planning" too extensive to discuss here) were designed to break capitalism in Japan. What was to replace it? Again, whether by accident or design, the theorists in Washington and Tokyo produced a solution of which the Communists could take the maximum advantage. This solution was the introduction of the most advanced kind of labor laws and the wide-spread unionization of labor—all this in a country where labor relations had been based on highly developed and socially responsible paternalism including unemployment insurance and arbitration of disputes; and where neither workers nor employers had any idea of Western concepts of labor relations.

The Labor Standard Law promulgated on April 5, 1947, forced on an impoverished Japan labor standards even higher than those enjoyed in the United States. For example, a labor contract with one company provided for a closed shop, a short work week, dismissal rights, cost of living bonuses, a union share in the profits and union approval of changes among company directors, inspectors and advisers. In some unions, full time union officials were paid by the company, and union headquarters and secretarial staff provided by the company.

All through 1946, unions called a long series of strikes of every kind—sit down, slowdown, walkout, etc. In many instances, unions seized plants, operated them and sold the products. The unions termed this "production management." Newspapers were likewise seized by the unions and turned into Communist organs. The labor division of SCAP had forced the repeal of laws by which, for example, strikers would be ousted from seized plants. Cowed employers did not even dare protest to SCAP against these seizures.

General MacArthur felt that his hands were tied. It was his own labor division which had sponsored this union activity. The Post-Surrender Directive instructed him that he could "prevent or prohibit strikes or other work stoppages only when you consider that these would interfere with military operations or directly endanger the security of the occupying forces." Furthermore, the directive instructed MacArthur that if changing the "feudal and authoritarian tendencies" of the Japanese government involved the use of force by the Japanese people he could "interfere only where necessary to ensure the security of your forces." The unions could also cite a far reaching declaration by the Far Eastern Commission establishing union rights.

In this situation, the Communists moved quickly into key unions, particularly in transportation and communications, and the Japanese CIO is now largely Communist-dominated. In January 1947, the Communists working through the unions moved to a showdown with the occupation by proclaiming a general strike. According to G-2 files, the committee heading this strike was actively encouraged by General Derevyanko, then head of the Russian Mission in Japan. General MacArthur decided that the threat of a general strike allowed him to intervene, despite the provisions of the Post-Surrender Directive. The strike was called off after MacArthur issued a written order forbidding it.

How did the Communists establish themselves so rapidly in Japan? The chief factor was the release of their leaders from jail by the American authorities acting on directive SCAPIN 93, Oct. 4, 1945. SCAPIN 93 was based on the Post-Surrender Directive. At about this same time, the Japanese Communists in Chinese Communist territory in Yenan were given the opportunity to return to Japan. This action was taken under the basic reparation directive SCAPIN 927 which in turn was based on the Potsdam Declaration. Under this directive, Sanzo Nosaka, the number two Communist and the link between the Russian and the Japanese Communists, was returned to Japan.

In answer to a direct query in August, 1948, SCAP stated that Nosaka was returned to Japan in the normal manner under SCAPIN 927. However, according to Kyuichi Tokuda, the present head of the Japanese Communist Party, Nosaka was specially flown from Korea to Tokyo in a plane of the Troop Carrier Command. Other sources state that orders for the flight originated with John Emmerson of the State Department, at that time assistant to George Acheson. Emmerson is further reported to have suggested that Nosaka be made Premier of the new Japanese Government which was being formed at the time.

Emmerson and other occupation officials personally aided the release from jail of Japanese Communists and received them in their offices with every show of cordiality. These actions probably played a considerable part in fostering the widespread Japanese delusion that the U.S. actually wanted Japan to go Communist.

Chapter 9, page 172

Another paper that influenced Higgins and others was written by W.W. "Duke" Diehl, who was at the American Embassy. A draft of the paper, accompanied by a note asking for review and comments, was sent to Higgins in mid-September 1949.

THE OCCUPATION OF JAPAN:
AN APPRAISAL REVIEW

A military occupation of Japan began in September 1945. Four years later, in September 1949, it is continuing. Appropriately, the initial considerations related to disarmament, reparations and the relation of both to elimination of war potential. A democratization program was developed to include extension of suffrage, a new constitution, new teaching materials and a shift to the 6-3-3 school system. Continuously through the early period leaders in business and finance suspected of militaristic leanings were purged from public office and positions of trust. From the beginning food, materials and medicines were imported for the prevention of disease and unrest. In 1949 industrial recovery became a recognized objective. This called for further imports of industrial raw materials as part of the over-all program of restoring industrial activity and foreign trade to some goal percentage of the arbitrary base period 1930-1934 and aiming at a balanced economy or a significant degree of economic self-sufficiency, by some specified time, such as the year 1953.

Since from 1945 there had been inflation from shortage of commodities, uncontrolled note issue and liberal borrowing potentialities, it was considered advisable to implement the recovery effort with an austerity program. In the spring of 1949 the budget was balanced, note issue was curtailed and rationalizing of government and industry was begun. The curtailment of currency in circulation and the increase of unemployment was designed to dry up the domestic market, and permit an all out use of labor and resources in building up manufacture for export. At just this time the export market began to deteriorate. Export contracts were canceled and new business became increasingly hard to find. As a result, during the summer and early autumn of 1949 manufacturers began to refuse to take up their full allocations of coal and other materials because of lack of business and lack of funds and the materials began to accumulate in storage places in quantities taxing the facilities. Thus in September 1949 the wheels of Japan's industry are turning more and more slowly and an industrial depression is taking form. The mounting unemployment and the return of thousands of indoctrinated repatriates have given a new lease on life to the militant Communist Party which is making an aggressive bid for political power.

PREWAR DEVELOPMENT

The economic problems of pre-war Japan and the social framework within which solutions were sought, have been ably delineated by a number of competent observers both Japanese and American. Notable among the latter are P.S. Treat, K.S. Latourette, J.E. Orchard, H.G. Moulton and Thorstein Veblen. There is among all a high degree of unanimity regarding the basic issues in the development of modern Japan.

At the beginning of modernization Japan was a feudal state, following paternalistic practices, tribal customs and devout observances in a pattern solidified by centuries of observance. No industrial revolution occurred, and therefore there was no gradual change in customs and community life such as takes place in the evolution from handicrafts to machine production. Instead western techniques were borrowed and grafted directly on to the existing structure bringing about a modern industrial plant but effecting no change in the traditional customs and relationships of the community nor in the reactions and habits of thought of the people.

Potentially a feudal state is a war making state. It is based upon force of arms and has an understandable predilection toward nationalism and conquest. Japan's fast progress in industry and trade in the latter part of the 19th century brought her into conflict with nations already on the scene. This fact and the pressure of a rapidly increasing population led to beginnings of militarism in the 1890s and to an increasing emphasis in the years that followed on an industrial plant capable of supporting a large war effort and on a steadily rising direct military budget.

Japan's industry grew during the first three decades of the 20th century to a point at which the country ranked among the leading industrial nations of the earth. The factors which made this possible were several. Through owned and controlled overseas areas Japan had ready access to essential industrial raw materials. These materials were carried to Japan in her own ships, and the products of industry were again carried out to the markets of the world by a Japanese merchant marine. A large supply of cheap industrial labor was available in the home islands to process materials at low cost. Desirable industries were at all times aided liberally by government subsidies.

So it was that at the beginning of World War II Japan ranked among the leading industrial economies of the world. But untouched in the background was the feudal state and the social practices and customs which it implied. The industrial plant in steel, chemicals, power, transportation and other elements was extensive and, to a degree, artificial, as they had been developed with partial regard to complementing the military machine and without sole emphasis on economic justification.

POSTWAR SITUATION

The end of the war found Japan cut off from its raw materials sources, its foreign market lost and its merchant marine destroyed. The once cheap labor had become considerably less cheap because of extensive unionization, and for the same reason the number of industrial disputes had risen abruptly—disputes which were practically non-existent under the paternalistic prewar conditions. The pressure of population was intensified by a decline in the death rate, a rise in the birth rate and addition to the population of repatriates from abroad. As of September 1949 population stood at nearly 83 millions persons in the 4 home islands—an area smaller than California.

For a time it was possible for Japan to conclude foreign trade contracts. This was the period of postwar world shortages when the population of the great industrial countries were spending freely to satisfy deferred needs. But—four years after the conclusion of hostilities—this postwar boom began to peter out in one country after another. Then capacity was released; then business men began to look abroad for orders to offset the slump at home. This brought American and

British business men, and those of many other nationalities, into direct competition with personnel trying to sell the output of the postwar industry of Japan.

Complications existing all during the Occupation, but intensified in 1949, were the financial difficulties of many of the nations regarded as possible large customers for Japanese merchandise. In Britain's defense of the pound, dollar purchases were cut to the bone, yet certain exports were maintained regardless of cost to hold specific markets. India and Pakistan curtailed Japan purchases in going along with the sterling bloc. The Philippines' dollar credits approached exhaustion and they could purchase more only after a new loan. While a number of Latin American countries signed trade agreements, these were simply promises to buy or sell when commodities were available and the price right—a consummation based on common sense and hardly requiring a written agreement.

Tariffs too played a part in preventing profitable expansion of Japan's foreign trade. Since the U.S. had once been a large customer the attempt was made to develop this market again. But American business men were not receptive to this competition. In the cases of crab meat, woolen gloves and several other commodities Washington received urgent and immediate requests for tariffs that would equalize costs and stop the flow. And in all of the former combatant nations a part of public opinion has leaned to the view that Japanese merchandise was unfair competition and that the war had not been fought to restore the prewar competitive relationships.

Even during the period of world shortages Japan's foreign trade had not been impressive. From September 1945 thru March 1949 exports totalled $688 million dollars. In the same period imports, excluding imports into Japan for the direct support of Occupation Forces, amounted to 1,783 million dollars.

The progress of industry during this time was measured by an index of industrial production for which the base period was 1930-34. The significance of the index can be questioned on the ground that the economy of the base period was an entirely different thing than the postwar economy. However, for whatever the index is worth it rose from about 20 in late 1946 to over 70 in mid-1949, reflecting the activity incident to filling requirements of the domestic economy executing work orders for the Occupation Forces and manufacturing for export.

The first evidences of slow-down were visible in the Spring of 1949. Manufacturers began refusing delivery of full coal allocations. The reasons given were shortage of funds and lack of business. Since there was not enough activity to warrant consumption of the basic industrial fuel, there also was not enough for the consumption of other industrial materials. As coal accumulated so too did coke, iron ore, lead, tin, chrome and other materials essential to industry. At the same time retail sales declined leaving stores and warehouses overloaded with merchandise.

A vigorous industrial revival is needed to start up activity again, and to begin consumption of accumulated materials. Where and how can this develop? With growing unemployment and decreasing purchasing power, there appears little likelihood of any increase in domestic demand adequate to start the wheels turning particularly in view of the stocks. A solution might appear if export orders were to increase substantially and set the heavy export industries in motion. But how can such export business be obtained? Only, of course, by selling competitively in world markets. Can Japan do this?

THE INDUSTRIAL PLANT

In light of the foregoing considerations let us look at the industrial plant. Developed during a period of national expansion with assured supply of raw materials, cheap labor and adequate shipping; and subsidized in part for policy reasons, the industry stands today cut off completely from the economic advantages which enabled it to grow and prosper.

Not only are the former markets gone but the task of recapturing them becomes extremely difficult with an industry for which raw materials must be brought long distances in bottoms owned by others and then processed by labor which is higher cost than before the war. In other words, Japan, once one of the lowest cost producers among the industrial nations has lost this valuable advantage. The industrial plant today is an anachronism—its economic justification has ceased to exist. The industrial plant of Japan cannot even be thought of as an aggregation of industries. Industry implies a balanced production process. Today the industrial plant of Japan is a mere conglomerate of manufacturing capacities. These capacities are far greater than needed for supplying the needs of the domestic economy for fabricated products and far too expensive to operate to enable them to compete successfully in world markets.

What is to be done with this capacity? How can it be made to contribute in some degree to the welfare of the population? What sort of a reorientation is needed and in what direction?

POLITICAL CONSIDERATIONS

For a moment let us look at the major political development of the 4 year period. In that time the Communists have completed the conquest of the bulk of China and have openly aligned themselves with Russia. Through all Southeastern Asia including Indonesia, Malaya, Siam, and India there are active Communist parties and occasional outbreaks of armed violence.

Thus the Red tide has partially surrounded Japan and Japan has become a focal front line point in the Cold War. Informed political opinion holds that it will be essential for the U.S. to remain in Japan for some years to come.

Such a continuance of the Occupation is to deny Russia the use of Japanese manufacturing capacity, deny her the use of the islands as an advance base and deny her the use of the manpower as an attack weapon. Such a program, too would aim at economic stability as a deterrent to the spread of Communism among the Japanese.

If these are solid reasons for planning a long Occupation how can this be done at the lowest cost to the American taxpayer and at the greatest benefit to the American and Japanese economies?

The costs of the Occupation to date have been heavy. In addition to the $1 billion deficit in foreign trade alluded to above there have been the expenses of maintaining the Department of the Army establishment and related items, to a total of perhaps another $2 billion. It is fruitless at this juncture to question value received for these expenditures. But it is pertinent to recognize that the American Congress and the American people are beginning to show an understandable interest in the current budget requests. More searching questions are being asked regarding the uses for which funds are

sought. Press comment is appearing more frequently specu-
lating on the probable costs and duration of the occupation of
Japan. Some of the early budgets were justified by integration
into a program calling for a balanced economy by 1953. But
this was so hedged about with exceptions, hypotheses, and
definitions that it was meaningless and the course of economic and political affairs in the Far East has since removed
all possibility of a balanced economy by 1953 on any assumption except that operating deficits be made up by U.S. dona-
tions.

Since the 'balanced economy' concept no longer has value
it should be abandoned. There has been no responsible suggestion that the U.S. withdraw completely from Japan. It is
too generally recognized that in the present shape of world
affairs this would be politically inexpedient as well as inhu-
man. If then, Japan is enough of an asset to the U.S. to warrant
plan for a long Occupation the time has come for the fact to
be recognized, the costs to be balanced against the benefits
and a plan developed in which the size of, and reasons for, the
total financial commitment, are made clear.

PLAN FOR FUTURE OCCUPATION

Once it has become apparent that continued occupation
is in the national interest a number of considerations present
themselves. If the U.S. is to be the nation at interest—the
economic and political 'big brother'—then the need for such
international bodies as the Far East Commission and the
Allied Council, and the presence of British military ceases
except for political considerations.

On the assumption that the democratization program has
been completed, the resources surveyed adequately, the public
health and welfare indoctrination completed and government
reforms instituted, entire GHQ sections can be disbanded
with mission completed. On the assumption that many of the
tight economic controls of scarcity days are no longer required
many economic, financial and business functions could be
turned over completely to the Japanese, freeing a large number
of American personnel previously engaged in these functions.

As noted above a number of leading business men, finan-
ciers and economists—men who had led Japan's modernization and expansion in the prewar years—were purged from

office. Some of these men are known internationally for top notch brains and ability. In the event that a relaxation of the purge were feasible their return to active life would lend valuable assistance to the Japanese government and business.

With the return of business and financial activities to the Japanese a solid rationalization program is forced by free economic pressures. Plants which have no economic justification will be closed or converted to the manufacture of products for which markets exist.

Conceivably with the turn-back of controls to the Japanese some relaxation of purge directives can be effected in individual instances. This would make available to the new postwar Japanese state some of the brains and ability which led the modernization of the economy before the war.

These shifts from control are only the beginning. Japan may be politically important to the U.S. for a number of years to come. A certain sized annual expenditure is required. The smaller this is the better and the nearer Japan can come to a condition of self support the better. Since there are many practical obstacles to a restoration of the prewar trading position, such restoration can be nothing more than a hope for the distant future. The immediate problem then is to maximize Japan's dollar sales and minimize the annual requirement for U.S. funds.

This problem can be approached in this way. Let there be a unit of the Department of the Army with responsibility for trade-promotion under any designation that seems suitable. The detail is to whether this unit could best operate alone or as an element of an inter-departmental Committee can be settled at a later stage with the many other organizational and administrative problems that would arise. For the moment let us refer to it as the Trade Promotion Division.

The TPD would prepare careful studies, adequately documented and supported by essential graphic and pictorial display. Trade Association and industry conferences would be held at which these statistical data would be used to depict for the American business groups the operating essentials of the corresponding Japanese industries. Thus TPD might hold a meeting with the Brush Manufacturers Association. The charts, maps, diagrams, perhaps movies, and printed material, would show the economic position of the industry and its marketing problems. The broad political and economic orientation of the U.S. toward Japan and the implications for the American taxpayer would be explained, and the place of the Japanese brush industry as a contributor to dollar income would be indicated. In the cases selected for this kind of liaison treatment all would fall in the group which needs American markets. Therefore, the final summary would end on a specific request for the cooperation of the Association in the solution of marketing problems.

Perhaps at this point the Brush Manufacturers Association would be invited to appoint a Marketing Advisory Committee to work with TPD.

The success of the invitation—the degree of enthusiasm with which it is embraced—will depend upon the skill with which the preliminaries are conducted. These require diplomacy and frankness and must convey the thought that the leading industries are being asked to help government toward a solution of marketing problems of basic national significance.

Once a Marketing Advisory committee has agreed to work with TPD the objective becomes one of finding outlets for certain types of Japanese products. In cases where the Japanese products are unequivocally in direct competition with the American counterparts perhaps no solution may be possible. But in some industries there are bound to be situations which will require careful study. For example price ranges can be reviewed. Does a market exist, not directly competitive, in a price range below that served by American industry. In certain kinds of semi-luxury goods, perhaps a high price band exists in which a hand made Japanese product would not impinge upon machine made American items. At the same time quality might be explored. It is conceivable that products of certain defined qualities would be non-duplicatory and unobjectionable.

Relationships of a contractual nature represent another source of inquiry. It might be to the profit of some American industries to send some of their semi-finished products, or sub-assemblies to Japan for the next step, or for finishing, and then return them to the U.S. for sale. Profitable in some cases too might be the purchase by American concerns of the finished output of Japanese factories for importation and sale at home. The incidence of these possibilities and the ramifications of their development would be a joint responsibility of the TPD and the Advisory Committee.

Another responsibility in the program is that of simply providing useful answers to the question "How do I do business in Japan"?

In all: the program of the TPD would involve close, continuous liaison with American business. It would embrace all necessary editorial statistical and graphic aids. It would perhaps include some permanent displays and would certainly include a group of competent, effective public speakers. All effort would be centered on the mission: to reduce, through cooperative study, business antipathy to Japanese products, and to foster continuously the development of mutually profitable industrial and marketing relationships.

Concurrently with this activity aid in market data could be furnished the Japanese for the penetration of other marketing areas and assistance of some agreed upon proportions could continue to be rendered in advice and surveillance in finance, allocations, techniques, accounting, labor problems and related matters.

With the requirement of remaining in Japan for a period of years, and with the institution of a carefully thought-out trade development program, the size of the annual commitment of the U.S. should be known after a year of operation. This commitment must be balanced at the highest levels against the assets which it can assure a low cost modern industrial plant and a large reserve of trained manpower; a strong political and strategic position in this part of the world, and an effective check to the spread of Communism in Japan.

Higgins did have suggestions for Diehl.

1. Review, Prewar Development, Post War Situation, The Industrial Plant, Political Considerations, pages 1 to 9 are excellent.
2. The pages following offer in effect only one solution "Sales Promotion", whereas there must be other solutions to the problem such as the possibility of hauling freight in Japanese bottoms, barter arrangements with Communists controlled areas, etc.
3. The outlook presented is believed slightly over pessimistic. It is believed that if the responsibility is placed *on the Japanese* and they are permitted to completely rationalize their industries, they *can* be competitive in world markets and, if competitive, they will get their share of available trade.
4. The fact that the economy is saddled with the cost of the Occupation and the burden of reforms is not given sufficient importance. Any relaxation of controls and or lessening of reforms and Occupation costs will improve Japan's future prospects and enable her to approach self sufficiency. A "free economy" will automatically rationalize industry, develop initiative, restore confidence and encourage maximum utilization of indigenous resources and talent.

In 1951, Higgins made additional recommendations.

During the two and a half years since the attached was written many changes have taken place. In the 1949 Spring elections, the Communists obtained 36 seats in the Diets and became the second largest political party in Japan. This was partly due to the total collapse of the Social Democratic party and partly due to the encouragement and protection given the communists by officials of the occupation.

The communists reached the peak of their power during the spring and summer of 1949 at which time they planned to stage a bloody revolution in October, provided their "August offensive" proved successful. The "August offensive" was a reconnaissance in force to test the reaction of the public and SCAP and the strength of the Japanese Government to resist.

The president of the National Railways was murdered because he ordered the dismissal of several hundred employees on the instructions of SCAP and the Japanese Government to reduce the budget. Riots and strikes were staged in every prefecture, trains were derailed and police intimidated.

SCAP immediately took cognizance of the situation and issued a statement denouncing communism. For the first time the man on the street learned that the occupation did not favor communism. The Japanese Government took quick advantage of SCAP's stand and began a systematic crackdown and "purge" that has driven the party underground and brought their activities under control.

It is now generally believed that the danger of Communism from within Japan has passed, but we must be careful not to recreate the danger or to allow the pendulum to swing too far in the other direction causing a revival of Imperialism. Japan is now following a middle course which may finally lead her to some acceptable form of democracy. It is to be hoped that the terms of the peace treaty will not force her to depart from her present course.

A year later, Higgins described the events affecting policy since his first addendum.

December 1, 1952
Another year and a half has passed and changes have been taking place rapidly. The Peace Treaty has been ratified and a new election held in which the Liberal Party won an overwhelming victory. Japan is gradually working herself free from her former occupation influences and is attempting to shape her course as an Independent Nation.

However, the present situation is a very difficult one and needs to be handled with great care. Too bright a picture was painted by SCAP advisors who were overeager to demonstrate the success of their economic experiments. This has created a false impression abroad of a "Resurgent Japan" ready to take over the markets of the World. It has recreated the fear of unrestricted and subsidized competition and has resulted in a cry for high tariffs on the part of American Industry.

The truth of the matter is that Japan's industry is still operating below 50% of its capacity in spite of the much talked about "Korean War Procurement." The apparent prosperity is built on the quicksand of "Beer Halls, Prostitutes and Black-markets."

Mr. Yoshida, the Prime Minister, is playing a very "astute" game. He has a tough job on his hands. Many of his difficulties are a result of reform measures imposed on the nation during the occupation by Marxist Economists and "Dogooders." These reforms were all imposed in the form of laws which now must be changed. Other difficulties are a result of the personal feud within the Liberal Party for Political Control.

We need not fear the ultimate result. Japan wants to and intends to go along with the Democracies. Her verdict on Communism was rendered decisively in the first election since the end of the occupation when every Communist candidate for Congress was defeated. Under the former SCAP controlled election in 1948 the Communists won 36 seats in the Diet. Mr. Yoshita succeeded in whittling this down to 22 through "purges" between 1948 and the election last month (Nov. 1952). The Japanese people took care of the remaining 22.

I think most of the "anti-American" or "reactionary" measures being proposed are "trial balloons" or are for the accomplishment of some desirable objective by indirect means. We are being made very conscious of the results of our mistakes in the matter of rearmament, Labor Laws, school reforms, etc. but behind it all is a determination to reach the same goal we ourselves are striving for.

Chapter 11, page 198

The buildup of Army, Navy, and Air Force personnel and the rush
to bring their families to Japan at taxpayer expense bothered Higgins
especially after he had acquired land and began planning as part of
an effort to spur local private housing development. He wrote
Senator Harry Byrd, a budget watchdog in Washington about his
concerns.

April 11, 1955

Honorable Senator Harry F. Byrd
Senate Office Building
Washington, D.C.

Dear Senator Byrd:
   I am taking the liberty of addressing you on a matter of
concern to our government because of your great interest in
wasteful expenditures of Federal funds.
   My close observation of the situation here in Japan has led
me to the conclusion that the United States taxpayer's money
is not only being spent recklessly but in such fashion as to
build ill will and alienate a country that could and should be
one of our strongest allies.
   We have in Japan a number of conscientious and able
public servants, particularly in the State Department, but
their views too often apparently fail to get the attention of
persons in a position to act on them.
   Japan is today *spending* less than 2 per cent of its national
income on defense. Yet, we are being asked to reduce her share
of the defense costs and to carry an even larger share ourselves.
Our Army, Navy and Air Force continue to expand their
operations, and bring more families out to enjoy the soft
living. They give the appearance of staying permanently when
they should be "phasing out" on a set schedule.
   One thing is certain Japan will *never* assume the burden
of providing for its own security as long as we insist on
providing not only planes, ships, tanks, guns and ammunition at U.S. expense but in addition garrison two American
divisions in Japan. They will rearm for their own protection
over night the minute our forces pull out and not one minute
sooner. There is no justification whatever for our continuing

to featherbed Army personnel here just because they like duty in Japan.

We have talked too vociferously about how badly we need Japan. The Japanese are now convinced that we do and are playing the game against us. In my view, it is time to give serious consideration to ways in which we can give the Japanese an *incentive* to provide a larger share in its own defense. Under current U. S. policy such incentives are clearly lacking.

The opinion has been expressed (an opinion which I share) that a single representative of the General Accounting Office, armed with proper authority to examine the manner in which Army funds are being expended here could save many millions of dollars and increase the effectiveness of our efforts at the same time.

If you wish more specific information or if you have any questions I will do my best to supply the answers based on my close contacts with Japanese industry and Government. Respectfully yours,

W.L. Higgins

Chapter 11, page 198

Higgins also wrote a general about the housing situation.

April 12, 1955

General Maxwell D. Taylor
Commanding General
Far East Command
Pershing Heights, Tokyo

Dear General Taylor:
Some time ago I became interested in the problem of
supplying dependent housing for American Military personnel in the Yokosuka Navy area where there seemed to be an
acute shortage of suitable facilities.

After investigating the matter rather thoroughly and discussing it with the Japanese City and U.S. Navy officials there
appeared to be sufficient profit incentive to justify private
Capital investment.

I proposed to build prefabricated homes of good construction for rental to military personnel on a basis that would
amortize all costs with a reasonable profit in five years. The
land and utilities would be furnished, rent free, by the City or
private owners. At the end of the five year period the houses
would be turned over to the city, or owner, free of charge for
rental to Japanese.

Aside from the element of risk due to the uncertainty as
to the length of stay of our military forces in Japan there is an
additional risk in the fact that the military forces are requesting funds for Government furnished quarters which, if
granted, will create severe competition.

In spite of the risks involved I had decided to proceed as
soon as suitable land areas were made available. I felt that
there would always be some demand for housing, now totally
lacking, for fleet personnel not entitled to Government housing. However, a recent experience has made me doubt the
wisdom of proceeding with my plan.

I recently bought a house for investment purposes from a
Commander in the U.S. Navy at Atsugi on the representation
that it could readily be rented at a figure that made the
investment attractive. A Navy Captain wanted to rent the

house and was perfectly willing to pay the rental I asked which was well within his rental allowance and a fair price based on the value of the property and convenience to the tenant.

After all parties concerned were agreed on the price and terms and after I had spent considerable extra money on improvements to the property the Army Rent Control Board arbitrarily crossed out the agreed rental in the application for approval and inserted a rental representing a 12½% reduction. There was no suggestion that the selling price of the house be reduced correspondingly.

I question the legal right of the Army to control private rentals and to change agreements made between private individuals except as to offer impartial advice to discourage profiteering and other abuses.

It seems to me that private investments of the sort I have in mind should be encouraged as being in the best interests of the U.S. taxpayer who must bear the burden of the high cost of Government furnished quarters. If my investment in housing is going to be jeopardized by arbitrary control of the Army (I say arbitrary advisedly because of the manner in which inspections have been carried out and evaluations made) I had better look elsewhere for investment opportunity.

I would greatly appreciate a review of this problem from the standpoint of private investment and an opportunity to discuss it with the appropriate members of your command. Sincerely yours,

W.L. Higgins

Chapter 11, page 199

The history of Japan's economic recovery revealed some subsidizing of select products. Higgins's correspondence traced both sides of the issue. Japan Steel Works had retained two Americans as advisors: Higgins to represent them in Japan and a Mr. Fred Rich, representing them in New York. In 1955, Mr. Rich prepared a paper titled "Further Report on Japanese Economic Affairs," and sent the draft to Higgins. Higgins responded:

April 13, 1955

Mr. Frederic P. Rich
Delafield, Marsh & Hope
15 William Street
New York 5, N.Y.

Dear Mr. Rich:
    Mr. Kurihara was kind enough to give me several copies of your letter of March 14th to Senator Alexander Smith and I passed copies on to Mr. Diehl and Mr. Waring of the Embassy and to Mr. Clarence E. Meyer, FOA Chief. I have not had an opportunity to discuss the matter with Mr. Meyer or Mr. Waring but I have discussed it at some length with "Duke" Diehl. I will pass on to you some of Mr. Diehl's comment for your information.
    Last paragraph page two seems like a "dangerous generalization." It is true that by means of the link system and other devices Japan increased its export at the expense of the domestic economy. However, the domestic economy has enjoyed five years of unusual prosperity and readily withstood the strain. In fact the standard of living continued to rise, domestic production including home, office and factory construction remained at a high level.
    The practice of selling abroad at below cost is bad economics and bad practice, yet all nations resort to it including our own. The U.S. has poured out more than 20 billion dollars on aid, mostly grant aid and in the form of U.S. products. We now plan to move $3 billion in surplus agricultural products *below domestic cost*. It is a bad practice but the point is: the U.S. domestic economy is strong enough to finance loss sales abroad and so is (apparently) Japan.

As regards "dumping" the U.S. has had a customs man out here for a number of months quietly but thoroughly investigating charges of dumping in various industries including ceramics, textiles, cameras, light machinery etc. and he recently reported to the Embassy that he could find no conclusive evidence to support a charge of dumping based on below cost production.

In connection with the last paragraph page 4 Mr. Diehl points out that the Japanese government, for political reasons perhaps, is not properly informing the public of the true facts. When the opposition recently asked Finance Minister Ichimada why the Japanese government was paying *over half* of the cost of garrisoning our troops in Japan, his reply was: "That matter is being negotiated." This, in spite of the fact that he had before him at the time, all the figures showing that the U.S. is supplying over 70% of *all* Japanese defense costs. Mr. Diehl also points out, top paragraph page 5, that the Japanese Government never did intend to carry out the program of rearmament it talked about and changed. The attitude has constantly been against rearmament and statements to the contrary were only nodding assent to U.S. demands.

Mr. Diehl further questions the conclusions drawn in regard to shipbuilding costs. High costs estimated by the shipbuilders in many cases fail to reveal the true facts. In our own shipbuilding industry standard methods of accounting are followed and all costs are known. I doubt if the Japanese shipyards ever use the same method of accounting when estimating any two different jobs. True overhead may be 50% in a certain shop but the overhead figured will vary from 25%, if there is no work in the yard and the job badly needed, up to 250% if the yard is busy. It actually should be figured in reverse.

Many times estimates fail to reveal vast hidden assets, inflated and unreal costs to minimize taxes both corporate and personal, 3 sets of statements. When the U.S. Navy sends their accountants to a yard to carefully check the books an entirely different picture is revealed than that presented a private buyer.

Cost of ship repairing in the Yokosuka naval yard paying top Japanese wages are only a fraction of Stateside prices even when procuring materials in the Japanese market. Likewise the cost of ships built by National Bulk Carriers Corp. at Kure, using mostly Japanese materials and labor, are perhaps the lowest in the world.

Further comment: in traveling around the Orient where do you find any level of living comparable to that of Japan? Why do the nations of the world (including U.K., India and the U.S.) fear Japanese low production costs? Is it all groundless? The Japanese led the world in 1954 in textile production and export at a profit.

In regard to the proposed conference, Mr. Diehl points out that it can be arranged if the Japanese want it. He does not agree that there are irreconcilable differences on the problems of rearmament, trade with Red China, and encouragement of private American capital. He thinks that the Japanese are realistic and smart and the reason for these differences is lack of incentive for Japan to think our way and poor handling on our part.

I trust you will understand that I do not necessarily share all of the viewpoints expressed by Mr. Diehl. I am merely passing them on to you as I remember them from our conversation so that you will be fully informed of his reactions. As soon as I have been able to learn of the reactions of Mr. Waring and Mr. Myer I will pass them along to you also.
Kindest personal regards,
Sincerely yours,

W.L. Higgins

cc: Mr. S. Kurihara, Japan Steel Works, Ltd.

Mr. Rich replied, taking issue with Diehl's statement that Japan can "afford to effect foreign exchange sales below the cost of production." Up to this time, Japanese manufacturers had priced their goods at rock bottom prices.

Chapter 11, page 199

On October 13, 1955, Higgins noticed a story on Japanese naval history in the newspaper *Mainichi* about the gradual destruction of the memorial on Yokosuka Naval Base. He wrote the next day to his good friend, the mayor of Yokosuka, and enclosed a personal check for ten-thousand yen.

October 14, 1955

Mr. Y. Umezu, Mayor
Yokosuka City
c/o Yokosuka City Hall

Dear Mr. Umezu:

It is with a sad heart that I read the article in yesterday's Mainichi regarding the controversy over the disposition of the former Japanese Navy Flagship Mikasa.

When I first saw the Mikasa in 1946 she was still almost intact. The U.S. Naval authorities had not totally "demilitarized" her along with the military installations that had been used in the late war. Her guns and turrets and masts were intact. The furniture was still in the admiral's cabin and the bunks in the officers staterooms could have been slept in. She was beautiful, and a great monument to her glorious past.

The U.S. Naval authorities wanted to preserve her. Imbedded in concrete her guns inoperable, she could certainly do no harm to anyone. If, as a silent reminder, she inspired a spirit of pride and reassurance to the young people of Japan, certainly nothing could have been needed more badly following her first crushing defeat.

In spite of the U. S. Navy protests and on the insistence of the Russians, orders were finally issued by SCAP to completely demilitarize the battleship Mikasa. It was with reluctance and a heavy heart that we proceeded with the task. I was therefore very happy to learn some time ago of the proposal to restore the Mikasa to its former state but, at the same time, I am amazed at the objections to doing so on the part of some Japanese themselves.

I resent the reference in the Mainichi article to the "Uncle maltreatment". It was over "Uncle's" protest and at the insistence of the Russians that this great treasure was mal-

treated. These same Russians are probably behind the movement to scrap her entirely.

The article indicates that the future is in the hands of the
City of Yokosuka so I am enclosing my check in the amount
of 10,000 yen as a contribution to complete restoration of this
great ship.
Sincerely yours,

W.L. Higgins

Repeatedly, over five years, Higgins led a drive to finance the
restoration of this memorial, which meant as much to the Japanese
as the restoration of the USS Constitution meant to Americans. In
1957, the promotion of a movie caused Higgins to continue his
Mikasa efforts with the following:

May 27, 1957

Mr. Mitsugi Ohkura, President
Shin-Toho Motion Pictures Co.
Dai-Ni Tekko Bldg., Marunouchi
Chiyoda-ku, Tokyo

Dear Mr. Ohkura:

I was very much interested in reading the article in the
Japan Times this morning describing the success of your new
film "Emperor Meiji and the Great Russo Japanese War." If
possible I want to see the picture some time.

It has long been my opinion that the Japanese people are
in great need of inspiration and a revival of patriotism. The
world war and the occupation which followed had a crushing
effect on the spirit of your people. You are now struggling
desperately to recover economically and again become a world
power but recovery must start first in the hearts and minds
of your people and their leaders.

My reason for mentioning this is two fold. First, I want to
congratulate you on the success achieved by the film finan-
cially and secondly, I want to suggest that you seriously
consider producing more films along similar lines, films that
will restore the confidence and pride of your citizens in the
destiny of Japan.

You have so much to be proud of and so little to apologize for even in connection with your defeat in World War II. Your armies, your air force and particularly your navy fought bravely and extremely well. You can be very proud of that. You were defeated only by overwhelming odds in manpower and equipment. A glorious picture could be created of your defeat as well as your victory.

I am sure all fair minded Americans feel the same way I do. We do not think "Militarism" should be encouraged any more than communism but we do hope you will again become "patriotic" which, to us, means love of country, pride in its history, and confidence in its future.

My home is in Yokosuka. While on active duty with the U.S. Navy in 1947, I was ordered by SCAP to demilitarize the glorious warship "Mikasa" which then was and is a beautiful memory of Japan's former glory. This order was issued at the insistence of the Russian Delegate on the Allied Council. The order was carried out with heavy heart and I now get a sad feeling whenever I see the Mikasa without masts, guns or turrets; a cheap circus-like museum.

Isn't there something we can do to restore the Mikasa to its former state of beauty? It might contribute a great deal toward the restoration of confidence and pride in your people as well.

Again my congratulations on your success.

Sincerely yours,

W.L. Higgins

Chapter 11, page 199

When the occupation ended, Higgins and his friends talked and corresponded about the facts of Japan's occupation. Wally Higgins was also thinking about the future.

August 27, 1955

Mr. W. W. Diehl
American Embassy
Tokyo, Japan

Dear Duke:

Have you been reading the series of articles in the Asahi Evening News the past few days "Eight Who Helped Remake Japan"?

Theodore Cohen's footwork was the best. He very cleverly dodged the responsibility that he shared with Julia Stander for writing the Labor Law.

Gordon Walker's article in the Aug. 27 issue of *Mainichi* was excellent "MacArthur not Shidehara behind No War Clause." During my SCAP days of 1948 and 1949 everyone even remotely connected with SCAP knew that the Japanese had little or nothing to say about what went into the constitution and many of the subsequent laws.

Actually I think MacArthur should "gag" Whitney. I think his efforts to justify MacArthur's blunders are so transparent alabis [sic] that anyone can see they are pure alibis. Mr. Truman must have burst a blood vessel when he read that MacArthur was responsible for his decision to send troops into Korea.

Many thanks for your letter regarding Brig. Gen. White and Mr. Warren Webster. In view of their tight schedule I doubt if I will be able to see them but I will call Lt. Col. Haley as you suggested. They may be able to squeeze in ten minutes.

I had lunch with Admiral Gano Friday and I really tore J5 apart before realizing that J5 is perhaps under his jurisdiction. However, I only told the truth. He seemed a bit uneasy when I said J5 was created by Gen. Marquat only to hold jobs for the former SCAP "hangers on." Incidentally you probably saw the article about the "High Born Lady", and the ten million dollars. Frankly I don't think Marquat was that smart an operator.

What do you think will be the outcome of Shigemitsu's trip? It looks as if the cards are all stacked against him. Too bad—He personally is O.K. but the reinforcements sent to follow him won't help the cause.

You must read "Horizons" by Ivor Iganasoff in this morning's *Times* on the Singer deal (Aug. 27). He really lays it on the line.

I became so absorbed in "gossip" that I forgot my real reason for writing you. Does the Embassy keep a record of American Companies having direct representatives here and those companies having technical assistance agreements with Japanese companies? If so I would like to obtain an up to date list. An idea has been germinating in my mind for some time and I would appreciate your opinion.

The new tax law will make it quite impossible for some salaried representatives to remain in Japan without greatly increasing the cost to the companies. Those firms with competent Japanese affiliates in many cases do not need a full time representative here. My clients, Gulf Oil and Combustion Engineering, are two good examples. Note copy of letter just received from Gulf. C.E. is getting 70% of all the boiler business in the area—a full time representative could do no more.

I believe I could take on additional clients provided the responsibilities were limited to liaison work on a policy level. It is the detail of direct selling and engineering that takes the time and effort. The present full time representative or someone from the company could come out here about twice a year to check and consult for far less money than the amount needed to pay 75% in taxes. My remuneration could be kept at a minimum fee plus an expense account which would (probably) not be taxable.

I have several situations in mind where I feel certain the company would be just as well off under such an arrangement as now with a full time representative. Some of them have a hard time finding productive work to do. Of course, I could make a living a lot easier in the States but I am in a situation where I can't very well make such a move. I practically have to stay here. What do you think?

Will see you soon.

Sincerely,

W.L. Higgins

Chapter 11, page 200

Concerned about the potential disaster if American President Eisenhower visited Japan, Higgins wrote to Senator Frank J. Lausche.

June 8, 1960

Honorable Senator Frank J. Lausche
Senate Office Building
Washington 25, D.C.
U.S.A.

Dear Senator Lausche:

I am writing you on a very urgent and important matter. The proposed visit of President Eisenhower to Japan.

The thinking Japanese and the responsible American businessmen are greatly concerned over the plans for President Eisenhower to arrive in Japan on June 19th. We have all been hopefully awaiting the news that the trip would be postponed but latest news reports indicate that such will not be the case. We, therefore, must take some action to make the true situation known to responsible parties.

I earnestly request that you use all of the influence you can muster to discourage Mr. Eisenhower's present plans. His arrival in Japan on the 19th will be a disaster for Japan and America as well. Our Ambassador, for whom I have the highest personal regard, would concur if he would do less talking and more listening to the people of Japan.

You are no doubt well informed on the mass demonstrations that are being carried out daily by extremist groups in protest of the Revised Security Pact and the Kishi Government. Anti-Americanism has been and still is a minor factor but the leftist propaganda is succeeding in an effort to persuade the people that Mr. Eisenhower's visit is designed to bolster the Kishi government. The fact that the date of arrival coincides with the date of which the pact automatically becomes effective is used to support this claim.

It is even said that Mr. Kishi was "inspired by Washington" to seize the opportunity on May 19th to railroad the pact through the Diet with the opposition party absent. Mr. Kishi's entire career has been one of seizing opportunities. It is for that reason that he personally has never been popular with the people and has never been fully trusted by the responsible leaders of industry and business.

Responsible Japanese want the following things to happen in the following order:

1. Nothing should interfere with the approval of the Revised Security Pact which will become effective June 19th if the present Diet remains in session until that date.
2. The resignation of Mr. Kishi after the Pact is effective.
3. A new election.

If and when these things have taken place the Liberal Democratic Party will still be in power. They will lose some seats to the newly formed "middle of the road" Democratic Socialist Party. The Socialists will also lose seats to the Democratic Socialists, thus firmly establishing a third party. They consider this good for Japan.

This will restore Japanese politics to normal and is just what the present extremists fear most. If Mr. Eisenhower comes to Japan after the above has taken place he will be welcomed with open arms and open hearts. The Japanese people, in spite of the demonstrations, are friendly to America. They want to greet Mr. Eisenhower but they fear that the present anti-Kishi and anti-Pact demonstrations may increase in intensity and reach a very dangerous point the day of Mr. Eisenhower's arrival.

Even should violence and bloodshed be avoided Mr. Eisenhower would have no opportunity to "meet the Japanese people" which is the announced purpose of his visit. He would be kept insulated from the people by a force of over 20,000 police now being mobilized for the purpose. Should violence break out, and the chances are more than even that it will, Mr. Eisenhower would be blamed personally as he was by Khruschev at Paris. It would break his heart and do great harm to our position in Japan and the Far East. He can accomplish no good by coming at this time and he runs a great risk of doing much harm.

I am not an alarmist and I still have great faith in the wisdom and stability of the Japanese people. They will work out their problems in their own way. Let's not give the minority radical element a chance to use our mistakes to gain their ends.

I must apologize for the length of this letter but I feel that some explanation must be given for my fears and the apprehension of Americans and pro-American Japanese. If the true facts were reported I am certain that the Administration would not be stupid enough to persist in the present plan. Respectfully yours,

W.L. Higgins

Chapter 11, page 202

July 3, 1960

Honorable Senator Frank J. Lausche
Senate Office Building
Washington 25, D.C.
U.S.A.

Dear Senator Lausche:

Thank you very much for your letter of 22nd June. I fully understand that your busy schedule does not permit a detailed reply to my letter nor is one expected. My letters to you are intended only as reports on the situation here as seen by one U.S. citizen and are for information only. Acknowledgement is appreciated but no comment or lengthy reply is required.

I feel compelled to write one more letter which I had hoped would be one of reassurance. My personal belief is that the crisis has passed and that the violent actions will give way to more orderly processes to restore the government to normal. My belief is based upon talks with many Japanese, on perusal of the Japanese and English Newspapers, and on the fact that the Japanese stock market has fully recovered from the two crashes caused by the "Haggerty Incident" and cancellation of the President Eisenhower's visit.

Another reassuring factor is the widespread and enthusiastic interest of Japanese business and professional men in such wholly democratic movements as Rotary, Lions, etc. I am currently vice president of the Yokosuka Rotary Club. We have 55 members and have a club attendance record of nearly 100%. It was 100% for three years. There are now over 360 clubs in Japan with a total membership of nearly 15,000.

When you consider the fact that, once each week, the leading businessmen in 360 communities all over Japan are meeting socially, conducting meetings in strict accordance with democratic Stateside procedure, singing their national anthem and Rotary songs and discussing world wide problems rationally, it is hard to believe that the country is in a stage of anarchy or that the government is in danger of collapse.

The thing that disturbs me most now is the near panic expressed by some Americans here in Japan and the kind of reporting that may result. Some of our Embassy personnel seem to be suffering from a case of the "jitters" from watching the thousands of demonstrators outside the Embassy being deployed in platoons, snakedancing and singing the "international". This is understandable but they lose sight of fact that, at this same time, the student demonstrations were being billed by the travel agencies as a tourist attraction and the offices all around the embassy are doing business as usual.

The U.S. Military are confined to their bases during the days of demonstrations and can judge only from newspaper reports and watching T.V. Naturally, they too are apprehensive. The unfortunate thing is that official reports reaching Washington may reflect a distorted picture from these official sources.

One of the hardest lessons I have had to learn in order to "get along" in Japan was to forget the U.S. way of doing things. To let my employees and associates work out Japanese problems their own way. For years I worked up a lather and frequently "blew my top" because my gardener or driver or some other employee did things the "wrong way". I finally surrendered and let them do it their way. Results have always been just as good and many times better and I have learned to relax.

Why didn't we get excited about Communism in Japan in 1948 and 1949? It was much stronger then than it is now. The Communist party was recognized as an official body and they had 36 seats in the Diet. When the Communist led labor unions called a general strike for May day 1949 General MacArthur realized for the first time that he had created a "Frankenstein". As Supreme Commander of the Allied Powers in Occupied Japan he forbad demonstrations and ordered the strike canceled. The Japanese man in the street was astonished and bewildered. We had been preaching democracy and freedom and now we autocratically forbade demonstrations. Until then the Japanese were convinced we wanted Communism. This was an abrupt about face. It was undemocratic. They could not understand our direct action and our preaching democracy while acting in an autocratic manner.

The recent political crisis is (or was) very similar. The communists have come from underground in recent years and have regained some of their hold on the Government and industry. They were again building up to a "reconnaissance in force" with the final goal the overthrow of the government.

However, the present government is not a SCAP dictatorship. The Japanese consider it must be handled in a "democratic manner" and that direct action is undemocratic. Now, I am getting into deep water and I will have to refrain from going any further in justifying or explaining their reasoning. The only thing I can add is that I am convinced that they will work this thing out to our complete satisfaction if we let them do it in their own way.

There are stormy seas ahead for Japan but never lose sight of the fact that they want Communism even less than we do. They will never surrender to the principles of Communism. I do not rule out the possibility of further demonstrations. The next "cause" will probably be "U.S. Bases in Japan" but I think future demonstrations will lack force now that they have been exposed to public scrutiny.

They have had to face disaster and crises throughout their long history and they seem to have learned that they can survive best by "rolling with the punch" instead of meeting it head on. One of my best Japanese friends who is one of Japan's ablest career diplomats, when I asked him in 1948 "what the Japanese thought of the U.S. Occupation?" answered me as follows: "We Japanese consider the occupation as just an interlude". They seem to be going in the wrong direction but I predict they will wind up in the right place.

Kindest regards.
Sincerely,

W.L. Higgins

Chapter 11, page 202

August 8, 1960

Honorable Senator Frank J. Lausche
U.S. Senate Office Building
Washington, 25, D.C.
U.S.A.

Dear Senator Lausche:

I know you must be extremely busy with Congress reconvening, election problems and the many unhappy circumstances developing around the world but I thought it would be refreshing for you to hear some encouraging news.

Here in Japan, if I read the barometer correctly, things have taken a decided turn for the better. The enclosed front page article from today's *Asahi Evening News* indicates a sudden jump in popularity for the new Ikeda government. Incidentally the *Asahi News* is generally slanted to the left so that the true situation might be even better.

A week ago the leading labor unions in Japan announced that they would back the Socialist party in the next elections but not the Communists. The Socialist Party and the main body of the Student Federation have likewise disassociated themselves from the Communists. The Socialists formerly welcomed Communist support but they have found that it is now costing them votes to do so.

In preparing for the coming elections the ruling Liberal Democratic Party is playing a very smart game although our politicians at home might consider their tactics as political suicide. Mr. Ikeda has adopted a "low posture" attitude of humility and is allowing the Socialists to "fight windmills". By keeping silent, the Liberal Democrats are avoiding controversial and sensitive issues before the election which leaves the Socialists no one to argue with but the in-between Social Democrats and the radical Communists.

The average voter is apathetic. He knows little or nothing of Political issues. His background is founded in a natural fear and hatred of Russia and he still remembers when it was a criminal offense to discuss politics in public. He usually votes the way someone in a higher position or the neighborhood "boss" tells him to. After the election he may even forget who he voted for. He never writes to his Congressman or Senator so that a representative may not know how his constituents feel about issues.

The Liberal Democratic strategy is to "sit tight" for several months when the elections will be held. It seems to be paying off as the opposition is losing ground daily in their efforts to "bait" the government into debate on such issues as the Security Pacts, U.S. bases in Japan and other sensitive issues.

The outlook now is for about a ⅔ majority for the Liberal Democrats in the next elections which will give them the power necessary to do what previous governments were unable to do. They know what should be done and, after the election, I look for a wholesale revision of unworkable laws and rigid enforcement of all laws on the books. This will be accepted without question as being a mandate from the people. Demonstrations will be crushed and the governments actions will have the popular support which until now has been lacking. A year from now Japan will present quite a different political picture. This does not necessarily mean that Japan will be more pro-American. It does mean that Japan will be more anti-Communist.

There may be a lot of "wishful thinking" in the above but it is the way I see the picture at this time.

Kindest Personal Regards.

Sincerely yours,

W.L. Higgins

Chapter 11, page 204

An article by Higgins appeared in the October 1961 issue of *Challenge* magazine.

COMMENT ON EMPLOYEE MOTIVATION
By W.L. Higgins

I was recently asked to address a group of U.S. Forces labor managers and supervisors on the subject of "Employee Motivation." The questions asked following my talk indicated a lively interest in this subject and an apparent unawareness of some of the factors governing employee motivation in Japan. I, therefore, decided to prepare an article for publication in the hope that (someone might read it and) it might help to explain some of the difficulties experienced by foreigners in dealing with Japanese labor problems.

The first thing we, as foreigners must do if we wish to understand the Japanese labor situation, or any other facet of Japanese life, is to completely forget our past experiences. We must not base our appraisal of Japanese situations on our own standards and practices. Rather we must keep in mind the fundamental differences in culture and historical background. We must accept the fact that our way, even though proven successful at home may not be the only way and it may not be at all suitable for the Japanese system. It would sometimes appear that the Japanese succeed best when doing things in a manner that is exactly opposite to our way.

Employee Motivation is a product of tradition, social background, education and employment practices. Generally the Japanese employee is more concerned with security and prestige than with high income or successful accomplishment. An employment contract in Japan is considered by employee and employer alike as a lifetime contract and the worker is trained for a permanent future in the company from the beginning of his employment until he retires.

Changing jobs to better oneself or for higher wages is unthinkable. Likewise dismissals for inefficiency or lack of effort are very rare. This permanent type of employer-employee relationship is well suited to the Japanese family type social system and it has produced a fully employed and stable work force. In one plant with 3,337 workers investigation disclosed that there were only 83 discharges per year over a five year period and these included regular retirements, resignations for bad health, resignations to become head of the family on the death of the father, etc.

By contrast the American labor force is highly mobile. Workers and even executives change jobs at will. Workers are subject to dismissal regardless of length of service if business falls off or the boss thinks someone else can do the job better, or for any one of a hundred reasons. "Cross fertilization" of talents is considered to be healthy for a business and ever increasing efforts are made to fit the man to the job. The American worker has been forced to learn to be self sufficient, self reliant and to accept responsibilities which seem difficult for Japanese. The high mobility of American labor results in a rather high rate of unemployment even in good times. The rate will generally vary between 5 and 6% of the total work force as compared to 1% in Japan.

The early history of American industrial expansion is one of ruthless exploitation of labor giving rise to strong labor unions. The original goal of the union was to increase wages so the worker could provide for his own security and the future of his family. This background has developed a work force that is highly individualistic.

In Japan, the hiring of employees and their future progress in the company are based on the *Nenko-Joretsu* system. Translated this means "a system in which the order of value is decided according to length of service." In other words the income of the Japanese employee throughout his career is based upon his age or length of service rather than upon his ability or the results he may be able to produce. Initial employment is based strictly on educational background but future salary increases take into account family needs and age rather than ability and results.

Employment examinations are held every fall throughout the nation for students who will graduate and start working the following spring. A strong preference is expressed by applicants for positions with the larger industrial and commercial companies which offer the maximum security and where the pay scale is generally a little higher than in the smaller enterprises.

WAGE DIFFERENTIALS UNDER THE
NENKO-JORETSU SYSTEM

The following table represents the average spread in starting wages and subsequent increases. In the following table the index of 100 is used to represent the starting salary of a male junior high school graduate (age 15).

Male Wages	Age 22	Age 25	Age 30
College Graduate	187 (first wage)	244	379
High School Graduate	188 (after 4 yrs.)	235	337
Junior High School Graduate	198 (after 7 yrs.)	238	315

Female Wages	Age 22	Age 25	Age 30
High School Graduate	165	210	250
Junior High School	160	200	230

MINIMUM & MAXIMUM WAGE BASED ON
EDUCATIONAL BACKGROUND

	Minimum (Starting Salary)	Maximum (Last Salary at 55)
Junior High School Graduate	100 (age 15)	550
Senior High School Graduate	110 (age 18)	710
College Graduate	187 (age 22)	870

In summary...

The trends seem obvious. Productivity in the U.S. is increasing at a 2% rate annually whereas wages are being boosted at a 3½% rate. A continuation of this ratio can result only in inflation and non-competitive prices. In Japan the cost of production is decreasing year by year as a result of productivity increases averaging 9% and wage increases averaging only 5%. In the final analysis the basic law of economics will operate.

I predict for Japan a gradual merger of the old and new employment systems and for America a slow down in the rate of wage increases but an increase in fringe benefits and closer employee-employer relations. In the end, the two competitive economies will not be so far apart in their labor relations as they now appear to be.

Chapter 11, page 205

The Japanese approach to patents was unlike the American system. When the president of the United Inventors & Scientists of America wrote to W.L. Higgins on April 26, 1965, for information on joint ventures between Japanese and American inventors, Higgins was glad to share his observations.

> I enclose "Patent and Trademark Regulations of Japan", which provides Japanese and Foreign inventors about the same legal protection as the patent laws of the United States. However, in Japan as in any other country including America, the only real protection against a violation of patent rights lies in the good faith and responsibility of the contracting parties. I know of no violations on the part of responsible Japanese firms. The larger firms are generally oriented to Western business methods and standards of ethics. Smaller and newer companies have been known to engage in unethical practices due to lack of knowledge or irresponsible leadership. I could cite many instances that were directly instigated by avaricious American so-called businessmen. They would bring a model to a small Japanese manufacturer and guarantee to buy his entire factory output at a fixed price, not telling who owned patent rights.

The large Japanese firms, Higgins found, were tough negotiators. The Ministry of International Trade and Industry, Higgins found, caused more difficulties. After several years of mutually profitable success between Mitsubishi and Combustion Engineering, the Japanese firm asked to shorten the period of the agreement or change terms and royalties. But CE's management hung tough, pointing out it would be unfair to other licensees.

Higgins found that it was MITI, the Japanese government agency, that was holding up approval of Mitsubishi's request for approval of C.E.'s "Raymond" technology.

He sent the translation of "Blue-Eyed Executives" to Don Walker at Combustion.

The plot unfolded through these letters:

May 5, 1955

D.S. Walker

Dear Higgins:

Thanks so much for your letter of April 29. Rest assured we read the translations which you sent me with interest and definite concern. It seems strange that here is a country which caused us much pain and heartache—a country that we are trying to help come back economically and morally and are accepting as if nothing ever happened—can now be influenced by such sheer Communistic propaganda. Facing that, we must now realign our thinking.

You mentioned the Raymond application...would it help if we held up all shipments of all Raymond products to Japan? They have only begun to scratch the surface so far as receiving our know-how in this highly technical field is concerned. Anticipating this we have refused to give our Licensees the information on the pressure mill which they are practically screaming for. Here I am adhering to the letter of the understanding...nothing goes to a Licensee unless it has been cleared by our Engineering Department and proven by field operation. What suggestions have you insofar as pushing the Raymond line through? The information they have in their hands at the moment is an infinitesimal part of the whole, and I see no reason why we should continue to act in good faith anticipating Governmental approval.

Along a second line, we have been working with Westing-house in the last few days on the unbelievable confusion and detailed information that your equivalent of the Hartford Boiler & Inspection group in Japan has asked for. You will remember the difficulties we had with the structural steel on Kansai and Kyushu. Evidently this was engendered by those two companies. However, now the Boiler Inspection Association of Nippi is asking us for information that we would not even give a Licensee. We have gone along with these people just far enough...we have a meeting at 2:30 this afternoon to determine policy. Mr. Akins of the Westinghouse Electric has even been asked for the calculations from which they design the turbine. We have been asked for stresses and all that. Someone inadvertently permitted the negatives of the X-rays to be sent to Japan, and frankly we are getting not only fed up, but disturbed. Mr Akins is suggesting that we send someone over to explain to them that a Hartford stamp is practically sacrosanct in this country and throughout the rest of the world. Evidently they have never heard of the Hartford Inspection or an ASME Code, for that matter.

Pete Ainsworth suggested that we invite one of this Inspection Group over to show how we handle these things, and the fact that there is a single .004 tool mark on the inside of a drum shell should not cause the drum's rejection. I pointed out that one Japanese engineer would never take the responsibility of accepting these three jobs, and that it would be necessary to send over an entire Committee.

This leads into the thinking that if our Licensees are beginning to insist that even after we took a $400,000 price reduction on these two jobs, that they must be paid their pound of flesh in the form of royalty, then we certainly are not going to stand the price of the entourage. If Mitsubishi wants to draw out of the reverse royalty due to some future date on these boilers, then this may be a solution, but our contract calls for furnishing boilers to Westinghouse...not Kansai or Kyushu...in accordance with the ASME code and Hartford Inspection.

It is my personal belief that it is high time somebody stops being nice. Have you any suggestions?
D.S. Walker

In his answer, Higgins gave a background of America's and Japan's mistakes in the post-war decade and then explained:

In our approach to our own problem we must not forget that we have perhaps the most reliable and trustworthy company in Japan as licensee. I still have no reason to believe that they do not represent our best interests (at least to the best of their ability).

Some companies have used MITI objections as an excuse to gain concessions but the fact that Mitsubishi succeeded in changing the royalty rate on parts from 2½ to 5% is evidence of their sincerity as this really took a lot of "doing." We must give Mitsubishi every benefit of the doubt because without her unqualified support our efforts with MITI will be to no avail.

I would definitely withhold the release of any important technical data until ratification. In doing this you are more than justified. Many recent examples can be cited of violation of licenses, trade marks and of other unethical practices.

In regard to holding up all shipments of all Raymond products to Japan, I do not feel qualified to advise on this point. Doing so might work a hardship on the customer and generate hard feelings. On the other hand it might be helpful if the customer has an influence with the Government. The principle thing is to keep pressure on Mitsubishi and make them realize that time is an important factor. They may be inclined to let matters "take their course" and under present conditions I do not think it wise for me to contact MITI directly.

After reading over the typed version of my rather hastily written "blast" (in giving background history of the occupation) the thought occurred to me that you might think me bitter because I too was "purged" for my anti-communist attitude. I was the first member of SCAP to publicly expose the influence of communism in the newly formed labor unions. Also that you might gain the impression that the present leaders of Japan were vindictive.

Mr. Hatoyama is a practicing Christian, a Mason, and thoroughly oriented to Western ways. I do not believe he harbors any grudge against the U.S. Mr. Shigemetsu is well known to me personally and I am sure he has a complete understanding of our position, our motives, and our sympathies. I doubt if anyone is more sympathetic to our ideas but he will always act in the best interests of Japan. I am sure that neither of these men are vindictive.
W.L.H.

The issues between Mitsubishi and Combustion Engineering were soon resolved through Higgins's efforts.

Chapter 11, page 206

Wally Higgins wrote this explanation of *zaibatsu* and shared it with many curious people.

ZAIBATSU

Of the old *zaibatsu*, Mitsubishi Shoji came closest to achieving its former position as a fully integrated cartel. Decentralized by order of SCAP in 1947, Mitsubishi began (after the signing of the peace treaty) to gradually regain control over its former affiliates through exclusive trading agreements with manufacturing companies and the purchase of equity stocks in these firms. This was relatively easy to accomplish because of the lack of sales and business talent in the organizations of most manufacturers. By 1960 Mitsubishi controls (or is affiliated with) 27 companies covering such diversified fields as fuel importing and processing, ferrous and non-ferrous metals production, textiles, petrochemicals, food processing, paper, leather and rubber production, banking, real estate and insurance.

Mitsui Bussan, the second of the pre-war Big Three *zaibatsu*, is also trying to regain control over all of its former members. Mitsui has not succeeded to the same extent as Mitsubishi because some of its affiliates, such as Tokyo Shibaura Electric (Toshiba), have developed their own strong sales organizations, and because of the strong competitive position of other trading companies and banks. Through mergers and stock control, Mitsui is entering such new fields as petrochemicals, oil refining and atomic energy. Mitsui interests are also penetrating the heavy industry field formerly dominated by Mitsubishi.

Sumitomo, the third of the Big Three, has entered the heavy industry field by acquiring Uraga Dock (shipbuilding) and Meidensha (heavy electrical machinery).

These mergers are marked by the formation of holding trusts comprising a group of many industries—mining, shipbuilding, manufacturing, chemicals, oil refining, transportation and banking—with each component diversifying its own output.

Politically, the new *zaibatsu* have little influence except through campaign contributions, much like American industry. Moreover, they are still controlled to a great extent by the Ministry of International Trade and Industry (the omnipresent "MITI") and the Ministry of Finance. No import or export license, no loan, no trade agreement or licensing arrangement can become effective without "MITI" approval. This approval is generally given on a basis that follows the *zaibatsu* pattern, being protectionist, committed to limiting competition while preserving all companies, the weak as well as the strong, and distribution of work as widely as possible.

Chapter 11, page 206

The following text is taken from Higgins's initial 1960 typewritten manuscript.

WHAT IS JAPAN?

A peculiar title but one that suggests itself as a result of the many questions being asked in letters from friends and business associates in America since the recent political unrest in Japan became front page news. The many conflicting reports and erroneous opinions expressed about the political situation here have prompted me, for the first time to "write a book" or in some manner attempt to "set the record straight."

Japan is a land of great contrast and strong traditions. It is a land of cherry blossoms and "honey buckets," of tea ceremony and suicide, of jets and oxcarts, of courtesy and rudeness, of kabuki and jazz. One need only to turn a corner and step backward one hundred years. While enthusiastically embracing the new, they tenaciously hold on to old traditions as evidenced by their many festivals and ceremonies. One can say Japan is fifty years behind in its progress or on a par with the most advanced countries of the world. One can say that its economy is sound or that it is bankrupt, that its politicians and statesmen are immature or that they are the smartest in the world. Abundant evidence can be found to support almost any view pro or con.

What then is the true situation? I have been asking myself this question now for fifteen years, during which time I have been closely associated with the people and their problems first in the capacity of military governor for the Navy area, later as a member of General MacArthur's staff and, for the past ten years, as a private businessman representing both American and Japanese companies.

I do not know what Japan was like before the war but I am told that its people were perhaps the most honest and law abiding in the world. Theft, rape and major crimes were almost unknown. The Yen was the second or third strongest currency in the world, indicating a stable and prosperous economy. There was no unemployment and no poverty. Employers took care of their workers as if members of the family. Young people traditionally took care of their elders.

There was security from the cradle to the grave—perhaps the greatest "social security system" the world has ever known.

By contrast today, after fifteen years of "democracy," people find it necessary to lock their houses at night, sex crimes and theft are common, and increasing rapidly. The whole nation seems to be pleasure mad. Forces of law and order are openly defied and reverence for Emperor, church and family seem to have been cast aside. Minority groups demonstrate in open violation of the law.

What is responsible for this great change? Material damage caused by the war has all but been repaired. The people have more food, more clothing, more of everything than ever before. There is little surface evidence of the fact that Japan, only fifteen years ago, was prostrate, a defeated nation, requiring a dole for its very existence. The wounds on the body seem to have healed completely but the soul is still sick.

We landed in Japan from a troop ship under full combat conditions. It was over a month after the surrender, but the commanders were taking no chances of meeting some physical resistance from suicide groups. No civilians were to be seen on our route to our billeting area, a distance of several miles. Police only lined the route at intervals of about fifty yards, their backs to the road. We were told that all women and children had been evacuated to the country to escape slaughter by the "barbarians".

Our billets were in charge of Kamikaze volunteers, men and women who had bravely volunteered for the jobs. It was several days before the women and children began to come out of hiding. They were amazed to find the "invaders" friendly and concerned over their welfare. (Incidentally, our combat troops who originally occupied Japan were magnificent in their conduct.) Soon the word spread and when units advanced further inland they were greeted as conquering heroes coming back home. The Japanese had expected the worst. The women, including the one I later married, were drilled with pointed bamboo spears to repel attacks. They were overwhelmed at the kind treatment. Every American was regarded as a god and could do no wrong. Our judgment was considered infallible and SCAP orders were executed without protest and with great eagerness even when they seemed strange to the Japanese concept of things. There was never any protest or act of violence against the occupation during the six plus years of occupation.

General MacArthur as Supreme Commander of the Allied
Powers was a soldier. He asked for economic and political
advisors to implement the post war surrender directive given
him by Washington and they soon began to arrive in boatloads. Many of them were "unreformed new dealers" some
were Communists or fellow travellers and some were well
meaning reformers. But most of them seemed to believe in a
socialized state. Many of these advisors were placed in positions of great authority. This was a perfect opportunity for
them to try out all of their "crack pot" ideas in the guise of
"democracy". The postwar surrender document prepared in
Washington by men experienced in Far Eastern Affairs was a
very commendable and workable document but its implementation was placed in the hands of young and inexperienced
persons who proceeded to carry out the letter and spirit of the
directive with great zeal and with many embellishments. This
was their great opportunity to prove their theories. The young
man who was in complete charge, a virtual dictator, over the
vast chemical industry of Japan had never had a days business
experience. He went into the Army directly from college and
after being tzar of the chemical industry three or four years
went back to finish college.

As a result Japan was saddled with a constitution written
by SCAP and adopted by a reluctant government. A labor law
written by SCAP giving benefits and controls to labor that no
other country in the world had. A land reform law, an education law and other laws that, however, well intended, were
not suited to the Japanese way of life. These laws were mildly
protested by the Japanese government then in power but
seldom, if ever, were Japanese suggestions adopted. One case
was reported of a SCAP official stopping the hands of the clock
in the Japanese Diet thus preventing the Diet from recessing
until a particularly objectionable bill was passed.

During the occupation SCAP played the role of dictator
which the Japanese readily accepted and understood. To them
it only meant serving under a U.S. dictator instead of under
Tojo. The thing they could not understand was our preaching
"Democracy." They were confused. The Communists were
also talking "Democracy" and their brand seemed little different than ours.

It is possible that had we offered Democracy as a way of
life for the Japanese and made an effort to "sell" it to them

instead of jamming it down their throats, they would have accepted it quite readily. They have never wanted any part of Communism. They were "ripe" for democracy but they feel that they had no chance to express a choice. The laws were imposed upon them and not submitted to them for popular vote.

The first official act of the occupation was to free all political prisoners. There were no communists in Japan at the time of the surrender. They were in jails in Manchuria. Mr. Nozaka, Moscow trained #1 communist, was flown from Manchuria in a U.S. Government plane to Tokyo and made an advisor to SCAP. The communist party was legalized and built up by SCAP as an "opposition party". This policy was so successful that in 1949 it became the second strongest political force in Japan with 36 seats in the National Diet. Then it exploded.

The Communist Party had become so strong that they planned a bloody revolution to take over control of the Government in October of 1949. A reconnaissance in force in the form of demonstrations, strikes and riots were staged all over Japan in April to test the resistance of the Japanese Government and SCAP and a general strike was ordered for May first. General MacArthur then became alarmed and declared that there would be no general strike. Investigation disclosed proof of the planned revolution and the party was driven underground. Action taken by SCAP was certain and swift. As Supreme Commander of the Occupying Forces, such decisive action was possible.

When General MacArthur realized he had created a "Frankenstein" and cracked down on the Communists, the Japanese man on the street was amazed. This was a direct about face. Until then, the Japanese thought we were in favor of Communism as a policy for Japan. They also could not understand how such arbitrary action could be taken by an authority preaching "Democracy".

Under the constitution, the present government has no such dictatorial power but must treat riot and insurrection in a "democratic manner". Every attempt to revise the constitution and strengthen the power of the police has met with violent opposition of the same hard core of communists who were in power in 1949. The dangers of the communist buildup were repeatedly pointed out by leading Japanese Government officials who predicted the possible results but their suggestions were disregarded. These facts are documented in "The Political Orientation of Japan," a U.S. Government publication compiled by the Government Section of SCAP.

One of the greatest mistakes of the occupation was the wholesale "purge" of all capable men in high positions in Banking, Business, Manufacturing, Education and Government. Under the postwar surrender document it was intended to purge the leading militarists, government officials and those "directly responsible" for leading Japan into war. As implemented by SCAP the purge was extended to include hundreds of friends of America who happened to occupy positions of responsibility. An article appeared in the Jan. 27, 1947 issue of *Newsweek* which questioned the wisdom of the wholesale purge of Japan's leaders by categories and predicted the inevitable result.

The "third team" (minus the real leaders) proved wholly inadequate to the task of running the country. Little or no economic progress was made in spite of the hundreds of millions of dollars the U.S. was contributing to "priming the pump" until the business leaders were "unpurged" and took up the reins of business and finance around 1950.

In 1948 I visited the coal mines of Kyushu where there was a minor jurisdictional labor dispute. My purpose was to learn why the mines were not producing the quotas set by SCAP and to arbitrate the dispute. The unions had interpreted the labor law as giving them control over production quotas. The union quota for the mine was less than the quota set by the Government and SCAP. The union was exercising "production control" by keeping the manager of the mine a virtual prisoner in his office and stopping work when the daily quota was reached. All officers of the union were card carrying communists. This was a fact quite easy to establish, as the party was recognized as a favored political party and it was almost an honor to carry a membership card.

It is to be noted that "Uncle Joe Stalin" never criticized the Occupation of Japan until the action taken by SCAP in 1949. All of the laws seemed to fit pretty well into his pattern. There were frequent strikes and demonstrations and labor always won. It was illegal to fly the rising sun flag and to sing the National Anthem of Japan but the demonstrations were thick with red flags and the "International" was thought by some to be the new national anthem.

Coal is Japan's only major natural resource so it was natural for SCAP to place great emphasis on coal production as a means of economic recovery. Coal Mining had always been considered the job of slave labor. High wages, free housing, and all kinds of extra bonuses were offered labor to go into Coal Mining. The result was whole families on mine payrolls, and production per man at an all time low roughly 1/25th of the U.S. standard. The ultimate result has been prices that are not competitive and a bankrupt industry today—the one real bad spot in Japan's economy.

The coal companies have been trying desperately to rationalize their industry to make coal competitive with other fuels but every effort to do so has been defeated by the radical element that still controls the unions. An arbitration board was finally set up to settle the long drawn out Miike Coal Mine dispute and both sides agreed to abide by the decision of the neutral board.

The board decided in favor of the management pointing out that the company had been losing money and markets and could no longer afford the luxury of featherbedding and special privilege. Labor is now trying to renege on its agreement.

All of the blame for the present situation cannot be placed on the Communists or on SCAP made laws, or on mistakes of U.S. diplomacy. Actually, SCAP did an outstanding job of carrying out the provisions of the U.S. Post War policy, which was designed to eliminate Japan forever as a potential enemy and make Japan an agrarian economy. The big mistake was in not modifying the implementation when our policy changed and we began to recognize the value of Japan to our own future security. We must bear our share of the blame but much of the trouble lies in the failure of successive Japanese Governments to take aggressive action. There has been a decided lack of leadership. Each government was looked upon as a "caretaker government" until the "old pros" could be unpurged or brought back into power. When the "old pros" finally did get their chance, they proved to be too old to take the strain of modern day politics and they failed.

In addition to destroying Japan's economic capacity to rearm, SCAP was directed "to encourage and show favor to "(a) policies which permit a wide distribution of income and ownership of the means of production and trade (b) the development of organizations of labor, industry and agriculture organized on a democratic basis". So effectively were these directives carried out that we were allocating raw materials under the Garioa [sic] Fund to over two hundred small bankrupt paint manufacturers and over two hundred soap manufacturers. Before the war there were perhaps twenty such manufacturers, all of them big and prosperous.

The "Democratization" of business and of labor was a noble experiment but that, plus the purge of all able business talent, made it quite impossible for the economy to get "off the ground." It was not until after the business leaders were "unpurged" and took over the reins that the economy began to recover. The Korean War helped greatly but the biggest factor in recovery was the availability of the first string players. All of our pump priming had been used to keep the economy merely alive.

In summary, it seems to me that the reasons for the present political unrest are quite clear. They are not understood by foreigners only because no one seems willing to focus attention on the real causes. Those responsible for the "great experiment" remain silent. Without the background and knowledge of what happened under the occupation and also what happened 100 years ago in molding the Japanese character it is naturally quite difficult to understand. The Japanese still hesitate to point out the facts but they will readily agree when asked specifically. The strange thing to me is that the situation has been kept under control as well as it has. The successive Japanese Governments have done a marvelous job of keeping some semblance of control under the circumstances. They have done so by "nibbling away" little by little when the opposition was looking the other way and by compromise and promise. The "demonstrations" are generally desperate efforts on the part of the Socialists and Communists to discredit the majority and win support for their cause. They have learned that Japan is basically conservative and Democratic and they can never win in a fair election. But their violent actions have now "backfired" and they are losing instead of gaining public support by their violent tactics.

Now for the first time a solution is in sight. The violence and irresponsible actions of the minority groups have focused public attention on the problem. The present new Government or one to follow in the very near future will have a clearer mandate from the people. Evidence is increasing of the probability that Mr. Ikeda's party will win a ⅔rds majority in the next election. It will then be able to revise necessary laws with public support, until now lacking, and will be able to bring the situation under control. Changes necessary cannot be made without amendment to the Constitution which requires a ⅔ majority. The leaders of Japan have not lost their "touch" altogether. They know and have known for a long time what is necessary but they must handle it in their own way, not by the direct action we would advocate.

Japan in less than 100 years emerged from a feudal clan to the position of one of the great world powers. The brains, energy and determination responsible for that progress is now beginning to put the "show back on the road." One of the wisest of Japan's statesmen said to me during the early days of the occupation that "Japan regards the occupation only as an interlude, a pause in her forward progress. I predict that great progress will be made during the next few years. Japan, like the rest of the world, is turning to the younger generation. The new Ikeda cabinet is composed mostly of younger men. Ikeda may be the leader Japan has been looing for. If he fails they may turn to an even younger man, possibly Mr. Miki who has the potential but who has not yet emerged as a front page figure. Business leaders have appeared in abundance. The economy is "bursting out all over". When they find a strong leader to take over the reins of Government nothing will stop them. We may have to get out of our easy chairs again to meet their competition.

A friend who had his 2000 acres of farm land in Hokkaido taken over by the Government under the Land Reform Law. He told me the other day that the farmers who had "inherited" his lands for almost nothing had even moved in on the small marginal tracts that had been left to him and, after developing the tracts, consider them their own while he is left with no income to pay the taxes.

I asked him "How do you feel about losing everything and having to go to work for a living and he replied *"Shikata-ga-nai!"* (It cannot be helped.) Anyhow, I alone was hurt while 2000 farmers have benefited. They own their own farms and most of them have television, running water, and many things they did not dream of before so frankly "I feel quite good about it."

In all fairness I must point out our efforts to bring Democracy have not all been in vain. Some of the reforms have been beneficial and others will work out in time. When Japan has recovered from her bad case of indigestion from swallowing too much in one gulp she will emerge as a strong Democratic country and a valuable asset to the free world.

Bibliography

Craig, William. *The Fall Of Japan*. New York: The Dial Press, 1967

Hersey, John. *Hiroshima*. New York: Alfred A. Knopf, 1946

Higgins, Raymond A. *Training And Developing Your Team*. Homewood, Illinois: Business One Irwin, 1993

Manchester, William. *American Caesar*. Boston: Little, Brown & Co., 1978

Masatsugu, Mitsuyuki. *The Modern Samurai Society*. New York: AMA-COM, 1982

Reischauer, Edwin O. *Japan*. New York: Alfred A. Knopf, 1946, revised 1964

Reischauer, Haru. Matsukata. *Samurai and Silk*. Cambridge: Belknap Press, 1986

Welch Jr., Robert H. *May God Forgive Us*, Henry Regnery Co., Chicago, 1952

Jndex

D

E

Shobara 71
Shogun's 102, 125
short snorter 18-20, 119-120
Showa Aircraft Company 192
Sixth Army 23-24
Social Democratic Party 121
Socialists 304
soda plant 122
Soviet 176
Soviet Union 165
stabilization 163, 191
  program 167
Stars and Stripes 172
State Department 160, 243
State-War-Navy Coordinating
  Committee 242
  See SWNCC
steaks 64
steam power 191
steel 173, 247, 257
  plants 55
Stockpile Bill 156
Strike Study 144
Strike, Clifford S. 144, 247
strikes 157, 188, 253-254, 265,
  301-302
submarines 54, 56
  midget suicide 47
subsidies 173
sugar cane 22
Suntory 55, 64, 180
supply ships 55, 64, 71-72
Supreme Commander of Allied
  Powers 83-84, 87, 91, 94, 118,
  122, 125, 132, 139, 142-143,
  147-152, 157-159, 163-164,
  166-169, 171-173, 175, 177, 188,
  191-193, 199, 201-202, 234, 245,
  248, 250, 252-254, 265-267,
  295-296, 300-303
  See SCAP
surrender 18-19, 26-27
SWNCC 242
  See State-War-Navy Coordinating
  Committee
swords 65

synthetic oil 247
synthetic rubber 247

T

Takeda Chemical Company 88, 90
Takehara 55, 61
Takenugii Mine 157
Tanabe 72-73
tariffs 173, 258, 266
Taylor, General Maxwell 198, 270
Taylor, Pitt 18
telephone system 121
Tenth Corps 25-26, 28, 43, 80
textiles 122, 169, 296
"The Occupation of Japan: An
  Appraisal" 172
Thirty-fourth Infantry Division 77
tin 259
Toda Manufacturing Company 100
Tokitsumaru 95
Tokuyama 85, 88-89, 91-93
Tokyo 23, 82-85, 94, 107, 117,
  139, 143-144, 148, 150, 155,
  157, 164, 177, 191, 198, 224
Tokyo Bay 18, 27, 115, 212
Tokyo Mitsui Club 159
Tokyo Reserve Officers of the Naval
  Service Club 151
Tokyo Shibaura Electric 296
Toshiba 296
tourism 218
Toya Cotton Spinning Mills 100
Toyota 223
trade 303
trademark 292
transportation 254, 257, 296
Truman Administration 165
Tsujimoto, Yoshio 194
tunnels 72, 115-116, 136, 212
Twentieth Century Fund 195
Twenty-fourth Division 73
typhoon 40, 59, 111

About the Author

Raymond A. Higgins was born in Elizabeth, N.J., in 1924. The third of Wallace Higgins's six sons, he entered the Army Air Corps on June 19, 1943, immediately after graduating high school in Mentor, Ohio. He served on a heavy bomber air crew as a navigator-flight officer. He was discharged on Nov. 19, 1945.

With help from the GI Bill, Higgins earned a B.S. in agriculture and M.S. in marketing at Ohio State University. He was an assistant professor of marketing at Michigan State University. For eleven years, he served as director of education for the Super Market Institute (now the Food Marketing Institute). Higgins then joined the Armour Grocery Products Company (now Dial Corporation), as Director of Sales Training, a position he held for 25 years until his retirement in 1989. He is now a management training consultant.

Higgins's first book was *The Sales Manager's Guide to Training and Developing Your Team* (1993, Irwin Professional Publishing/Professional Society of Sales and Marketing Trainers). He has written hundreds of booklets for managers and salespeople.

He is a member of the Japan-America Society of Phoenix, the Professional Society of Sales and Marketing Training, Optimist International, Sales Professionals of Phoenix and the Western Michigan University Curriculum Committee.

Higgins's two half-brothers from his father's second marriage live in Atlanta. Victor Katsumi Higgins, 47, produces films for American and Japanese TV. His 1991 film, *Time Bridge of Fifty Years*, for Tokyo Television Network, due to be re-released this year, is about a Japanese-American astronaut whose spacecraft goes into a time warp and ends up in Japan during WWII. It includes scenes in a reconstructed version of the Kotani house. Ernest Makoto Higgins, 43, is a travel agent for Japanese groups touring the U.S.

Raymond Higgins lives in Phoenix with his wife, June.

To order a copy of *From Hiroshima With Love* for yourself, a friend or even a service buddy, fill out this form or call today.

❏ Please send me *From Hiroshima With Love*

Name _____

Address _____

City _____ State _____

Zip Code _____ Phone _____

Ship to:

Name _____

Address _____

City _____ State _____

Zip Code _____ Phone _____

Send $18.95 for each book you wish to order. Add $4 for shipping of the first book, $1.50 for each additional book. Allow 1–2 weeks for delivery. Make checks payable to VIA Press.

Please send me _____ books at $18.95 _____

Shipping _____

Tax (Arizona residents: add 1.29 per book) _____

TOTAL

❏ Check enclosed ❏ **VISA** ❏ **MasterCard**

Card # _ _ _ _ _ _ _ _ _ _ _ _ _ _ _ _ _ _ exp. ___/___

Please autograph my copy to

_____

Call **1-800-284-2669**

or send your order and check to VIA Press
1 E. Camelback, Suite 550, Phoenix, AZ 85012-1650